EXTRAPOLATION, INTERPOLATION, AND SMOOTHING OF STATIONARY TIME SERIES

EXTRAPOLATION, INTERPOLATION, AND SMOOTHING OF STATIONARY TIME SERIES

With Engineering Applications

by Norbert Wiener

THE M.I.T. PRESS
MASSACHUSETTS INSTITUTE OF TECHNOLOGY
CAMBRIDGE, MASSACHUSETTS

First MIT Press paperback edition, 1964

ISBN 978-0-262-23002-5 (hc : alk. paper), 978-0-262-73005-1 (pb)

PREFACE

Largely because of the impetus gained during World War II, communication and control engineering have reached a very high level of development today. Many perhaps do not realize that the present age is ready for a significant turn in the development toward far greater heights than we have ever anticipated. The point of departure may well be the recasting and unifying of the theories of control and communication in the machine and in the animal on a statistical basis. The philosophy of this subject is contained in my book entitled *Cybernetics.** The present monograph represents one phase of the new theory pertaining to the methods and techniques in the design of communication systems; it was first published during the war as a classified report to Section D_2, National Defense Research Committee, and is now released for general use. In order to supplement the present text by less complete but simpler engineering methods two notes by Professor Norman Levinson, in which he develops some of the main ideas in a simpler mathematical form, have been added as Appendixes B and C. This material, which first appeared in the *Journal of Mathematics and Physics*, is reprinted by permission.

In the main, the mathematical developments here presented are new. However, they are along the lines suggested by A. Kolmogoroff (Interpolation und Extrapolation von stationären zufälligen Folgen, *Bulletin de l'académie des sciences de U.R.S.S.*, Ser. Math. 5, pp. 3–14, 1941; cf. also P. A. Kosulajeff, Sur les problèmes d'interpolation et d'extrapolation des suites stationnaires, *Comptes rendus de l'académie des sciences de U.R.S.S.*, Vol. 30, pp. 13–17, 1941.) An earlier note of Kolmogoroff appears in the Paris *Comptes rendus* for 1939.

To the several colleagues who have helped me by their criticism, and in particular to President Karl T. Compton, Professor H. M. James, Dr. Warren Weaver, Mr. Julian H. Bigelow, and Professor Norman Levinson, I wish to express my gratitude. Also, I wish to give credit to Mr. Gordon Raisbeck for his meticulous attention to the proofreading of this book.

Norbert Wiener

Cambridge, Massachusetts
March, 1949

*Published by The M.I.T. Press, Cambridge, Massachusetts

CONTENTS

CONTENTS

INTRODUCTION

0.1 The Purpose of This Book

This book represents an attempt to unite the theory and practice of two fields of work which are of vital importance in the present emergency, and which have a complete natural methodological unity, but which have up to the present drawn their inspiration from two entirely distinct traditions, and which are widely different in their vocabulary and the training of their personnel. These two fields are those of time series in statistics and of communication engineering.

0.2 Time Series

Time series are sequences, discrete or continuous, of quantitative data assigned to specific moments in time and studied with respect to the statistics of their distribution in time. They may be simple, in which case they consist of a single numerically given observation at each moment of the discrete or continuous base sequence; or multiple, in which case they consist of a number of separate quantities tabulated according to a time common to all. The closing price of wheat at Chicago, tabulated by days, is a simple time series. The closing prices of all grains constitute a multiple time series.

The fields of statistical practice in which time series arise divide themselves roughly into two categories: the statistics of economic, sociologic, and short-time biological data, on the one hand; and the statistics of astronomical, meteorological, geophysical, and physical data, on the other. In the first category our time series are relatively short under anything like comparable basic conditions. These short runs forbid the drawing of conclusions involving the variable or variables at a distant future time to any high degree of precision. The whole emphasis is on the drawing of some sort of conclusion with a reasonable expectation that it be significant and accurate within a very liberal error. On the other hand, since the quantities measured are often subject to human control, questions of policy and of the effect of a change of policy on the statistical character of the time series assume much importance.

In the second category of time series, typified by series of meteorological data, long runs of accurate data taken under substantially uniform external conditions are the rule rather than the exception. Accordingly

1

quite refined methods of using these data for prediction and other related purposes are worth considering. On the other hand, owing to the length of the runs and the relative intractability of the physical bases of the phenomena, policy questions do not appear so generally as in the economic case. Of course, as the problem of flood control will show, they do appear, and the distinction between the two types of statistical work is not perfectly sharp.

0.3 Communication Engineering

Let us now turn from the study of time series to that of communication engineering. This is the study of messages and their transmission, whether these messages be sequences of dots and dashes, as in the Morse code or the teletypewriter, or sound-wave patterns, as in the telephone or phonograph, or patterns representing visual images, as in telephoto service and television. In all communication engineering—if we do not count such rude expedients as the pigeon post as communication engineering—the message to be transmitted is represented as some sort of array of measurable quantities distributed in time. In other words, by coding or the use of the voice or scanning, the message to be transmitted is developed into a time series. This time series is then subjected to transmission by an apparatus which carries it through a succession of stages, at each of which the time series appears by transformation as a new time series. These operations, although carried out by electrical or mechanical or other such means, are in no way essentially different from the operations computationally carried out by the time-series statistician with slide rule and computing machine.

The proper field of communication engineering is far wider than that generally assigned to it. Communication engineering concerns itself with the transmission of messages. For the existence of a message, it is indeed essential that variable information be transmitted. The transmission of a single fixed item of information is of no communicative value. We must have a repertory of possible messages, and over this repertory a measure determining the probability of these messages.

A message need not be the result of a conscious human effort for the transmission of ideas. For example, the records of current and voltage kept on the instruments of an automatic substation are as truly messages as a telephone conversation. From this point of view, the record of the thickness of a roll of paper kept by a condenser working an automatic stop on a Fourdrinier machine is also a message, and the servo-mechanism stopping the machine at a flaw belongs to the field of communication engineering, as indeed do all servo-mechanisms. This fundamental unity of all fields of communication engineering has been obscured by the traditional division of engineering into what the Germans call *Starkstromtechnik* and *Schwachstromtechnik*—the engineering of strong currents and the engineering of weak currents. There has been a tendency to identify this split with that between power and communications engineering. As a result of the consequent division of personnel, the communications problems of the power engineer are often handled by a technique different from that which the ordinary communications engineer employs, and useful notions such as that of impedance or voltage ratio as a function of the frequency are often much neglected.

This is still further accentuated by the wide difference in the frequency range of interest to the telephone engineer and to the servo-mechanism engineer. Ordinary passive electric circuits have time constants of a small fraction of a second. For time constants of seconds or minutes, passive circuits require impedances of orders of magnitude not at all to be realized by the conventional technique of inductances and capacities. This difference in technique has often blinded the communications and the power engineers to the essential unity of their problems.

It is, of course, true that the main function of power engineering is the transmission of energy or power from one place to another together with its generation by appropriate generators and its employment by appropriate motors or lamps or other such apparatus. So long as this is not associated with the transmission of a particular pattern, as for example in processes of automatic control, power engineering remains a separate entity with its own technique. On the other hand, in that moment in which circuits of large power are used to transmit a pattern or to control the time behavior of a machine, power engineering differs from communication engineering only in the energy levels involved and in the particular apparatus used suitable for such energy levels, but is not in fact a separate branch of engineering from communications.

0.4 Techniques of Time Series and Communication Engineering Contrasted

Let us now see what are the fields from which the present-day statistician and the present-day communication engineer draw their techniques. First, let us consider the statistician. Behind all statistical work lies the theory of probabilities. The events which actually happen in a single instance are always referred to a collection of events which might have happened; and to different subcollections of such events, weights or probabilities are assigned, varying from zero or complete improbability (rather than certainty of not occurring), to unity or complete probability (rather than certainty of occurring). The strictly mathematical theory corresponding to this theory of probability is the theory of measure, particularly in the form given by Lebesgue. A statistical method, as for example a method of extrapolating a time series into the future, is judged by the probability with which it will yield an answer correct within certain bounds, or by the mean (taken with respect to probability) of some positive function or norm of the error contained in its answer.

0.41 The Ensemble

In other words, the statistical theory of time series does not consider the individual time series by itself, but a distribution or *ensemble* of time series. Thus the mathematical operations to which a time series is subjected are judged, not by their effect in a particular case, but by their average effect. While one does not ordinarily think of communication engineering in the same terms, this statistical point of view is equally valid there. No apparatus for conveying information is useful unless it is designed to operate, not on a particular message, but on a set of messages, and its effectiveness is to be judged by the way in which it performs on the average on messages of this set. "On the average" means that we have a way of estimating which messages are frequent and which rare or, in other words, that we have a *measure* or probability of possible messages. The apparatus to be used for a particular purpose is that which gives the best result "on the average" in an appropriate sense of the word "average."

0.42 Correlation

Another familiar tool of the statistician is the theory of correlation. If $x_1, \cdots, x_n$ are the numbers of one set and $y_1, \cdots, y_n$ the numbers of another set, the coefficient of correlation between the two is

$$\frac{\sum_1^n x_i y_i}{\sqrt{\sum_1^n x_j{}^2 \sum_1^n y_j{}^2}} \tag{0.421}$$

This quantity must lie between -1 and 1. Mathematically it is to be interpreted as the cosine of the angle between the two vectors $(x_1, \cdots, x_n)$ and $(y_1, \cdots, y_n)$. When this quantity is nearly ± 1, there is a strong degree of direct or reverse linear dependence between the x_k's and y_k's. On the other hand, if this quantity is nearly 0, a low degree of linear dependence between the x_k's and y_k's is indicated. This correlation coefficient has been normalized by the denominator which has been adopted. For many purposes it is useful to consider the numerator $\sum_1^n x_i y_i$ as the correlation.

In time series the correlations which chiefly come into play are those between a certain sequence of values and the same or another sequence of values under a shift in time, time being represented by the index of the data to be correlated. If this is a sequence $\cdots, x_1, x_2, \cdots, x_n, \cdots$ we take the correlation

$$\varphi_j = \lim_{N \to \infty} \frac{1}{2N+1} \sum_{k=-N}^{N} x_{k+j} \bar{x}_k \qquad (0.4215)^*$$

to be the so-called auto-correlation coefficient of the sequence $\cdots$, $x_1, x_2, \cdots, x_n, \cdots$, and similarly we take

$$\lim_{N \to \infty} \frac{1}{2N+1} \sum_{k=-N}^{N} x_{k+j} \bar{y} \qquad (0.422)$$

to be the cross-correlation coefficient of the x sequence with the sequence $\cdots, y_1, y_2, \cdots, y_n, \cdots$. These auto-correlation coefficients and cross-correlation coefficients are of course functions of the lag j. It will be seen that the auto- and cross-correlation coefficients are independent respectively of a shift in the time origin for the sequence of x's alone or the pairs of x and y sequences. Where we are dealing with continuous data instead of discrete data the sequence $\cdots, x_1, x_2, \cdots, x_n, \cdots$ has as an analogue the function $f(t)$, where the variable t corresponds to the subscript of the x. As an analogue of the auto-correlation in the discrete case we obtain the quantity

$$\varphi(\tau) = \lim_{T \to \infty} \frac{1}{2T} \int_{-T}^{T} f(t+\tau) \overline{f(t)} \, dt, \qquad (0.424)$$

which we also call the auto-correlation. Similarly the quantity

$$\lim_{T \to \infty} \frac{1}{2T} \int_{-T}^{T} f(t+\tau) \overline{g(t)} \, dt \qquad (0.425)$$

is termed the cross-correlation of f and g. We shall see that these quantities bear an intimate relation to the theory of spectra or periodograms and that they are quite as significant for the electrical engineer as they are for the statistician.

---

* In this book sections and equations are numbered by a flexible system analogous to the Dewey Decimal System, which permits the inclusion of other sections and equations as they are needed.

0.43 The Periodogram

The process of obtaining the auto-correlation coefficient of a given sequence or function preserves certain information concerning the sequence or function and discards certain other information. The information preserved is such as to throw away all relations of phase of the frequency components and to preserve all information concerning their frequencies and amplitudes. For example when

$$f(t) = \sum a_n e^{i\lambda_n t} \tag{0.431}$$

we shall have

$$\lim_{T \to \infty} \frac{1}{2T} \int_{-T}^{T} f(t + \tau)\overline{f(t)}\, dt = \sum |a_n|^2 e^{i\lambda_n \tau}. \tag{0.432}$$

Thus the information given by the auto-correlation coefficient is of the same nature as the information given by the so-called periodogram of a sequence or function, in which we give the square of the amplitude of every trigonometrical component as the function of the frequencies by disregarding phase relations. However, the periodogram of a function in the narrowest sense, originally given to it by Sir Arthur Schuster, is concerned only with that part of the function which is actually the sum of a discrete set of trigonometric terms. The present author[†] has developed a form of periodogram theory in which not only the lines in the spectrum of a function of a sequence play a role but also that residue which is left after the removal of all sharply defined lines. More of this will be found in our first chapter. The periodogram theory as thus extended will be found to cover exactly the same ground as the theory of the auto-correlation coefficient. Similarly, an extension of this periodogram theory for pairs or other sets of several functions will be found to lie in close relation with the theory of cross-correlation.

As will be indicated by our discussion in Chapter I, one of the operations which is often performed on time series is the search by these methods or others for certain hidden periodicities. Except in a few cases when certain enthusiasts have taken these periodicities as ultimate realities, the purpose of the search for hidden periodicities is in some way to aid the extrapolation of time series either into the past or into the future. While this is the main purpose behind the periodogram analysis which plays so large a part in statistical literature, it is doubtful that we can find anywhere a thoroughly satisfactory statement of how such periodograms can be most effectively used in prediction. What we shall do in the present volume is to make a direct attack on the prediction

---

† Generalized Harmonic Analysis, *Acta Mathematica*, Vol. 55, pp. 117–258, 1930.

problem in which many of the same notions as those found in periodogram analysis will play a part, but we shall approach the question from the standpoint of determining the optimum method of prediction rather than from that of giving an independent weight to the problem of search for hidden periodicities.

The history of periodogram analysis is rather interesting in the light that it throws on the question of the bond between statistical theory and communication engineering. The method of periodogram analysis is due to the late Sir Arthur Schuster and had its origin in his researches in optics and in particular on the problem of coherency and incoherency in light. This statistical theory goes back to a physical origin closely related to communication engineering.

0.44 Operational Calculus

We now come to notions which belong to the repertory of the communications engineer as distinguished from the statistician. One of the first of these pieces of technique is the method of studying an electric circuit by ascertaining its response to an instantaneous switching on of a voltage or application of a current. This method, much pursued by the late J. B. Carson of the American Telephone and Telegraph Company, is perhaps the only method which is equally familiar to communications and to power engineers. As such it has played a large role in existing servo-mechanism technique. The functions obtained for these switching transients satisfy elementary systems of differential equations with constant coefficients and elementary initial or terminal conditions.

Equations of this sort have interested mathematicians from early times, because of the simple way in which many operators with constant coefficients are compounded, this composition amounting to a multiplication in elementary algebra, if we treat the differential operator d/dt as a quasi-number. While methods of this sort are at least as old as Laplace, the credit for developing them into a practical technique for circuit computation is unquestionably due to the late Oliver Heaviside. From about 1900 until 1930, Heaviside's methods dominated the whole of communications engineering technique, and their rigorous mathematical justification was a moot question in engineering circles. Towards the end of this period, however, several avenues of approach for the rigorous mathematical justification of the formal Heaviside calculus were found, and with this it came to be appreciated that Heaviside's work belonged directly together with the theory of the Laplace and Fourier integrals. The construction of a comprehensive table of Fourier transforms by Drs. Campbell and Foster of the Bell Telephone Laboratories almost at once replaced the Heaviside calculus by the classical

Fourier integral theory as the method of choice in communications engineering. This place the latter still holds.

0.45　The Fourier Integral; Need of the Complex Plane

If $f(t)$ is a function defined over the infinite interval then under certain circumstances the expression

$$g(\omega) = \frac{1}{\sqrt{2\pi}} \int_{-\infty}^{\infty} f(t)e^{-i\omega t}\, dt \tag{0.451}$$

exists, where ω also lies anywhere on the infinite line. Under certain somewhat more restricted circumstances not only does $g(\omega)$ exist but

$$f(t) = \frac{1}{\sqrt{2\pi}} \int_{-\infty}^{\infty} g(\omega)e^{i\omega t}\, d\omega. \tag{0.452}$$

The functions $f(t)$ and $g(\omega)$ are said to be Fourier transforms, each of the other, and the representation

$$f(t) = \frac{1}{2\pi} \int_{-\infty}^{\infty} e^{i\omega t}\, d\omega \int_{-\infty}^{\infty} f(s)e^{-i\omega s}\, ds \tag{0.453}$$

is said to be the Fourier integral representation of $f(t)$. There is a satisfactory Fourier integral theory which does not move from the axis of real values of ω. On the other hand, the study of $g(\omega)$ in a complex half-plane or even in the entire complex plane has proved to be very fruitful in electrical circuits. This was clearly seen by Bromwich, Doetsch, Wiener and others.‡ The use of the complex plane is intimately allied to the fact that physically applicable operators of engineering allow us to work with the past of our data, but not with their future. A somewhat different way of stating what amounts to the same thing is to assert that, in the discussion of vibrating systems, the position of singularities of certain associated functions expressed in the complex plane will determine whether these systems have oscillations which die out to zero or which grow to infinity. These considerations are familiar to everyone who has worked in filter theory, but they are far from familiar to the average statistician and have, until recently, played no part in the classical development of the theory of time series.

0.5　Time Series and Communication Engineering—The Synthesis

We are thus confronted with two groups of techniques, each of which is intrinsically relevant both to time-series work and to communications

‡ For these and other articles on this topic see Harold Jeffreys, *Operational Methods in Mathematical Physics*, 2nd Ed., Cambridge University Press, 1931, Bibl. pp. 114–117.

engineering. Methods involving probability theory and correlation are part of the traditional stock in trade of the statistician, but, on the other hand, the use of the complex plane is quite foreign to his training. The complex plane of function theory has a long history in communication technique, but statistical methods do not, and, as things stand at present, a man may be a practiced communications engineer without even being aware of their existence. Fourier methods belong partly to the repertory of each, for they occur in the theory of the periodogram and in the operational calculus, but they have been applied neither by the statistician nor by the communications engineer with a full awareness of their power. It is the purpose of this book to introduce methods leading from both these existing techniques and fusing them into a common technique which, in the opinion of the author, is more effective than either existing technique alone.

0.51 Prediction

Let us now consider some of the things which we can do with time series or messages. The simplest operation which we can perform is that of extrapolating them or, in other words, of prediction. This prediction, of course, does not in general give a precise continuation of a time series or message, for, if there is new information to come, this completely precludes an exact estimate of the future. In accordance with the statistical nature of time series, they are subject to a statistical prediction. This means that we estimate the continuation of a series, which, within certain limitations, is most probable, or at any rate the continuation of a series which minimizes some statistically determinable quantity known as the error. This consideration also applies to whatever other operations we can perform on time series.

0.52 Filtering

The next important operation on time series is that of purification or filtering. Very often the quantity which we really wish to observe is observable only·after it has been in some way corrupted or altered by mixture, additively or not, with other time series. It is of importance to ascertain as nearly as possible in an appropriate sense, that is, in a statistical sense, what our data would have been like without the contamination of the other time series. This may be the complete problem before us; or it may be combined with a prediction problem, which means that we should like to know what the uncontaminated time series will do in the future; or we may allow a certain amount of leeway in time and ask what the uncontaminated time series has done at a certain past epoch. This problem comes up in wave filtering. We have a message which is a time series, and a noise which is also a time series. If we seek that which we know concerning the message, which is not bound to a specific origin in time, we shall see that such information will generally be of a statistical nature; and this will likewise be true of our information of the same sort concerning the noise alone, or the noise and the message jointly. While this statistical information will in fact never be complete, as our information does not run indefinitely far back into the past, it is a legitimate simplification of the facts to assume that the available information runs back much further into the past than we are called upon to predict the future.

The usual electrical wave filter attempts to reproduce a message "in its purity," when the input is the sum of a message and a noise. In case the measure of the purity of a message is the mean power of its perturbation, and the apparatus allowed to us for filtering is of linear character, the desired statistical information concerning the noise and the message alone will be that furnished by their spectrum or periodogram. The extra information required concerning the two together is exactly that which may be derived from their cross correlation.

While the pure filtering problem is clearly distinguishable from the prediction problem, mixed problems involving elements of both are of great importance. The filter problem as we have described it is that in which a message is to be imitated without a time delay. In practical circuit problems, a uniform delay is not undesirable if it is not excessive, and the theory must be adapted to this fact. Indeed, good filter performance depends on the introduction of a delay. If the delay is negative, the performance suffers, but, on the other hand, the filter becomes a filtering predictor, which is often a useful instrument.

The problem of filtering may occur on a very different time level in mechanical circuits:—for example, if data are put into a circuit by the operation of a manual crank, it will frequently occur that cranking errors are in some way superimposed on the true data and must be eliminated to prevent the harm they may do to the future interpretability of these data. Even in statistical time series given purely numerically, it is not always possible to eliminate errors in the collection of the data values, and it is often necessary to resort to a mathematical method intended to minimize the effect of these errors after the data have been collected.

0.53 Policy Problems

The time-series problems of prediction and filtering have one aspect in common which we may cover by saying that they are extrinsical. They operate on data which have been collected completely, and do not give us direct information as to how these data might have been altered if we had made some humanly possible variation in the system in which these data occurred. Opposed to this use of time series, or at least apparently opposed, is what we may call the intrinsic study of time series. For example, we may wish to ascertain how certain series dealing with the economics of a country might have been changed if a different system of taxation had been adopted, or we may wish to know the expected effect of a new dam in a river system on the statistics of floods. Questions of this sort are often called questions of policy. Let it be noted that in the long run questions of policy, although they depend on what we may call the dynamics rather than the kinematics of the systems to which they pertain, deal with a dynamics which, after all, itself can only be determined statistically. In this sense, what is an intrinsic problem for a single series or a small collection of series may prove to be an extrinsic problem if we are dealing with a sufficiently complicated multiple time series. Thus the distinction between extrinsic and intrinsic problems, while important, may not be considered absolute.

0.6 Permissible Operators: Translation Group in Time

The theory of the proper treatment of time series involves the selection of certain operators on time series from among all possible operators, or at least from a subsidiary class of possible operators. One requirement on such operators is immediate. If we are dealing with any field of science where long-time observations are possible and where experiments can be repeated, it is desirable that our operations be not tied to any specific origin in time. If a certain experiment started at ten o'clock today would give a certain distribution of results by twelve o'clock, then we must expect that if this experiment is carried out under similar conditions at ten o'clock tomorrow, by twelve o'clock we should get the same distribution of results. Without at least an approximate repeatability of experiments, no comparisons of results at different times are possible, and there can be no science. *That is, the operators which come into consideration are invariant under a shift in the origin of time.* These shifts can be combined in such a way that the result of two consecutive shifts is a shift, while the inverse of a shift is a shift. In mathematical language, they constitute a *group*, known as the translation group in time. In other words, the allowable operators must be invariant with respect to the translation group in time. We shall assume that, even where this is not strictly the case, as may occur in economic data owing to the extreme variability of their background, some attempt has been made to eliminate the trends and drifts before the methods of this book are applied.

0.61   Past and Future

Not every operator invariant under the translation group is allowed. We have said already that, while the past of a time series is accessible for examination, its future is not. That means that our operators must have an inherent certain one-sidedness. In the case of linear operators, an adequate theory of these one-sided operators is in existence. In the general non-linear case, much remains to be done in this direction.

0.62   Subclasses of Operators

We have just spoken of linear operators. In this connection, the operators which are allowed to us for a given task of prediction or filtering or policy prescription are not always the complete class of all conceivable operators. Either in order to facilitate computation or on account of the present imperfection of engineering techniques of realization we may have to restrict ourselves to a much narrower class. One such restricted class is that of all linear operators; or, better stated, all linear operators depending only on the past and invariant under translation. This is a class for which the theory and computation are particularly easy, and it is also a class for which adequate electrical and mechanical realizations are at hand. However, there are times when we may not be at liberty to restrict ourselves to this task, as well as times in which, for reasons of technical convenience, we may not have this full class at our disposal.

Even the class of linear operators invariant under a translation in time and not referring to the future of a function is a class containing widely diverse members. For example, the operators on $f(t)$ yielding

$$f(t); \quad 3f(t-5); \quad f'(t-2); \quad \tfrac{1}{2}f'(t) + \tfrac{1}{2}f(t);$$

$$\int_0^\infty f(t-s)e^{-s}\,ds$$

are all examples of such operators. On the other hand, the operators yielding

$$[f(t)]^2; \quad \frac{f'(t)}{f(t)}; \quad \int_0^\infty \int_0^\infty f(s)f(t)K(s-t)\,ds\,dt$$

are not linear; that yielding

$$\int_{-\infty}^\infty f(t-s)e^{-s^2}\,ds$$

depends in fact on the future of $f(t)$; and that yielding

$$tf(t)$$

is not invariant under the translation group, since

$$(t + 5)f(t + 5) \neq tf(t + 5).$$

0.7 Norms and Minimization

The task of determining the best operator for a particular purpose depends on the definition of "best." One very general type of such definitions is that in which we assign a certain quantity as the error of performance of our operator, and then seek to choose our operator from the admissible class in such a way that the error it produces is as small as possible. Thus the best operator for prediction will be that which minimizes the numerical measure of the difference between the actual future of a time series and its predicted future. This numerical measure should itself not be tied to an origin in time and should be a single quantity even though the difference which it measures is that between two functions.

The numerical measure of an error we shall call its *norm*. The desired conditions for a norm are the following:

First, the norm must always be a positive quantity, or zero.
Second, the norm must be positive whenever an error exists and zero whenever an error does not exist.

The simplest types of norm to fulfill these conditions are what we may call the *quadratic* norms. Such a norm depends upon the error in such a way that when we multiply the error by $\pm A$ we multiply its norm by A^2.

The quadratic norm of a voltage which is a function of the time is, on a proper scale, a quantity of the nature of *power*. The quadratic norm of the error of a message determines the power of the correcting message. It is this that gives quadratic norms their physical importance.

These norms are not the only ones which are possible. For example, we may have third- or fourth-power norms.

We thus have specified the problem of prediction or filtering or policy-prescription control as the selection of an operator from among a certain admissible class, in such a way that some "error quantity" (which estimates the degree by which our statement of the problem is not perfectly solved) shall be minimized. If a minimization problem is carried out in a system of a finite number of degrees of freedom, it belongs to the ordinary differential calculus. If the system of operations over which we have to minimize is more extensive than such a system (of a finite number of degrees of freedom), the problem of minimization belongs to the calculus of variations of Euler and Lagrange or, at any rate, to one of its extensions. Let it be noted that the more general minimization problems which may arise in the work under discussion go well beyond the calculus of variations as it is commonly defined at present, since the quantity our problem requires us to minimize may be determined, not by a function which is in the ordinary sense defined in a space of a finite number of degrees of freedom, but by a functional operation involving the entire past of the functions with which we are dealing and not reducible to one which is restricted to a space of a finite number of degrees of freedom.

0.71 The Calculus of Variations

Every minimization problem demands a set of variable entities (numbers, vectors, functions) over which the desired minimization is to be performed. The set of functions afforded for minimization purposes should have at least this one property, that the sum of any two functions or operators should also belong to the set. Let us then symbolically represent such an operator by the symbol Op and another operator which we shall call its variation by the symbol δOp. Let us consider the restricted class of operators given by Op $+$ $\epsilon\delta$Op. In this the quantity ϵ is a real quantity which may be varied at will. Let the norm of the error resulting from the use of Op $+$ $\epsilon\delta$Op be n(Op $+$ $\epsilon\delta$Op). If we are to select Op in such a way that n(Op $+$ δOp) is to be a minimum when δOp $= 0$, we must a fortiori minimize n(Op $+$ $\epsilon\delta$Op) at $\epsilon = 0$ for every choice of δOp. Note that it does not immediately follow that to minimize n(Op $+$ $\epsilon\delta$Op) for every choice of ϵ will result in a complete solution of the minimization problem with a free choice of the operator throughout our entire field of operators, but this limited minimization is "at least" necessary. This minimization, depending on ϵ, is of the same nature as the familiar minimizations of functions of a single variable which we find in the classical differential calculus. In the ordinary calculus, if we are minimizing a quantity having everywhere a derivative which is continuous, and if we can in one way or another eliminate from consideration the boundary values of our parameter, then the minimum of our dependent quantity is attained at a point where its derivative with respect to the independent quantity vanishes. Such a point is called a stationary point. It is, of course, not true that every stationary point is even a local minimum or maximum in the sense that it is a minimum or maximum for near-by values. It is even less true that a local minimum or maximum need be an absolute minimum or maximum. If, however, we have other evidence for the existence of one and only one minimum in the interior of the region considered, and if we have found a stationary point in this region, then the stationary point must be the minimum in question. *Therefore, the first stage in the investigation of minima is the search for stationary points.*

In the present case, this leads to the system of equations

$$\frac{d}{d\epsilon} n(\text{Op} + \epsilon\delta\text{Op}) = 0 \quad \text{when} \quad \epsilon = 0 \quad (0.711)$$

for all admissible δOp.

This system of equations may often be reduced to a single equation in which δOp does not appear explicitly. However, as we have stated above, such an equation must be supplemented by a further investigation to determine whether it yields a solution which is a true absolute minimum. Furthermore, there will be cases in which the equation has no solution satisfying the conditions which we have originally set up for the class of functions in terms of which the original minimization was to have been performed. In other words, we may have accidentally selected a class of operators which permits us to make the norm of our error as near its minimum value as we wish, but will not permit it actually to assume this value. It may or may not be possible to remove this difficulty by assuming a more comprehensive class of admissible operators to begin with. Even if this cannot be done, this does not mean that the whole problem of minimization has become trifling. In the absence of a true optimum method of determining a prediction or filtering operator, it is often of practical value to determine an operator which will produce as the norm of the error a value arbitrarily near its minimum. In many cases this can be done by tying up the minimization problem with a related problem having slightly differing conditions, in which a true minimum exists. We shall have occasion to do exactly this.

0.8 Ergodic Theory

Before taking up concrete prediction or filtering problems, it is worth while to discuss the general statistical nature of time series and certain statistical parameters relative to such series. If a time series is not tied down to a specific origin in time and is conceived to run from minus infinity to infinity in time, then any statistical distribution of such series will not be affected by a shift of the origin of time. This means that such a shift comprises a transformation of one time series into another time series which in general alters the individual series and changes any set of time series for which a well-defined probability exists into another set of different time series, but with the same probability. Without here entering upon the analytic refinements essential to a definition of Lebesgue measure, it may be said that Lebesgue measure is a technical term for a concept agreeing in all essential characters with probability, and that we have a situation in which every shift in our time scale by a real additive constant (or an integer additive constant, as the case may be) generates a probability-preserving (or measure-preserving) transformation of a set of contingencies into itself.

We are thus confronted with the identical situation contemplated by the so-called ergodic theorem of Professor G. D. Birkhoff. The term "ergodic" has an interesting history in the literature of statistical mechanics. The problem with which it is associated is that of the relation between phase averages and time averages. It was essential for the statistical mechanics of Willard Gibbs that some means be found to identify averages concerning the consecutive positions of a dynamical system of a certain sort with averages concerning all systems at a certain energy level. The first method suggested for making this identification was to assume that such a system in time would assume all positions compatible with the energy level in question. This assumption, however, is completely inadequate to the conclusions drawn from it; and, even worse, it can never be satisfied save in trivial cases. The suggested weakened hypothesis, that the system in course of time passes arbitrarily near every possible position, is not contradictory but is inadequate to the derivation of any significant conclusion. The correct theorem of Birkhoff, in the language of probability, reads as follows: Let Σ be a set of contingencies of finite probability. Let T be a transformation turning a contingency P into a contingency TP, and let it leave the set of contingencies Σ unaltered. If Σ_1 is a set of contingencies contained in Σ, for which a probability exists, and $T\Sigma_1$ is the set of its transforms by T, let the probability of Σ_1 be the same as that of $T\Sigma_1$. Let $|F(P)|$ have an average over Σ. Then, except for a set of contingencies P of zero probability, the limit

$$\lim_{N \to \infty} \frac{1}{N+1} \sum_{n=0}^{N} F(T^n P) \qquad (0.80)$$

will have a definite value.

In this case we have been considering the transformation T and its powers. It is possible to introduce the notion of the fractional powers of a transformation T. Let T^λ be a measure preserving transformation no matter whether the value of λ is positive, negative, or zero, so long as it is real. Let $T^\lambda(T^\mu P)$ always be equal to $T^{\lambda+\mu}P$. Let us make an auxiliary assumption, of interest only to the pure mathematician, to the effect that $T^\lambda P$ is measurable in both λ and P. Let $\int_\Sigma |F(P)| \, dV_P < \infty$, where dV_P signifies integration with respect to volume for the point P. Then Birkhoff's theorem is to the effect that the limit

$$(0.8005)$$

will almost always exist in the sense that the probability that a point P should lie in a set for which this limit does not exist is 0.

To go back to the discrete case, let us consider the time series $\cdots$, $a_{-n}, \cdots, a_0, \cdots, a_n, \cdots$. In this time series let the particular numbers themselves depend upon some quantity α which we shall call the parameter of distribution and which we shall take to lie between 0 and 1. In other words, let us not consider the individual time series $\{a_n\}$, but rather a statistical distribution of time series $\{a_n(\alpha)\}$. Let any set of time series for which this parameter of distribution α lies on a set S_1 (of values with probability p) go into another set for which the parameter α lies on a set S_2 (of values with the same probability p), when each a_n goes into a_{n+1}. In a language often used in statistical theory we shall say that the time series is *stationary*. Furthermore, let the average of $|a_0{}^2|$ with respect to the parameter α be finite. Then Birkhoff's theorem for the discrete case tells us that, except for a set of values of α of zero probability, the so-called auto-correlation

$$\lim_{N \to \infty} \frac{1}{2N+1} \sum_{n=-N}^{N} a_{n+k}\bar{a}_n \qquad (0.801)$$

will exist (for all k) and be finite.

If we have two distinct time series, that of the a_n's and a similar one of the b_n's dependent on the same parameter of distribution α, and if the means with respect to α of $|a_0|^2$ and $|b_0{}^2|$ both are finite, and if the same transformation of α generates the change of a_n into a_{n+1} and the change of b_n into b_{n+1}, then, except for a set of values for α of zero probability, the cross-correlation between the a's and the b's

$$\lim_{N \to \infty} \frac{1}{2N+1} \sum_{n=-N}^{N} a_{n+k}\bar{b}_n \qquad (0.803)$$

will also exist (for all k) and be finite.

The notion of stationary time series will apply as well to continuous series of data as to discrete series of data. A continuous time series dependent on a parameter α may be written in the form $f(t, \alpha)$. Let us consider the case in which

$$f(t + \tau, \alpha) = f(t, T^\tau\alpha),$$

where the transformation T^τ preserves probability in α. Let

$$\int_0^1 |f(0, \alpha)|^2 \, d\alpha < \infty. \qquad (0.804)$$

shown

the limit

$$\lim_{T \to \infty} \frac{1}{2T} \int_{-T}^{T} f(t + \tau, \alpha)\overline{f(t, \alpha)} \, dt \qquad (0.806)$$

will exist and have a definite finite value. Similarly, an analogous result to (0.803) will hold when we consider two continuous stationary time series dependent on the same parameter of distribution.

At this point there is a new matter which deserves a little discussion. It is a well-known fact of measure theory that a denumerable set of contingencies of zero probability, that is, a set of contingencies which can be exhausted by an arrangement in $1, 2, 3, \cdots$, order, adds up to a set of contingencies which is itself of zero probability. From this it follows that, if we prove the limit (0.801) to exist except for a set of cases of zero probability for each k independently, then it exists except for a set of cases of zero probability for all k's simultaneously. If, however, we refer to formula (0.806), it does not follow that, if that limit exists for almost all values of α for each τ independently, it exists for almost all values of α simultaneously for all values of τ. Nevertheless it can be proved mathematically that the limit (0.806) does, in fact, exist for all τ at the same time, for almost all α.

Let us remark that stationary time series have properties other than those of auto-correlation coefficients which may be proved to exist for almost all values of α by means of the ergodic theory. For example let

$$f(t + \tau_1, \alpha)f(t + \tau_2, \alpha) \cdots f(t + \tau_n, \alpha) \qquad (0.808)$$

be absolutely integrable over the range $(0, 1)$ of α. The average

$$\lim_{T \to \infty} \frac{1}{2T} \int_{-T}^{T} f(t + \tau_1, \alpha) \cdots f(t + \tau_n, \alpha) \, dt \qquad (0.8085)$$

will exist for almost all values of α. It may be shown that quantities such as (0.808) constitute in a certain sense a complete set of parameters of a stationary time series, but in this book we shall not deal with this remark in any detail.

A particular class of measure-preserving transformation of α into itself is that in which no set of values of α (of probability other than 1 or zero) is transformed into itself under the transformation T or the set of transformations T^λ, respectively. Similarly, in the continuous case we may have a situation where no set of values of α of measure other than 1 or zero is transformed into itself by all the transformations T^λ. In these cases the transformation T is said to be *ergodic* or *metrically transitive*. If T is an ergodic transformation, and F is a function whose absolute value is integrable, then, except for a set of values of P of probability zero, we may show that

$$\lim_{N \to \infty} \frac{1}{N+1} \sum_{0}^{N} F(T^n P) = \int_{\Sigma} F(P) \, dV_P.$$ **(0.809)**

Similarly, if T^λ represents an **ergodic group of measure-preserving transformations** such that

$$T^\lambda(T^\mu P) = (T^{\lambda+\mu} P)$$ **(0.8091)**

and

$$\int_{\Sigma} F(P) \, dV_P = A,$$ **(0.8092)**

then for almost all elements P we have

$$\lim_{T \to \infty} \frac{1}{T} \int_{0}^{T} F(T^\lambda P) \, d\lambda = A.$$ **(0.8093)**

It may thus be shown that in the ergodic case we have

$$\lim_{T \to \infty} \frac{1}{T} \int_{0}^{T} F(T^\lambda P) \, d\lambda = \lim_{T \to \infty} \frac{1}{T} \int_{-T}^{0} F(T^\lambda P) \, d\lambda$$

$$= \lim_{T \to \infty} \frac{1}{2T} \int_{-T}^{T} F(T^\lambda P) \, d\lambda,$$ **(0.8094)**

for almost all elements P. It may also be shown that in the non-ergodic case the measure-preserving transformation may in a certain sense be resolved into ergodic components. From this it is not hard to conclude that formula (0.8094) is also valid in the non-ergodic case for almost all elements P. Thus in the case of auto-correlation coefficients we almost always have

$$\lim_{T \to \infty} \frac{1}{2T} \int_{-T}^{T} f(t + \tau, \alpha) \overline{f(t, \alpha)} \, dt$$

$$= \lim_{T \to \infty} \frac{1}{T} \int_{-T}^{\text{lesser of } (0, -\tau)} f(t + \tau, \alpha) \overline{f(t, \alpha)} \, dt,$$ **(0.8095)**

in the sense that the probability that α be a value for which this is not true is zero. This enables us to make the inductive inference from an expression

$$\lim_{T \to \infty} \frac{1}{T} \int_{-T}^{\text{lesser of } (0, -\tau)} f(t + \tau, \alpha) \overline{f(t, \alpha)} \, dt,$$ **(0.8096)**

determined only by the past of the function $f(t, \alpha)$, to an auto-correlation

$$\lim_{T \to \infty} \int_{-T}^{T} f(t + \tau, \alpha) \overline{f(t, \alpha)} \, dt,$$ **(0.8097)**

which strictly involves an investigation of both the past and the future. We shall find this conclusion of vital importance in the process of prediction, as well as the exactly similar conclusions for pairs of functions, f and g, and for the discrete case.

0.81 Brownian Motion

Let us now look for examples of stationary time series as they are found in nature. For such stationary time series to be really interesting from the standpoint of communication engineering, it is essential that their future be only incompletely determined by their past. This immediately excludes such time series as are generated by the solutions of the wave equations or similar partial differential equations in systems where some sort of analyticity is presupposed for the instantaneous data. For a long time all physical time series were supposed to be of this sort. However, with the progress of the microscope, it became obvious that small particles sustained in a liquid or gas were subject to a random motion whose future was largely unpredictable from its past.§ If a particle is kicked about by the molecules of gas or liquid, it describes a path which may be characterized approximately in the following way: The X, Y, and Z components of the motion of the particle are completely independent each of the other. Taking any single component, the amount of change which it is likely to make in a given time has a distribution completely independent of the amount of change which it makes in an interval of time not overlapping this. The distribution of this amount of change in a given time is what is known as Gaussian; that is, the probability that the displacement of the particle in time t should lie between x and $x + dx$ will be of the form

$$\frac{1}{\sqrt{2\pi\rho t}}\, e^{-x^2/2\rho t}\, dx, \tag{0.811}$$

where the quantity ρ depends upon the medium in which the particle is suspended as well as the mass and size of the particle and the temperature. The theory of this ensemble of functions has been given by the present author,‖ and it appears that, although the ensemble is not strictly a time series in that the origin of reference changes with the time, there are related to it time series having the ergodic property. If in a Brownian motion we consider not the position at a given time but instead sets of positions at more than two times, and then take only their differences, then the distribution of Brownian motions over an appreciable

§ J. Perrin, *Les atomes*, 4th Ed., Paris, 1931.
‖ Generalized Harmonic Analysis, *Acta Mathematica*, Vol. 55, 1930.

interval is unchanged by a shift in the origin of time. Therefore, if we take any property of a Brownian motion independent of the absolute position of this motion, we shall generate a time series having the ergodic property.

A particular example of this results from the response of a linear resonator to a Brownian input. ¶ We shall present the harmonic analysis of the response of a resonator to the Brownian motion and thus shall generate a definite form of statistical ensemble, subject to a specific theory of anticipation or filtering.

0.9 Summary of Chapters

There are other theories of random distribution besides the Brownian theory, which likewise are subject to definite techniques of analysis. In the discrete case the ensemble of sequences $\{a_n\}$ (where each a_n is uniformly distributed over some interval, in complete independence of all other a_m's, and the transformation T changes a sequence by adding 1 to the index n of each term) is an example in point. Again, in the continuous case, the Poisson distribution (which may be described as the distribution of bullet holes on a remote target, when taken in the one-dimensional case on an infinite line) yields a distribution of patterns which is invariant under time translation and serves as the basis of a prediction or filtering theory. These instances will be discussed in Chapter I, together with a large number of other mathematical notions which are indispensable for a comprehension of what is to follow. These cover in particular much material from the author's book, *The Fourier Integral* (Cambridge, 1933); his joint Colloquium tract with the late R.E.A.C. Paley, *Fourier Transforms in the Complex Domain* (New York, 1934); and his memoir, Generalized Harmonic Analysis, in *Acta Mathematica* (1930). In the present book, proofs are in general not given, but the main significant results are summarized.

Chapter II of this text is devoted solely to the discussion of the prediction problem for a single stationary time series. We shall discuss both continuous and discrete series and shall illustrate them by a number of examples. We shall show (a) that a certain method which we present is an optimum linear method for minimizing a mean square prediction error, and that the only statistical parameter which is required concerning the time series on which it operates is the auto-correlation coefficient of the series. We shall further show (b) that the result is an absolute optimum in comparison with any alternative method, linear or non-linear, when the time series to which it applies is obtained as the response of a linear

¶ We shall have something to say of non-linear resonators, but at present their theory is far from complete.

resonator to a Brownian input, as for example by the response of a linear electric circuit to a shot effect. Actually to avoid duplication of material we shall chiefly discuss (a) in Chapter II and (b) in Chapter III. We shall discuss the technical difficulties of the prediction problem in the presence of disturbing lines in the spectrum or of other non-absolutely continuous parts of the spectrum, or when the past of the function to be predicted completely determines its future; and in at least one case we shall observe how the validity of a long-time prediction changes with a change of the auto-correlation coefficient. We shall also consider how the prediction problem is altered when the predicting operator is built up as the sum of a denumerable or finite set of multiples of previously assigned operators.

In Chapter III we proceed to the filter problem, which we treat along the same lines as we use for the prediction problem in Chapter II. Except for the detailed changes of formulas, there is little difference between the steps taken in designing a prediction filter (or a filter with lead) and a predictor which has no specified filtering function. In the case of a filter with lag the design problem is a little more complicated. The filter with lag is the conventional type, because where a modest, uniform phase shift is not objectionable, more precise results can be obtained by a lagging filter than by a non-lagging filter. In the case of the lagging filter we are faced with the additional problem of simulating a lag operator $e^{-i\beta\omega}$ by a rational function.* The problem of realization takes one into the theory of equivalent networks as developed by Guillemin and others. In the design of the general four-terminal network, it is not enough to realize the transfer voltage ratio. There is also the question of the matching of input and output impedances with those of the circuits out of which and into which the filter works. Important as these problems are, they carry one far away from the general considerations of this tract and may best be treated elsewhere.

With the restriction to the determination of the characteristic of a filter as a rational function, we may still say much that is concrete on the design of filters according to our method. The filter with very great delay, and its intrinsic error; the effect of lag on improving filter characteristics, and the method whereby this lag should be decided; the algebraic computation of the characteristic of a filter, and the basis for determining this—all these can be handled in terms of rational voltage ratios, without pursuing the theory of equivalent structures into any detail. We shall also have something to say on the filter whose function

---

* The emphasis put on rational functions here is of course not a matter of mathematical formalism alone, but is of essential importance in the actual realization in the field of a finite electrical or mechanical structure.

is to detect a very faint message in the presence of a nearly overwhelming noise.

Up to this point, we have been considering predictors and filters for use in time series consisting of single numerical sequences of data, whether these sequences be discrete or continuous. In Chapter IV, we proceed to consider multiple time series and, in particular, double time series, both from the point of view of filtering and from that of prediction, with greater emphasis on the latter point of view. Such series occasionally make their appearance in engineering applications of the theory, but they are most conspicuous in the statistical applications, both economico-sociological and meteorologico-geophysical, since in both instances the relative lead of one time series with respect to another may well give much more information concerning the past of the second than of its own. For example, on account of the general eastward movement of the weather, Chicago weather may well be more important in the forecasting of Boston weather than Boston weather itself. Accordingly, we give much prominence here to the discrete case of forecasting. The methods of this chapter, as might easily be anticipated, make much use of the method of undetermined coefficients and of the linear equations (in a finite number of variables) to which these give rise.

Prediction and filtering do not exhaust the capacity of our methods. They may be applied whenever an ideally desirable linear operation on a statistically uniform time series is in fact not strictly realizable, although an approximation may be realized. Two problems of this sort are those of obtaining a derivative of the first or of higher order from data that have been corrupted by additive errors of known spectrum and known statistical relation to the message, and that of interpolating a continuous function between the discrete values of a time series of known statistical character. The first of these applications is of very practical use in the design of servo-mechanisms, where a derivative computed on too short a base of Δt will be so erratic as to be of no value, while a derivative computed on too long a base will discard much valuable information. The interpolation problem is interesting as leading to a formula identical in appearance with that employed for extrapolation. These matters are taken up in Chapter V, our last chapter. At the end of the entire discussion, we give a table of Laguerre functions.

The unity of this book is methodological. It represents an attempt to use Fourier methods so as to take significant advantage of the way in which "before" and "after" enter into the translation group in time. It does not pretend to have drained this field dry. It is the hope of the author that those to whose attention it comes, and who find either new pure mathematical developments connected with the topics discussed or new fields of application in which the methods may be useful, will bring them to his attention. This applies to any criticisms of the entire book, either in what concerns the validity of its mathematical methods or in the appropriateness and usefulness of its applications to engineering or statistics.

CHAPTER I

RÉSUMÉ OF FUNDAMENTAL MATHEMATICAL
NOTIONS

1.00 Fourier Series

The realization of the objectives which we have stated at the end of
the introductory chapter will require a fairly elaborate mathematical
technique. This technique is available in the literature and in particular
in two books in which the author has participated. The first of these is
his book, *The Fourier Integral*,* and the second (done in collaboration
with the late R.E.A.C. Paley of Cambridge University) is entitled,
Fourier Transforms in the Complex Domain.† As will be seen, the word
"Fourier" appears in the titles of both books. We have already stated
that the intrinsic invariance of our problems with respect to a translation
in time, combined with their linear character, makes a recourse to Fourier
theory inevitable. However, the conventional textbooks on Fourier
developments devote much more time to what is to us the secondary
case of the Fourier series than to the Fourier integral; and, even in the
case of the Fourier integral, they fail to treat of its extension to functions
which, instead of tending to zero as their argument becomes infinite,
keep up the same average power level over an infinite time.

Since this chapter is a résumé of the existing theory, it may be better
for the reader who first approaches the subject to use it for purposes of
reference only, proceeding directly to Chapter II, and when in the course
of the argument a notion comes up which demands reference to a syllabus
of formulae, to return to the appropriate part of Chapter I. It would
have been perfectly possible to eliminate this chapter from the treatment
of our subject, for those readers to whom an adequate mathematical
library was available, containing the texts already mentioned. Since,
however, in the majority of cases in which this volume will be of use
such libraries will not be available, and since the books referred to are
not sufficiently generally used in routine mathematical education to
enable us to assume that any large fraction of the readers of this work
will possess them as relics of their own mathematical training, we have
no alternative but to present this chapter in full.

* Cambridge, 1933.
† American Mathematical Society Colloquium Publication, Vol. 19, 1934.

We repeat that, owing to the very nature of the problems considered, this book makes extensive use of methods of Fourier or trigonometrical analysis, and that this is due to the fact that these problems are not tied to any origin or epoch but are invariant under a displacement of time, in the sense that, if we start a time series late by the interval of time T, we shall also start any prediction, or the result of any filtering, late by the same time interval T. This statement simply asserts the repeatability of our methods and is indeed a necessary condition for the existence of any scientific theory whatever. A scientific theory bound to an origin in time, and not freed from it by some special mathematical technique, is a theory in which there is no legitimate inference from the past to the future. If scientific investigation were a game with the world, in which all rules were subject to a future revision unknown to us, it would scarcely be a game worth playing. A dependence on starting time connotes such a change in the rules.

This mode of invariance under a translation of the origin in time is indeed shown by Newtonian laws of mechanics, the laws of heat flow, the laws of electrical flow, the Maxwell equation, etc. It is expressed by the fact that they lead to differential equations with coefficients constant in the time.

Besides this general property of the objectives of this book, we shall here confine ourselves to *linear* problems of filtering or prediction. We are thus interested in additive classes of functions, which are not tied to any fixed origin in time. Here we deal with phenomena where added causes produce added effects. An extremely simple class of this sort is the set of functions

$$ae^{i\omega t}$$

for

$$ae^{i\omega(t+\tau)} = ae^{i\omega\tau}e^{i\omega t}.$$

Indeed these two properties, that of invariance and that of linearity, are completely diagnostic of the field in which a linear analysis into trigonometric terms $e^{i\omega t}$ is appropriate.

The simplest representation of a function by linearly additive trigonometric terms is that found in the theory of Fourier series. Let $f(t)$ be a (possibly complex valued) integrable function defined over the interval $(-\pi, \pi)$.‡ Then, formally, its approximation by a Fourier series will be

$$\frac{1}{2\pi} \sum_{-\infty}^{\infty} e^{int} \int_{-\pi}^{\pi} f(x)e^{-inx}\, dx \cong f(t). \qquad (1.000)$$

‡ Any interval may be chosen, but this is a convenient normalization of the desired interval.

This formal series need not converge everywhere, and, even if it should fail to converge anywhere, it may still be useful. If the square of the modulus of f as well as f itself is integrable, and we form the quadratic norm

$$\int_{-\pi}^{\pi} \left| f(t) - \sum_{-N}^{N} a_n e^{int} \right|^2 dt = \epsilon_N, \qquad (1.0005)$$

this will have the expansion

$$\int_{-\pi}^{\pi} |f(t)|^2 dt - 2\mathrm{R} \left\{ \sum_{-N}^{N} a_n \int_{-\pi}^{\pi} \overline{f(t)} e^{int} dt \right\}$$
$$+ \sum_{m=-M}^{N} \sum_{n=-N}^{N} a_m \bar{a}_n \int_{-\pi}^{\pi} e^{i(m-n)t} dt; \qquad (1.001)$$

and since

$$\int_{-\pi}^{\pi} dt = 2\pi; \qquad \int_{-\pi}^{\pi} e^{i\nu t} dt = \frac{e^{i\nu\pi} - e^{-i\nu\pi}}{i\nu}$$
$$= 0 \text{ if } \nu \text{ is an integer other than } 0, \qquad (1.0015)$$

this expansion (1.001) may be written

$$\int_{-\pi}^{\pi} |f(t)|^2 dt - 2\mathrm{R} \left\{ \sum_{-N}^{N} a_n \int_{-\pi}^{\pi} \overline{f(t)} e^{int} dt \right\} + 2\pi \sum_{-N}^{N} |a_n|^2$$
$$= \int_{-\pi}^{\pi} |f(t)|^2 dt - \frac{1}{2\pi} \sum_{-N}^{N} \left| \int_{-\pi}^{\pi} f(t) e^{-int} dt \right|^2$$
$$+ 2\pi \sum_{-N}^{N} \left| a_n - \frac{1}{2\pi} \int_{-\pi}^{\pi} f(t) e^{-int} dt \right|^2. \qquad (1.002)$$

This expression is by inspection a minimum when and only when

$$a_n = \frac{1}{2\pi} \int_{-\pi}^{\pi} f(t) e^{-int} dt \quad (-N \leq n \leq N), \qquad (1.0025)$$

where it should be noted that the value of a_n is the familiar Fourier coefficient and is independent of N. This minimum remainder value will then be

$$\int_{-\pi}^{\pi} |f(t)|^2 dt - \frac{1}{2\pi} \sum_{-N}^{N} \left| \int_{-\pi}^{\pi} f(t) e^{-int} dt \right|^2, \qquad (1.003)$$

which is always positive as it is the integral of the square of a modulus. Clearly this minimum expression will decrease as N becomes infinite. That it will decrease to zero may not be immediately concluded but may be proved to be true. This fact is known as the Parseval theorem and is equivalent to the fact that a_n as prescribed in (1.0025) minimizes the expression set up by (1.0005) as $N \to \infty$.

An extremely important mathematical lemma which is useful and may now be discussed is that of Schwarz. Let $f(t)$ and $g(t)$ be real, integrable, and of integrable absolute square over the interval $-\pi$ to $+\pi$. Then the quadratic polynomial in λ

$$\int_{-\pi}^{\pi} [f(t) + \lambda g(t)]^2 \, dt = \int_{-\pi}^{\pi} [f(t)]^2 \, dt + 2\lambda \int_{-\pi}^{\pi} f(t)g(t) \, dt$$
$$+ \lambda^2 \int_{-\pi}^{\pi} [g(t)]^2 \, dt \quad (1.0035)$$

is always positive or zero regardless of the value of λ, and the equation

$$\int_{-\pi}^{\pi} [f(t)]^2 \, dt + 2\lambda \int_{-\pi}^{\pi} f(t)g(t) \, dt + \lambda^2 \int_{-\pi}^{\pi} [g(t)]^2 \, dt = 0 \quad (1.004)$$

cannot have distinct real roots. If we write the equation

$$c + b\lambda + a\lambda^2 = 0$$

the discriminant $b^2 - 4ac$ cannot be positive, and

$$\left[\int_{-\pi}^{\pi} f(t)g(t) \, dt \right]^2 \leq \int_{-\pi}^{\pi} [f(t)]^2 \, dt \int_{-\pi}^{\pi} [g(t)]^2 \, dt. \quad (1.0045)$$

As an immediate consequence, even if $f(t)$ and $g(t)$ are complex,

$$\left| \int_{-\pi}^{\pi} f(t)g(t) \, dt \right| \leq \left\{ \int_{-\pi}^{\pi} |f(t)|^2 \, dt \int_{-\pi}^{\pi} |g(t)|^2 \, dt \right\}^{\frac{1}{2}}. \quad (1.005)$$

This is the *Schwarz inequality*.

Let us now apply the Schwarz inequality to a convergence problem of interest in the study of Fourier series. Up to the present we have been treating the Fourier series as a purely formal expression without any regard to whether it converges or not. We shall use the Fourier series and other similar trigonometrical developments to represent physical quantities as functions of the time t or whatever other variable we indicate by t. Now it is obvious that no physical quantity can be observed for a single precise value of t. No watch or other chronometer is accurate enough to isolate an instant, but can only isolate a small but positive interval of time. Thus all functions of t are for the physicist averages over small ranges of t rather than values at a precise point of t. Therefore it is important to discuss how such averages behave and how they can be expressed in terms of the formal series (1.000). Now we have shown that, if $f(t)$ is integrable and of integrable absolute square, we shall have

$$\lim_{N \to \infty} \int_{-\pi}^{\pi} \left| f(t) - \frac{1}{2\pi} \sum_{-N}^{N} e^{int} \int_{-\pi}^{\pi} f(x)e^{-inx} \, dx \right|^2 dt$$
$$= \lim_{N \to \infty} \epsilon_N = 0. \quad (1.0055)$$

Thus, by the Schwarz inequality, if $g(t)$ is also integrable and of integrable absolute square

$$\lim_{N \to \infty} \int_{-\pi}^{\pi} \left\{ f(t) - \frac{1}{2\pi} \sum_{-N}^{N} e^{int} \int_{-\pi}^{\pi} f(x) e^{-inx} \, dx \right\} g(t) \, dt = 0. \quad (1.006)$$

That is,

$$\int_{-\pi}^{\pi} f(t) g(t) \, dt = \lim_{N \to \infty} \frac{1}{2\pi} \sum_{-N}^{N} \int_{-\pi}^{\pi} g(t) e^{int} \, dt \int_{-\pi}^{\pi} f(x) e^{-inx} \, dx. \quad (1.0065)$$

In other words, the series

$$f(t) \cong \frac{1}{2\pi} \sum_{n=-\infty}^{n=\infty} e^{int} \int_{-\pi}^{\pi} f(x) e^{-inx} \, dx, \quad (1.007)$$

while it has not been shown to converge, does in fact yield a convergent series when multiplied term by term with $g(t)$ and integrated; and this new series converges to the integral of the product of f with g. In particular we may confine our attention to a $g(t)$ differing from zero only over a small interval. Thus all local averages of the formal series (1.000) converge to the corresponding local averages of $f(t)$. As we have pointed out, this is all that we need to make a practical employment of the Fourier series for $f(t)$.

The partial sum of this series may be written

$$\frac{1}{2\pi} \sum_{-N}^{N} e^{int} \int_{-\pi}^{\pi} f(x) e^{-inx} \, dx$$

$$= \frac{1}{2\pi} \int_{-\pi}^{\pi} f(x + t) \frac{\sin\left(N + \frac{1}{2}\right)x}{\sin \frac{1}{2}x} \, dx.$$

Closely related to this, there is a quantity known as the *Cesaro partial sum*, which may be written

$$\frac{1}{2\pi} \sum_{-N}^{N} \left(1 - \frac{|n|}{N} \right) e^{int} \int_{-\pi}^{\pi} f(x) e^{-inx} \, dx$$

$$= \frac{1}{2\pi N} \int_{-\pi}^{\pi} f(x + t) \frac{\sin^2 \frac{1}{2} N x}{\sin^2 \frac{1}{2} x} \, dx. \quad (1.008)$$

Both partial sums represent weighted averages of $f(x)$ with the points in the neighborhood of $x + t$ weighted especially heavily. In both cases the total weight of all points around the circle is 1, as we see by

$$\frac{1}{2\pi} \int_{-\pi}^{\pi} \frac{\sin\left(N + \frac{1}{2}\right)x}{\sin \frac{1}{2}x} \, dx = \frac{1}{2\pi N} \int_{-\pi}^{\pi} \frac{\sin^2 \frac{1}{2} N x}{\sin^2 \frac{1}{2} x} \, dx = 1. \quad (1.0085)$$

There is however, this important difference: the weighting for the ordinary sum assumes both positive and negative signs, with the total absolute weight becoming infinite, while the weighting of the Cesaro sum is non-negative, so that the total absolute weighting is the same as the total weighting and is 1 in all cases. Thus the Cesaro partial sum of the Fourier series of a non-negative function is also non-negative.

It will be seen that the coefficients of a Fourier series are given as integrals. When the function $f(x)$ is as continuous, save perhaps for a finite number of finite jumps, the sort of integration used is that given in the ordinary textbooks. However, there are many cases in which it is desirable to represent in a formal Fourier series a function corresponding to the sum $\sum\limits_{-\infty}^{\infty} a_n e^{int}$ for which we know only that $\sum\limits_{-\infty}^{\infty} |a_n|^2$ converges. In order to do this we must adopt an extension of the usual notion of integration. There is one notion of integration and just one which fits the needs of the case, and that is the definition given by Lebesgue. This is not the place for a general exposition of the theory of integration, but it may be said that Lebesgue's form of the integral has all the ordinary properties which are desirable in an integral. For example, if two functions have an integral, then their sum has an integral, and the integral of the sum is the sum of the integrals of the two functions taken separately. If a sequence of functions tends boundedly to a limit function, and if all the approximating functions have integrals, then the limit function has an integral which is the limit of the integrals of the approximating functions. A non-negative function, if it has an integral at all, has a non-negative integral. Again, an increasing sequence of functions which is such that the sequence of their integrals remains bounded tends "almost everywhere" to a limit function whose integral is the limit of the integrals of the approximate functions.

Let it be noted that the expression "almost everywhere" means this: two functions that are identical almost everywhere differ by a function, the integral of whose modulus is zero, and may be considered for practical purposes as the same function.

It is not only true, on the basis of this definition, that, if $f(t)$ is integrable and of integrable absolute square, then

$$\lim_{N \to \infty} \int_{-\pi}^{\pi} \left| f(t) - \frac{1}{2\pi} \sum_{-N}^{N} e^{int} \int_{-\pi}^{\pi} f(x) e^{-inx} \, dx \right|^2 dt = 0, \quad (1.0087)$$

but it is also true that, if $\sum\limits_{-\infty}^{\infty} |a_n|^2 < \infty$, then there exists a function $f(t)$ integrable and of integrable square modulus, such that

$$\lim_{N \to \infty} \int_{-\pi}^{\pi} \left| f(t) - \sum_{-N}^{N} a_n e^{int} \right|^2 dt = 0. \quad (1.0088)$$

This function will be determinate "almost everywhere"; but as a single point is a set of measure zero it may be changed at any single point whatever.

The theorem we have just cited is known as the *Riesz-Fischer theorem*. Strictly speaking, it is an immediate deduction from another of less specific appearance, known as *Weyl's lemma*. This latter asserts that, if $\{f_n(t)\}$ is a sequence of integrable functions of integrable square modulus over (a, b), and

$$\lim_{m, n \to \infty} \int_a^b |f_m(t) - f_n(t)|^2 \, dt = 0, \qquad (1.0089)$$

then there exists a function $f(t)$, integrable and of integrable square modulus, such that

$$\lim_{n \to \infty} \int_a^b |f(t) - f_n(t)|^2 \, dt = 0. \qquad (1.0090)$$

By applying this to the sequence

$$f_n(t) = \sum_{-n}^{n} a_k e^{ikt}, \qquad (1.0091)$$

the Riesz-Fischer theorem follows.

We shall find it convenient to write

$$f(t) = \underset{n \to \infty}{\text{l.i.m.}} \, f_n(t) \qquad (1.0093)$$

$$\lim_{n \to \infty} \int_a^b |f(t) - f_n(t)|^2 \, dt = 0. \qquad (1.0094)$$

Similar modes of writing will be used for the infinite or semi-infinite interval replacing (a, b), or a continuous variable replacing n. We shall write $f(t) \sim \sum_{-\infty}^{\infty} a_n \varphi_n(t)$ for $f(t) = \underset{N \to \infty}{\text{l.i.m.}} \sum_{-N}^{N} a_n \varphi_n(t)$.

1.01 Orthogonal Functions

The theory of Fourier series is but one chapter in the theory of sets of orthogonal functions. A set of functions $\varphi_n(t)$ is said to be normal and orthogonal over (a, b) if it consists of integrable functions for which

$$\int_a^b |\varphi_n(t)|^2 \, dt = 1; \qquad (1.010)$$

and if, whenever $m \neq n$,

$$\int_a^b \varphi_m(t)\overline{\varphi_n(t)} \, dt = 0. \qquad (1.011)$$

As in the trigonometric case, if $f(t)$ is an integrable function of integrable square modulus, the expression

$$\int_a^b \left| f(t) - \sum_1^N a_k \varphi_k(t) \right|^2 dt \tag{1.012}$$

is minimized by putting

$$a_k = \int_a^b f(t) \overline{\varphi_k(t)} \, dt. \tag{1.013}$$

Any set of functions $\psi_n(t)$, integrable and of integrable square modulus, may be used as the point of departure in forming a set of linear combinations φ_n of the ψ_n's which will be normal and orthogonal, and for which every ψ_n is a linear combination of a finite number of φ_n's, except at a set of points of zero measure.

To illustrate the process of forming orthogonal sets, let us start with $\psi_1(t)$, and let it be not equivalent to 0. Let us put

$$\varphi_1(t) = \frac{\psi_1(t)}{\sqrt{\int_a^b |\psi_1(t)|^2 \, dt}}. \tag{1.014}$$

Taking $\psi_2(t)$, if it is not equivalent to a multiple of $\psi_1(t)$, we put

$$\varphi_2(t) = \frac{\psi_2(t) - \varphi_1(t) \int_a^b \psi_2(t) \overline{\varphi_1(t)} \, dt}{\left\{ \int_a^b \left| \psi_2(t) - \varphi_1(t) \int_a^b \psi_2(t) \overline{\varphi_1(t)} \, dt \right|^2 dt \right\}^{\frac{1}{2}}}. \tag{1.015}$$

If ψ_3 is not equivalent to a linear combination of $\psi_1(t)$ and $\psi_2(t)$, we put

$$\varphi_3(t) =$$

$$\frac{\psi_3(t) - \varphi_1(t) \int_a^b \psi_3(t) \overline{\varphi_1(t)} \, dt - \varphi_2(t) \int_a^b \psi_3(t) \overline{\varphi_2(t)} \, dt}{\left\{ \int_a^b \left| \psi_3(t) - \varphi_1(t) \int_a^b \psi_3(t) \overline{\varphi_1(t)} \, dt - \varphi_2(t) \int_a^b \psi_3(t) \overline{\varphi_2(t)} \, dt \right|^2 dt \right\}^{\frac{1}{2}}};$$

$$\tag{1.016}$$

and so on.

A set of functions, whether normal and orthogonal or not, is said to be *complete* or *closed* if there is no function orthogonal to every function of the set. If a set of normal and orthogonal functions $\varphi_n(t)$ is not closed, and if $f(t)$ is not equivalent to zero and is orthogonal to every function of the set, we have of course

$$f(t) \neq \sum \varphi_k(t) \int_a^b f(t)\overline{\varphi_k(t)}\, dt. \qquad (1.017)$$

On the other hand, we always have for any $f(t)$

$$\int_a^b \overline{\varphi_j(t)} \left\{ f(t) - \sum_1^N \varphi_k(t) \int_a^b f(t)\overline{\varphi_k(t)}\, dt \right\} dt = 0; \qquad (1.018)$$

and if

$$\int_a^b \left| f(t) - \sum_1^N \varphi_k(t) \int_a^b f(t)\overline{\varphi_k(t)}\, dt \right|^2 dt \neq 0 \qquad (1.019)$$

the set is not closed but can be enlarged by adjoining another function. Thus, if a normal and orthogonal set is closed and $f(t)$ is any integrable function of integrable square modulus, then

$$\lim_{N \to \infty} \int_a^b \left| f(t) - \sum_1^N \varphi_k(t) \int_a^b f(t)\overline{\varphi_k(t)}\, dt \right|^2 dt = 0. \qquad (1.0193)$$

The definitions of closure, normality, and orthogonality may be applied to functions over a semi-infinite interval $(0, \infty)$ or the complete infinite interval $(-\infty, \infty)$, as well as to functions defined over a finite interval. The one change which has to be made is that the class of functions which are integrable and of integrable square modulus must now be replaced by functions of Lebesgue class L^2 of integrable modulus *over every finite interval* and of integrable square modulus over the infinite interval. For example, the function $1/\sqrt{1 + \omega^2}$ is integrable over every finite interval and of integrable square modulus over the whole range of ω, still

$$\int_{-\infty}^{\infty} \frac{d\omega}{\sqrt{1 + \omega^2}} = \infty. \qquad (1.0195)$$

With this change, Weyl's lemma holds for the infinite intervals, and the analogue of the Riesz-Fischer theorem holds for functions orthogonal over such intervals. The Schwarz inequality holds alike for finite and infinite intervals.

A set of normal and orthogonal functions particularly important for our purpose is that obtained by orthogonalizing the set of functions $x^n e^{-x} (0 \leq n < \infty)$ over the interval $(0, \infty)$. These functions are known as the *Laguerre functions* and, when divided by e^{-x}, as the *Laguerre polynomials*. We shall see at a later point how to compute them more expeditiously.

1.02   The Fourier Integral

We now come to a theory pertaining primarily to the infinite interval. Let $f(t)$ belong to L^2 over all t, and let

$$F_A(\omega) = \frac{1}{\sqrt{2\pi}} \int_{-A}^{A} f(t)e^{-i\omega t}\, dt. \qquad (1.020)$$

Then a theorem due to Plancherel§ asserts that there exists a function $F(\omega)$, likewise belonging to L^2, such that

$$\lim_{A\to\infty} \int_{-\infty}^{\infty} |\, F(\omega) - F_A(\omega) \,|^2\, d\omega = 0. \qquad (1.0205)$$

It further asserts‖ that

$$\int_{-\infty}^{\infty} |\, F(\omega) \,|^2\, d\omega = \int_{-\infty}^{\infty} |\, f(t) \,|^2\, dt, \qquad (1.021)$$

$$\lim_{A\to\infty} \int_{-\infty}^{\infty} \left|\, f(t) - \frac{1}{\sqrt{2\pi}} \int_{-A}^{A} F(\omega)e^{i\omega t}\, d\omega \,\right|^2 dt = 0. \quad (1.0215)$$

The function $F(\omega)$ thus defined is said to be the *Fourier transform* of $f(t)$.

If now $G(\omega)$ is the Fourier transform of $g(t)$, since the Fourier transform is additive, $F(\omega) + G(\omega)$ will be the Fourier transform of $f(t) + g(t)$; $F(\omega) - G(\omega)$, that of $f(t) - g(t)$; $F(\omega) + i\,G(\omega)$, that of $f(t) + i\,g(t)$; and $F(\omega) - i\,G(\omega)$, that of $f(t) - i\,g(t)$. Hence

$$\int_{-\infty}^{\infty} \{F(\omega)\overline{F(\omega)} + F(\omega)\overline{G(\omega)} + G(\omega)\overline{F(\omega)} + G(\omega)\overline{G(\omega)}\}\, d\omega$$

$$= \int_{-\infty}^{\infty} \{f(t)\overline{f(t)} + f(t)\overline{g(t)} + g(t)\overline{f(t)} + g(t)\overline{g(t)}\}\, dt;$$

$$\int_{-\infty}^{\infty} \{F(\omega)\overline{F(\omega)} - F(\omega)\overline{G(\omega)} - G(\omega)\overline{F(\omega)} + G(\omega)\overline{G(\omega)}\}\, d\omega$$

$$= \int_{-\infty}^{\infty} \{f(t)\overline{f(t)} - f(t)\overline{g(t)} - g(t)\overline{f(t)} + g(t)\overline{g(t)}\}\, dt;$$

$$\int_{-\infty}^{\infty} \{F(\omega)\overline{F(\omega)} - i\,F(\omega)\overline{G(\omega)} + i\,G(\omega)\overline{F(\omega)} + G(\omega)\overline{G(\omega)}\}\, d\omega$$

$$= \int_{-\infty}^{\infty} \{f(t)\overline{f(t)} - i\,f(t)\overline{g(t)} + i\,g(t)\overline{f(t)} + g(t)\overline{g(t)}\}\, dt;$$

§ See Titchmarsh, *Theory of Functions*, p. 436.
‖ See Wiener, *Fourier Integral*, p. 196.

$$\int_{-\infty}^{\infty} \{F(\omega)\overline{F(\omega)} + i\,F(\omega)\overline{G(\omega)} - i\,G(\omega)\overline{F(\omega)} + G(\omega)\overline{G(\omega)}\}\,d\omega$$

$$= \int_{-\infty}^{\infty} \{f(t)\overline{f(t)} + i\,f(t)\overline{g(t)} - i\,g(t)\overline{f(t)} + g(t)\overline{g(t)}\}\,dt. \quad (1.022)$$

We take the first of these equations as it stands, the negative of the second, the third multiplied by i, and the fourth multiplied by $-i$. We then add and normalize by dividing by four, thus obtaining

$$\int_{-\infty}^{\infty} F(\omega)\overline{G(\omega)}\,d\omega = \int_{-\infty}^{\infty} f(t)\overline{g(t)}\,dt. \quad (1.0225)$$

It results from this that a set of normal and orthogonal functions of t goes over, upon Fourier transformation, into a set of normal and orthogonal functions of ω. Similarly, t-closure goes over into ω-closure.

1.03 Laguerre Functions

A very interesting set of normal and orthogonal functions of ω is the set

$$l_n(\omega) = \frac{(1 - i\omega)^n}{\sqrt{\pi}(1 + i\omega)^{n+1}} \quad (n = 0, 1, \cdots). \quad (1.030)$$

Here

$$\int_{-\infty}^{\infty} |\,l_n(\omega)\,|^2\,d\omega = \frac{1}{\pi}\int_{-\infty}^{\infty} \frac{d\omega}{1 + \omega^2} = 1, \quad (1.0305)$$

and, on the other hand, if $m \neq n$,

$$\int_{-\infty}^{\infty} l_m(\omega)\overline{l_n(\omega)}\,d\omega = \frac{1}{\pi}\int_{-\infty}^{\infty} \frac{(1 - i\omega)^{m-n-1}}{(1 + i\omega)^{m+1-n}}\,d\omega = 0. \quad (1.031)$$

This we establish by Cauchy's theorem, since one half-plane of the integrand is free from singularities.

Let us now consider the function of t which is 0 for negative arguments, and which is $t^n e^{-t}$ for positive arguments. Its Fourier transform is

$$\frac{1}{\sqrt{2\pi}}\int_0^{\infty} t^n e^{-t} e^{-i\omega t}\,dt = \frac{n!}{\sqrt{2\pi}(1 + i\omega)^{n+1}}. \quad (1.0315)$$

Thus $l_n(\omega)$ may be expressed by the expansion

$$\frac{[2 - (1 + i\omega)]^n}{\sqrt{\pi}(1 + i\omega)^{n+1}} = \frac{2^n}{\sqrt{\pi}(1 + i\omega)^{n+1}} - \frac{2^{n-1}n}{\sqrt{\pi}(1 + i\omega)^n} + \cdots$$

$$+ \frac{2^{n-k}(-1)^k \dfrac{n!}{k!(n-k!)}}{\sqrt{\pi}(1 + i\omega)^{n-k+1}} + \cdots + \frac{(-1)^n}{\sqrt{\pi}(1 + i\omega)}. \quad (1.032)$$

Furthermore, $l_n(\omega)$ will be the transform of the function $L_n(t)$, which latter function will be 0 for negative values of t, while it will assume the value

$$L_n(t) = \left\{\frac{2^{n+\frac{1}{2}}t^n}{n!} - \frac{2^{n-\frac{1}{2}}n}{(n-1)!}\,t^{n-1} + \cdots + 2^{n-k+\frac{1}{2}}\frac{n!(-1)^k}{k![(n-k)!]^2}\,t^{n-k}\right.$$
$$\left. + \cdots + 2^{\frac{1}{2}}(-1)^n\right\}e^{-t} \quad (1.0325)$$

for positive arguments.

With the aid of these functions, it is very easy to give an approximate representation of any function of class L^2, over the interval $(0, \infty)$, in terms of a linear combination of functions which have rational Fourier transforms. The functions $L_n(t)$ are known as *Laguerre functions* and are the products of e^{-t} with polynomials known as *Laguerre polynomials*. Tables of them are given in Appendix A.

1.04   More on the Fourier Integral; Realizability of Filters

To return to the Fourier transform, properties determining the smoothness of a function generally correspond to properties determining the behavior of its Fourier transform at infinity. The Fourier transform of $-itf(t)$ is $F'(\omega)$, and the Fourier transform of $f'(t)$ is $i\omega F(\omega)$. In general, a function and its Fourier transform can not be simultaneously very small at infinity. More precisely, if for all t,

$$|f(t)| < \text{const } e^{-t^2/2}, \quad (1.040)$$

and if for all ω,

$$|F(\omega)| < \text{const } e^{-\omega^2/2}, \quad (1.0405)$$

then

$$f(t) = \text{const } e^{-t^2/2}. \quad (1.041)$$

Further, if for all t,

$$|f(t)| < \text{const } (1 + t^n)e^{-t^2/2}, \quad (1.0415)$$

and if for all ω,

$$|F(\omega)| < \text{const } (1 + \omega^n)e^{-\omega^2/2}, \quad (1.042)$$

then

$$f(t) = P(t)e^{-t^2/2}, \quad (1.0425)$$

where $P(t)$ is a polynomial of degree not exceeding n. If $f(t)$ vanishes for negative values of t, the integral

$$\int_{-\infty}^{\infty} \left|\frac{\log|F(\omega)|}{1 + \omega^2}\right| d\omega \quad (1.043)$$

must remain finite. Again, if $H(\omega)$ belongs to L^2 and

$$\int_{-\infty}^{\infty} \frac{|\log H(\omega)|}{1 + \omega^2} d\omega < \infty, \quad \text{and} \quad H(\omega) \geq 0, \qquad (1.0435)$$

then there exists a function $F(\omega)$, with $H(\omega)$ as its absolute value, which is the Fourier transform of a function $f(t)$ vanishing for negative values of t.

This last fact plays a very important part in the theory of filters. It states that, in any realizable network whatever, the attenuation, taken as a function of the frequency ω, and divided by $1 + \omega^2$, yields an absolutely integrable function of the frequency. This results from the fact that the attenuation is the logarithm of the absolute value of the transform of $f(t)$ which vanishes for negative t; or, in other words, because strictly no network can foretell the future. Thus no filter can have infinite attenuation in any finite band. The perfect filter is physically unrealizable by its very nature, not merely because of the paucity of means at our disposal. No instrument acting solely on the past has a sufficiently sharp discrimination to separate one frequency from another with unfailing accuracy.

1.1 Generalized Harmonic Analysis

The impedances or admittances or voltage transfer ratios of electric circuits are in many cases quantities possessing well-defined Fourier transforms. The messages transmitted by a communication circuit, if we idealize them, as we here do, in such a way that they are not tied to any origin in time, do not have such transforms. To cover these, or even to cover the analysis of sums of trigonometric terms of incommensurable frequencies, we need an extended concept of Fourier analysis. The author has succeeded in doing this,¶ and what follows represents a résumé of his results in this direction.

Let us start with a function $f(t)$, for which

$$\lim_{T \to \infty} \frac{1}{2T} \int_{-T}^{T} |f(t)|^2 \, dt = A. \qquad (1.10)$$

Then it is also true that

$$\lim_{T \to \infty} \frac{1}{2T} \int_{-T+a}^{T+a} |f(t)|^2 \, dt = A. \qquad (1.105)$$

¶ *Acta Mathematica*, Vol. 55, 1930, p. 273.

To prove this, let us observe that

$$\left| \frac{1}{2T} \int_{-T+a}^{T+a} |f(t)|^2 \, dt - \frac{1}{2T} \int_{-T}^{T} |f(t)|^2 \, dt \right|$$

$$\leq \frac{1}{2T} \int_{T}^{T+a} |f(t)|^2 \, dt + \frac{1}{2T} \int_{-T}^{-T+a} |f(t)|^2 \, dt$$

$$\leq \frac{1}{2T} \int_{-T-a}^{T+a} |f(t)|^2 \, dt - \frac{1}{2T} \int_{-T+a}^{T-a} |f(t)|^2 \, dt. \quad (1.11)$$

Now

$$\lim_{T \to \infty} \frac{1}{2T} \int_{-T-a}^{T+a} |f(t)|^2 \, dt$$

$$= \lim_{T \to \infty} \frac{2(T+a)}{2T} \frac{1}{2(T+a)} \int_{-T-a}^{T+a} |f(t)|^2 \, dt = A. \quad (1.115)$$

Similarly,

$$\lim_{T \to \infty} \frac{1}{2T} \int_{-T+a}^{T-a} |f(t)|^2 \, dt = A. \quad (1.12)$$

Thus, for the upper bound of oscillation at ∞,

$$\overline{\lim_{T \to \infty}} \left| \frac{1}{2T} \int_{-T+a}^{T+a} |f(t)|^2 \, dt - \frac{1}{2T} \int_{-T}^{T} |f(t)|^2 \, dt \right| \leq A - A = 0$$

$$(1.125)$$

from which our statement (1.105) follows at once.

Now let us assume that

$$\lim_{T \to \infty} \frac{1}{2T} \int_{-T}^{T} f(t+\tau)\overline{f(t)} \, dt = \varphi(\tau) \quad (1.13)$$

exists as a finite limit for every real τ. Then, if for a finite N we define

$$g(t) = \sum_{1}^{N} a_k f(t+\tau_k), \quad (1.135)$$

it follows that

$$\lim_{T \to \infty} \frac{1}{2T} \int_{-T}^{T} |g(t)|^2 \, dt \quad (1.14)$$

will always exist and be finite. In particular, both the real

$$\lim_{T \to \infty} \frac{1}{2T} \int_{-T}^{T} |f(t+\tau) \pm f(t)|^2 \, dt \quad (1.145)$$

and the complex

$$\lim_{T \to \infty} \frac{1}{2T} \int_{-T}^{T} |f(t+\tau) \pm i f(t)|^2 \, dt \quad (1.15)$$

quadratics will exist and be finite. Furthermore, the complex argument

$$f(t + \tau)\overline{f(t)} = \tfrac{1}{4}\{|f(t + \tau) + f(t)|^2 - |f(t + \tau) - f(t)|^2$$
$$+ i|f(t + \tau) + if(t)|^2 - i|f(t + \tau) - if(t)|^2\}. \quad (1.151)$$

Thus the integrals

$$\lim_{T \to \infty} \frac{1}{2T} \int_{-T+a}^{T+a} f(t + \tau)\overline{f(t)}\, dt = \lim_{T \to \infty} \frac{1}{2T} \int_{-T+a}^{T+a} \tfrac{1}{4}\{|f(t + \tau) + f(t)|^2$$
$$- |f(t + \tau) - f(t)|^2 + i|f(t + \tau) + if(t)|^2 - i|f(t + \tau) - if(t)|^2\}\, dt$$
$$(1.152)$$

and as before

$$= \lim_{T \to \infty} \frac{1}{2T} \int_{-T}^{T} \tfrac{1}{4}\{|f(t + \tau) + f(t)|^2 - |f(t + \tau) - f(t)|^2$$
$$+ i|f(t + \tau) + if(t)|^2 - i|f(t + \tau) - if(t)|^2\}\, dt$$
$$= \lim_{T \to \infty} \frac{1}{2T} \int_{-T}^{T} f(t + \tau)\overline{f(t)}\, dt.$$

Again, by the Schwarz inequality,

$$\frac{1}{2T} \int_{-T}^{T} f(t + \tau)\overline{f(t)}\, dt \le \frac{1}{2T} \sqrt{\int_{-T}^{T} |f(t + \tau)|^2\, dt \int_{-T}^{T} |f(t)|^2\, dt}.$$
$$\textbf{(1.153)}$$

Hence

$$\varphi(\tau) \le \varphi(0). \quad \textbf{(1.154)}$$

Thus in the vicinity of zero

$$\varphi(0) \ge \lim_{\epsilon \to 0} \varphi(\epsilon). \quad \textbf{(1.155)}$$

An example such as

$$f(t) = e^{it^2} \quad (1.156)$$

will show that the equality cannot in general be used to replace the inequality; for here

$$\varphi(0) = 1; \quad \varphi(\epsilon) = \lim_{T \to \infty} \frac{1}{2T} \int_{-T}^{T} e^{i(t+\epsilon)^2 - it^2}\, dt$$

$$= \lim_{T \to \infty} \frac{1}{2T} \int_{-T}^{T} e^{i(2t\epsilon + \epsilon^2)}\, dt \quad (1.157)$$

$$= \lim_{T \to \infty} \frac{e^{i\epsilon^2}}{2T} \cdot \frac{e^{2iT\epsilon} - e^{-2iT\epsilon}}{2i\epsilon} = \lim_{T \to \infty} \frac{e^{i\epsilon^2}}{2T} \frac{\sin 2T\epsilon}{\epsilon} = 0.$$

In those cases in which the function $\varphi(t)$ is discontinuous at $t = 0$ there is a discrepancy between two ways of measuring what we may consider the total power of the motion $f(t)$. Of course, $\varphi(0)$ is a measure of the total power of $f(t)$; but, if we attempt to specify that part of the power which lies between frequencies $-A$ and A and let A tend to ∞, we find the limit which we obtained will be the same as $\lim_{\epsilon \to 0} \varphi(\epsilon)$. In other words, if $\varphi(t)$ is discontinuous at the origin, then there is a portion of the energy which does not belong to any finite frequencies, and which in a certain sense we must associate with infinite frequencies. In the example given we have a function whose oscillation becomes of higher and higher frequencies the further we recede from the origin. It is therefore natural to consider a part, and in this case the whole, of the energy to be at infinite frequency. For the purpose of our future work, we wish to exclude this case, and correspondingly we wish to make $\varphi(t)$ continuous at the origin. That is

$$\varphi(0) = \lim_{\epsilon \to 0} \varphi(\epsilon). \tag{1.158}$$

Under all circumstances,

$$| \varphi(\tau) - \varphi(\epsilon + \tau) | = \left| \lim_{T \to \infty} \frac{1}{2T} \int_{-T}^{T} [f(t + \tau) - f(t + \epsilon + \tau)] \overline{f(t)} \, dt \right| \tag{1.159}$$

and by the Schwarz inequality

$$\leq \lim_{T \to \infty} \frac{1}{2T} \sqrt{\int_{-T}^{T} | f(t + \tau) - f(t + \tau + \epsilon) |^2 \, dt \int_{-T}^{T} | f(t) |^2 \, dt}.$$

That is, using R to denote "real part of"

$$\leq \sqrt{[\varphi(0) - 2R\{\varphi(\epsilon)\} + \varphi(0)]\varphi(0)}.$$

Thus, if $\varphi(t)$ is continuous at the origin, the difference $|\varphi(\tau) - \varphi(\epsilon + \tau)|$ tends to 0 as ϵ tends to 0, and $\varphi(t)$ is everywhere continuous. This case is so much the most important that we shall assume it without more ado in all the practical applications we make of $\varphi(t)$.

Let us proceed to find a weighing function $K(t)$ which is of limited total variation, and let

$$\int_{-\infty}^{\infty} \varphi(\tau + \alpha) \, d\overline{K(\tau)} \tag{1.16}$$

exist. This will have the value

$$\int_{-\infty}^{\infty} d\overline{K(\tau)} \lim_{T \to \infty} \frac{1}{2T} \int_{-T}^{T} f(t + \tau + \alpha) \overline{f(t)} \, dt$$

$$= \int_{-\infty}^{\infty} d\overline{K(\tau)} \lim_{T \to \infty} \frac{1}{2T} \int_{-T+\tau}^{T+\tau} f(t + \alpha) \overline{f(t - \tau)} \, dt$$

$$= \int_{-\infty}^{\infty} d\overline{K(\tau)} \lim_{T \to \infty} \frac{1}{2T} \int_{-T}^{T} f(t + \alpha) \overline{f(t - \tau)} \, dt. \tag{1.161}$$

There are many conditions under which the limit sign and the first integration may be interchanged. This will be the case, for instance, if K varies only over a finite interval, or if $f(t)$ is bounded, both of which occur frequently in practice. We shall here assume that one of these justifying conditions is fulfilled. Then

$$\int_{-\infty}^{\infty} \varphi(\tau + \alpha) \, d\overline{K(\tau)} = \lim_{T \to \infty} \frac{1}{2T} \int_{-\infty}^{\infty} d\overline{K(\tau)} \int_{-T}^{T} f(t + \alpha)\overline{f(t - \tau)} \, dt$$

$$= \lim_{T \to \infty} \frac{1}{2T} \int_{-T}^{T} f(t + \alpha) \int_{-\infty}^{\infty} \overline{f(t - \tau) \, dK(\tau)} \, dt. \quad (1.162)$$

In a similar way, and under similar conditions,

$$\int_{-\infty}^{\infty} d\overline{K(\tau)} \int_{-\infty}^{\infty} \varphi(\tau - \sigma) \, dK(\sigma)$$

$$= \int_{-\infty}^{\infty} d\overline{K(\tau)} \int_{-\infty}^{\infty} dK(\sigma) \lim_{T \to \infty} \frac{1}{2T} \int_{-T}^{T} f(t + \tau - \sigma)\overline{f(t)} \, dt$$

$$= \int_{-\infty}^{\infty} d\overline{K(\tau)} \int_{-\infty}^{\infty} dK(\sigma) \lim_{T \to \infty} \frac{1}{2T} \int_{-T+\tau}^{T+\tau} f(t - \sigma)\overline{f(t - \tau)} \, dt$$

$$= \int_{-\infty}^{\infty} d\overline{K(\tau)} \int_{-\infty}^{\infty} dK(\sigma) \lim_{T \to \infty} \frac{1}{2T} \int_{-T}^{T} f(t - \sigma)\overline{f(t - \tau)} \, dt$$

$$= \lim_{T \to \infty} \frac{1}{2T} \int_{-\infty}^{\infty} d\overline{K(\tau)} \int_{-\infty}^{\infty} dK(\sigma) \int_{-T}^{T} f(t - \sigma)\overline{f(t - \tau)} \, dt$$

$$= \lim_{T \to \infty} \frac{1}{2T} \int_{-T}^{T} dt \left| \int_{-\infty}^{\infty} f(t - \sigma) \, dK(\sigma) \right|^{2}. \quad (1.163)$$

It is easy to show that, if $\varphi(0)$ exists, or if even the considerably looser condition $\lim_{\epsilon \to 0} \varphi(\epsilon) < \infty$ obtains, then

$$\int_{-\infty}^{\infty} \frac{|f(t)|^{2}}{1 + t^{2}} < \infty. \quad (1.164)$$

Accordingly, we may show that the required generalized Fourier transform given by the limit-in-the-mean

$$G(\omega) = \operatorname*{l.i.m.}_{A \to \infty} \frac{1}{\sqrt{2\pi}} \left[\int_{-A}^{-1} + \int_{1}^{A} \right] \frac{f(t)e^{-it\omega}}{-it} \, dt$$

$$+ \frac{1}{\sqrt{2\pi}} \int_{-1}^{1} \frac{f(t)(1 - e^{-it\omega})}{it} \, dt \quad (1.165)$$

exists. This would be the integral of the Fourier transform of $f(t)$, with an appropriate choice of constant of integration, if such a transform existed.

A very important theorem concerning the function $G(\omega)$ is that, if $\varphi(\tau)$ exists and is continuous, it is identical with the quadratic average

$$\varphi(\tau) = \lim_{\epsilon \to 0} \frac{1}{4\pi\epsilon} \int_{-\infty}^{\infty} |G(\omega + \epsilon) - G(\omega - \epsilon)|^2 e^{i\omega\tau} d\omega. \quad (1.166)$$

From this it may readily be deduced that there exists a monotonically increasing function $\Lambda(\omega)$ of finite variation, generating as a transform

$$\varphi(\tau) = \frac{1}{\sqrt{2\pi}} \int_{-\infty}^{\infty} e^{i\omega\tau} d\Lambda(\omega). \quad (1.167)$$

This function $\Lambda(\omega)$, which we shall know as the *integrated spectrum* or *integrated periodogram* of $f(t)$, may be recovered from $\varphi(\tau)$ by the process

$$\underset{A \to \infty}{\text{l.i.m.}} \frac{1}{\sqrt{2\pi}} \left[\int_{-A}^{-1} + \int_{1}^{A} \right] \frac{\varphi(\tau) e^{-i\tau\omega}}{-i\tau} d\tau$$

$$+ \frac{1}{\sqrt{2\pi}} \int_{-1}^{1} \frac{\varphi(\tau)(1 - e^{-i\tau\omega})}{i\tau} dt = \Lambda(\omega) + \text{const.} \quad (1.168)$$

If $\Lambda(\omega)$ is modified by an additive constant in such a way that it vanishes when $\omega \to -\infty$, it then represents (on an appropriate scale) *the total power in the spectrum of $f(t)$ between $\omega = -\infty$ and the frequency ω. The word "power" is used instead of "energy," because the phenomenon represented by $f(t)$ is a continuing one, having a finite mean over all time, instead of a transient one, having a finite integral over all time. This power is positive over every region of frequency, and consequently $\Lambda(\omega)$ is monotonically increasing, but this increase may occur in several ways. If

$$f(t) = \sum_{1}^{n} f_k e^{i\Lambda_k t}, \quad (1.169)$$

then

$$\varphi(\tau) = \lim_{T \to \infty} \frac{1}{2T} \int_{-T}^{T} \sum_{j=1}^{n} \sum_{k=1}^{n} f_j \bar{f}_k e^{i(\Lambda_j t + \Lambda_j \tau - \Lambda_k t)} dt = \sum_{j=1}^{n} |f_j|^2 e^{i\Lambda_j \tau}, \quad (1.170)$$

and

$$\Lambda(\omega) = \sqrt{\frac{\pi}{2}} \sum_{j=1}^{n} |f_j|^2 \operatorname{sgn}(\omega - \Lambda_j), \quad \text{where } \operatorname{sgn} x = \begin{cases} 1 & \text{if } x > 0; \\ 0 & \text{if } x = 0; \\ -1 & \text{if } x < 0. \end{cases} \quad (1.171)$$

Accordingly, $\Lambda(\omega)$ thus defined is an ever-increasing step-function. A slightly more general case is that in which $\Lambda(\omega)$, though not a function having a necessarily finite number of steps, has at most a denumerable set of points of increase. We shall see that the Brownian motion, among other phenomena, will give rise to a $\Lambda(\omega)$ which is the integral of its averaged positive derivative, where we may accordingly write

$$\varphi(\tau) = \frac{1}{\sqrt{2\pi}} \int_{-\infty}^{\infty} e^{i\omega\tau}\Lambda'(\omega)\,d\omega. \tag{1.172}$$

Another type of $\Lambda(\omega)$, known from actual instances,[*] is continuous everywhere but grows over a set of points of Lebesgue measure 0 and is not absolutely continuous. Finally, $\Lambda(\omega)$ may be the sum of parts of any two of these types or of all three. The type which is most significant in prediction problems is that in which $\Lambda(\omega)$ is the weighted integral of its average derivative.

1.18 Discrete Arrays and Their Spectra

Parallel to this theory of the harmonic analysis of continuous phenomena not changing their scale with the increase of time there runs a theory of discrete phenomena. We start with a time sequence f_n, for which

$$\varphi_m = \lim_{N \to \infty} \frac{1}{2N+1} \sum_{n=-N}^{N} f_{m+n}\overline{f_n} \tag{1.180}$$

exists for every m. As before,

$$\varphi_m \le \varphi_0, \tag{1.181}$$

and

$$\sum_{-\infty}^{\infty}{}' \frac{|f_n|}{n} \sim \tag{1.182}$$

where the $\sum'$ indicates that the zero term is missing. Accordingly, the function $G(\omega)$, again given by the limit-in-the-mean

$$G(\omega) = \text{l.i.m.}_{N \to \infty} \frac{1}{\sqrt{2\pi}} \sum_{-N}^{N}{}' \frac{f_n e^{-in\omega}}{-in} + \frac{1}{\sqrt{2\pi}} f_0(\omega) \tag{1.183}$$

exists. We have likewise

$$\varphi_m = \lim_{\epsilon \to 0} \frac{1}{4\pi\epsilon} \int_{-\pi}^{\pi} |G(\omega + \epsilon) - G(\omega - \epsilon)|^2 e^{i\omega m}\,d\omega \tag{1.184}$$

and we may write

$$\varphi_m = \frac{1}{\sqrt{2\pi}} \int_{-\pi}^{\pi} e^{i\omega m}\,d\Lambda(\omega),$$

---

[*] See Wiener and Mahler, Spectrum of an Array, *Journal of Mathematics and Physics*, Vol. 6, 1927, pp. 145–163.

where $\Lambda(\omega)$ is a monotonically increasing function of limited total variation over $(-\pi, \pi)$. As before, $\Lambda(\omega)$ may contain discontinuous, absolutely continuous, and non-absolutely continuous parts. We shall have as before

$$\underset{N \to \infty}{\text{l.i.m.}} \frac{1}{\sqrt{2\pi}} \sum_{-N}^{N}{}' \frac{\varphi_n e^{-in\omega}}{-in} + \frac{1}{\sqrt{2\pi}} \varphi_0 \omega = \Lambda(\omega) + \text{const.} \quad (1.185)$$

In both the discrete and the continuous cases, the jumps of $\Lambda(\omega)$ represent what we think of physically as lines in the spectrum. Continuous spectra are familiar in spectroscopy, although the non-absolutely continuous variety does not seem to have put in its appearance there.

1.2 Multiple Harmonic Analysis and Coherency Matrices

Besides the problems concerning a single time series, spectroscopy has its problems of polarization, coherence, and the like, which concern several time series simultaneously. If $f_1(t), f_2(t), \cdots, f_n(t)$ are an array of functions, the generalization of $\varphi(\tau)$ will be the double array

$$\varphi_{jk}(\tau) = \lim_{T \to \infty} \frac{1}{2T} \int_{-T}^{T} f_j(t + \tau)\overline{f_k(t)}\, dt. \quad (1.20)$$

Here by symmetry

$$\varphi_{jk}(\tau) = \overline{\varphi_{kj}(-\tau)}. \quad (1.205)$$

We shall be able to write

$$\varphi_{jk}(\tau) = \frac{1}{\sqrt{2\pi}} \int_{-\infty}^{\infty} e^{i\omega\tau}\, d\Lambda_{jk}(\omega), \quad (1.210)$$

where

$$\Lambda_{jk}(\omega) = \overline{\Lambda_{kj}(\omega)}; \quad (1.215)$$

or, in other words, the matrix $\| \Lambda_{jk}(\omega) \|$ is *Hermitian*, as is the matrix $\| \Lambda'_{jk}(\omega) \|$, when the Λ_{jk} are absolutely continuous. The form

$$\sum_{j,k} \Lambda'_{jk}(\omega) a_j \bar{a}_k \quad (1.220)$$

is in general a positive definite Hermitian form. The problem of determining the principal axes of symmetry of this form reduces to the problem of determining linear combinations

$$g_j(t) = \sum_{j,k} a_{jk} f_k(t) \quad (1.225)$$

such that if

$$\psi_{jk}(\tau) = \lim_{T \to \infty} \frac{1}{2T} \int_{-T}^{T} g_j(t + \tau)\overline{g_k(t)}\, dt \quad (1.230)$$

and

$$\psi_{jk}(\tau) = \frac{1}{\sqrt{2\pi}} \int_{-\infty}^{\infty} e^{i\omega\tau}\, dM_{jk}(\omega); \quad M_{jk}(-\infty) = 0; \quad (1.235)$$

then

$$M_{jk}(\omega) = \begin{cases} 1 \text{ if } j = k; \\ 0 \text{ if } j \neq k. \end{cases} \quad (1.240)$$

We shall have

$$\| M_{jk}(\omega) \| = \| a_{jl} \| \cdot \| \Lambda_{lm}(\omega) \| \cdot \| \bar{a}_{mk} \|. \quad (1.245)$$

We shall call the matrix $\| \Lambda_{jk}(\omega) \|$ the *coherency matrix* of the set $\{f_j(t)\}$. If all terms outside the principal diagonal vanish, and only then, the various time series $f_j(t)$ are incoherent. The study of the state of polarization of light reduces to the study of the coherency matrix of two components at right angles.

The theory of coherency matrices is almost the same for discrete time series as for continuous time series.

1.3 Smoothing Problems

For both discrete and continuous time series, in view of the additional chapters of this book, a certain theory of approximation is desirable. The manipulations to come later on are much facilitated if φ_j is an expression which vanishes if $|j| > N$, or if $\varphi(\tau)$ is a function with a Fourier transform which is rational. In both cases, $\Lambda(\omega)$ must be monotonically increasing, or $\Lambda'(\omega)$ positive for all (ω). In the discrete case, this is secured by taking as our approximate φ_j the expression

$$\varphi_j \backsim \begin{cases} \varphi_j \left(1 - \dfrac{|j|}{N}\right) \text{ where } (|j| \leq N); \\ 0 \quad \text{where} \quad (|j| > N); \end{cases} \quad (1.30)$$

which will make the approximate $\Lambda'(\omega)$, or

$$\Lambda'(\omega) \cong \frac{1}{\sqrt{2\pi}} \sum_{-N}^{N} \varphi_n \left(1 - \frac{|n|}{N}\right) e^{-in\omega}, \quad (1.31)$$

non-negative. In the continuous case, we form

$$\Lambda'(\omega) \cong \frac{1}{\pi} \sum_{-\infty}^{\infty} e^{2in \tan^{-1} \omega} \int_{-\infty}^{\infty} \Lambda'(u) e^{-2in \tan^{-1} u} \frac{2}{1 + u^2}\, du, \quad (1.32)$$

or perhaps

$$\Lambda'(\omega)(1 + \omega^2) \cong \frac{1}{\pi} \sum_{-\infty}^{\infty} e^{2in \tan^{-1} \omega} \int_{-\infty}^{\infty} \Lambda'(u) e^{-2in \tan^{-1} u}\, du. \quad (1.33)$$

We then represent $\Lambda'(\omega)$ or $\Lambda'(\omega)(1 + \omega^2)$ by the approximate Fourier development

$$\Lambda'(\omega) \cong \frac{1}{\pi} \sum_{-N}^{N} \left(1 - \frac{|n|}{N}\right) e^{2in \tan^{-1}\omega} \int_{-\infty}^{\infty} \Lambda'(\omega) e^{-2in \tan^{-1}u} \frac{du}{1 + u^2},$$

or

$$\Lambda'(\omega)(1+\omega^2) \cong \frac{1}{\pi} \sum_{-N}^{N} \left(1 - \frac{|n|}{N}\right) e^{2in \tan^{-1}\omega} \int_{-\infty}^{\infty} \Lambda'(u) e^{-2in \tan^{-1}u} \, du. \quad (1.35)$$

As before, this will be ever positive, and, since

$$e^{2in \tan^{-1}\omega} = \left(\frac{1 + i\omega}{1 - i\omega}\right)^n, \quad (1.36)$$

it will also be rational. The same convergence factors which render $\Lambda(\omega)$ increasing will render $\sum_{j=1}^{n} \sum_{k=1}^{n} \Lambda'_{jk}(\omega) a_j \bar{a}_k$ positive as an Hermitian form.

1.4 Ergodic Theory

In order to produce examples of functions or sequences for which the functions or sequences $\varphi(\tau)$ or φ_j exist, let us appeal to ergodic theory, as presented in the Introduction. If, in particular, Σ is a set of elements P, and T is a measure-preserving transformation of Σ into itself, or if, more generally, T^λ is a measure-preserving group of such transformations, for which λ is real, and

$$T^\lambda(T^\mu P) = T^{(\lambda+\mu)} P, \quad (1.40)$$

then, if $F(P)$ is a function of class L^2 throughout this set, we have that in the discrete case

$$\varphi_m = \lim_{N \to \infty} \frac{1}{N+1} \sum_{n=0}^{N} F(T^{(m+n)}P) \overline{F(T^n P)}$$

$$= \lim_{N \to \infty} \frac{1}{2N+1} \sum_{n=-N}^{N} F(T^{(m+n)}P) \overline{F(T^n P)}, \quad (1.41)$$

or for the case of continuous phenomena

$$\varphi(\tau) = \lim_{A \to \infty} \frac{1}{A} \int_0^A F(T^{\tau+t}P) \overline{F(T^t P)} \, dt$$

$$= \lim_{A \to \infty} \frac{1}{2A} \int_{-A}^{A} F(T^{\tau+t}P) F(T^t P) \, dt. \quad (1.42)$$

In the first instance, the particular Σ set defined assures the existence of φ_m and $\varphi(\tau)$ throughout the set P (except those of Lebesgue measure zero) for a single m or τ. As we have indicated in the Introduction, the same statement may be shown to hold simultaneously for all m or τ, and the set of exceptional values of P remains of zero measure. In the continuous case, moreover, we have as before

$$\lim_{\epsilon \to 0} \varphi(\epsilon) = \varphi(0) \tag{1.43}$$

almost always. Thus the theory of generalized harmonic analysis which we have here stated is applicable to almost all orbits in ergodic theory. If the transformation T or the transformation group T^λ is metrically transitive (or ergodic, as it is now the fashion to call it), we shall have (almost always) that φ_m is given by the integral throughout the set Σ

$$\varphi_m = \int_\Sigma F(T^m P)\overline{F(P)} \, dV_\rho, \tag{1.44}$$

when discrete; and when continuous,

$$\varphi(\tau) = \int_\Sigma F(T^\tau P)\overline{F(P)} \, dV_\rho. \tag{1.45}$$

This relationship existing between the generalized harmonic analysis of this chapter and ergodic theory renders generalized harmonic analysis a most useful tool in communication engineering and in the study of time series.

One extremely important fact in ergodic theory, which we have already indicated as resulting from invariance of the translation group in time, is that, if G is integrable, then almost always

$$\lim_{N \to \infty} \frac{1}{N+1} \sum_{n=0}^{N} G(T^n P) = \lim_{N \to \infty} \frac{1}{2N+1} \sum_{n=-N}^{N} G(T^n P). \tag{1.46}$$

This allows us to identify averages made on the observable past of a time series with averages to be subsequently obtained from the now unattainable future. It is at precisely this point that the ensemble of time series, as contrasted with the individual time series, becomes important. This step (legitimate for the ensemble) is not legitimate for the individual series. It is this step which constitutes the logical process of induction.

1.5 Brownian Motion

Now let us turn to the theory of the Brownian motion. The fundamental formula behind this theory is that

$$\frac{1}{\sqrt{2\pi(t_1 + t_2)}} e^{\left(\frac{-x^2}{2(t_1 + t_2)}\right)} = \frac{1}{2\pi\sqrt{t_1 + t_2}} \int_{-\infty}^{\infty} e^{\left(\frac{-y^2}{2t_1} - \frac{(x-y)^2}{2t_2}\right)} \, dy. \tag{1.50}$$

This means that, if the quantity X has a Gaussian distribution, so that the probability that it lies between x and $x + dx$ is given by

$$\frac{1}{\sqrt{2\pi t_1}} e^{\left(-\frac{x^2}{2t_1}\right)} dx, \tag{1.51}$$

and if the quantity Y, completely independent of X, has likewise a Gaussian distribution, so that the probability that it lies between x and $x + dx$ is

$$\frac{1}{\sqrt{2\pi t_2}} e^{\left(\frac{-x^2}{2t_2}\right)} dx, \tag{1.52}$$

then the probability that the sum $|X + Y|$ lies between x and $x + dx$ will be

$$\frac{1}{\sqrt{2\pi(t_1 + t_2)}} e^{\left(\frac{-x^2}{2(t_1+t_2)}\right)} dx. \tag{1.53}$$

Now, in the Brownian motion, a particle moves in such a way that the distance traversed by the particle in one interval of time has a distribution independent of the movement of that particle in any non-overlapping interval of time and dependent only on the length of that interval of time. If the distribution of the X-distance traversed by the particle in an interval of time of length l is Gaussian, it can accordingly have only the form

$$\frac{1}{\sqrt{2\pi\rho l}} e^{\left(\frac{-x^2}{2\rho l}\right)} dx. \tag{1.54}$$

Let us normalize this by taking $\rho = 1$. The author has shown† that, if we take $x(0)$ to be 0, and we regard the probability that

$$x < x(t_2) - x(t_1) < x + dx \quad (t_1 < t_2) \tag{1.55}$$

as being

$$\frac{1}{\sqrt{2\pi(t_2 - t_1)}} e^{\left(\frac{-x^2}{2(t_2-t_1)}\right)} dx \tag{1.56}$$

then it is possible to map sets of functions $x(t)$, simultaneously satisfying conditions of the type

$$a_1 \leq x(t_1) \leq b_1; \quad a_2 \leq x(t_2) \leq b_2; \quad \cdots, a_n \leq x(t_n) \leq b_n;$$
$$t_1 \leq t_2 \leq \cdots \leq t_n \tag{1.57}$$

upon measurable sets of points on the line $0 \leq \alpha \leq 1$, in such a way that the probability of the simultaneous occurrence of any such set of con-

† See *Proceedings of the National Academy of Sciences*, Vol. 7, No. 9, pp. 253–260, September, 1921.

tingencies becomes equal to the measure of the set of corresponding values of α. In other words, if we write $x(t, \alpha)$ for the $x(t)$ corresponding to each α, and put $t_0 = 0$, we have, as a measure of the probability of each coincidence, the product

$$M = \frac{1}{(2\pi)^{n/2} \prod_{1}^{n} (t_k - t_{k-1})^{\frac{1}{2}}} \cdot \int_{a_1}^{b_1} dx_1 \cdot \int_{a_2}^{b_2} dx_2 \cdot$$

$$\cdots \cdot \int_{a_n}^{b_n} dx_n \exp\left(-\sum_{1}^{n} \frac{(x_k - x_{k-1})^2}{2(t_k - t_{k-1})}\right) \quad (1.575)$$

for the set of cases where $\{a_1 \leq x(t_1, \alpha) \leq b_1, \cdots, a_n \leq x(t_n\alpha) \leq b_n\}$, in which normalization is indicated by the partial product divisor, and the symbol exp designates the exponential function of a complex variable.‡ In this manner we may determine the integral (or average) of other functions of α, determined as functionals of $x(t, \alpha)$. This may be extended easily to include values of t on an infinite range from $-\infty$ to ∞. Here $x(-t, \alpha)$ and $x(t, \alpha)$ are taken to be projections of independent Brownian motions. In particular, if $f_1(t), \cdots, f_n(t)$ are a set of differentiable functions of class L^2, and such that $\int_{-\infty}^{\infty} |f_k(t)| \, dt < \infty$, and we define

$$\int_{-\infty}^{\infty} f_k(t) \, dx(t, \alpha) = -\int_{-\infty}^{\infty} x(t, \alpha) f_k'(t) \, dt, \quad (1.58)$$

then

$$\int_0^1 d\alpha \prod_1^n \int_{-\infty}^{\infty} f_k(t) \, dx(t, \alpha) = \sum \prod \int_{-\infty}^{\infty} f_j(t) f_k(t) \, dt \quad (1.583)$$

where the partial product $\prod$ is one in which every number from 1 to n inclusive appears just once as a j or a k, and the sum $\sum$ is taken over all such products. The result is 0 if n is odd.

The transformation of $x(t, \alpha)$ into

$$x(t + \lambda, \alpha) - x(\lambda, \alpha) = x(\beta) \quad (1.585)$$

will generate a transformation of α into β which will conserve measure on the line $(0, 1)$. Such a group as is formed by all these transformations for all values of λ will be exactly a case in which we may employ the ergodic theorems. It may be shown, as a result of the independence of non-overlapping intervals of t, that this group of transformations is

‡ See Whittaker and Watson, *Modern Analysis*, p. 581.

ergodic or *metrically transitive*. Thus almost always

$$\lim_{T \to \infty} \frac{1}{2T} \int_{-T}^{T} d\tau \prod_{1}^{n} \int_{-\infty}^{\infty} f_k(t + \tau) \, dx(t, \alpha) = \sum \prod \int_{-\infty}^{\infty} f_j(t) f_k(t) \, dt.$$

(1.587)

This gives us the spectrum of the response of a linear resonator to a Brownian input, since if

$$f(t) = \int_{-\infty}^{\infty} f(t + \tau) \, dx(t, \alpha),$$

(1.590)

then $\varphi(\tau)$ will almost always be

$$\varphi(\tau) = \int_{-\infty}^{\infty} f(t + \tau) \overline{g(t)} \, dt,$$

(1.593)

and

$$\Lambda'(\omega) = \frac{1}{\sqrt{2\pi}} \int_{-\infty}^{\infty} e^{-i\omega t} \, dt \int_{-\infty}^{\infty} g(t + \tau) \overline{g(t)} \, dt$$

$$= \sqrt{2\pi} \left| \frac{1}{\sqrt{2\pi}} \int_{-\infty}^{\infty} g(t) e^{-i\omega t} \, dt \right|^2$$

(1.595)

In words, *the response of a linear resonator to a unit Brownian motion input has the same distribution of power in frequency that its response to a single instantaneous pulse will have as a distribution of energy in frequency.*

It will be seen upon computation that the spectrum of

$$\int_{-\infty}^{\infty} g(t + \tau) \, dx(\tau, \alpha)$$

(1.597)

will be dependent only on $\left| \dfrac{1}{2\pi} \displaystyle\int_{-\infty}^{\infty} g(t) e^{-i\omega t} \, dt \right|$. From this fact alone, it does not necessarily follow that all the statistical parameters of the distribution of $\displaystyle\int_{-\infty}^{\infty} g(t + \tau) \, dx(\tau, \alpha)$ will depend only on the spectrum of the function, but that such is actually the case may be proven by (1.587). These functions generated by the response of a linear resonator to a Brownian input have their spectrum as their sole statistical parameter. In general, a function with a spectrum not belonging to such a restricted class has many other independent statistical parameters as well. This is one of the principal reasons why our theory, which secures only an optimum *linear* filter or predictor in the general case, secures an *absolutely* optimum one in this special class of inputs.

1.6 .Poisson Distributions

Another interesting type of random distribution is that of *Poisson*. Let us assume that on the infinite line $-\infty < x < \infty$ the probability that a given segment of length l does not contain a bullet hole is

$$e^{-Al} \qquad (1.60)$$

and that these probabilities are independent for non-overlapping intervals. It may be shown that these assumptions are consistent, and that the probability that a segment of length l contain exactly ν bullet holes will be

$$\frac{(Al)^\nu}{\nu!} e^{-Al}. \qquad (1.61)$$

As in the Brownian case, the contingencies of bullet-hole distribution may be mapped on a probability interval $(0, 1)$ of a parameter α. Only a set of values of α of zero measure will correspond to the cases in which some finite interval of the line contains more than a finite number of bullet holes. If the X-coordinates of all the bullet holes are $x_1(\alpha)$, $\cdots$, $x_n(\alpha)$, $\cdots$, and if we consider $x_n(\alpha)$ and integrals with respect to α, we shall have

$$\int_0^1 \sum_n f[x_n(\alpha)] \, d\alpha = A \int_{-\infty}^\infty f(x) \, dx \qquad (1.62)$$

whenever $f(x)$ belongs to the class of Lebesgue integrable functions over $(-\infty, \infty)$. Furthermore, if $f(x)$ and $g(x)$ are Lebesgue integrable and of class L^2 on the infinite line,

$$\int_0^1 \sum_n f[x_n(\alpha)] \sum_m g[x_m(\alpha)] \, d\alpha = A \int_{-\infty}^\infty f(x) g(x) \, dx$$
$$+ A^2 \int_{-\infty}^\infty f(x) \, dx \int_{-\infty}^\infty g(x) \, dx. \qquad (1.63)$$

The change of $\{x_n(\alpha)\}$ into $\{x_n(\alpha) + \lambda\}$ generates a measure-preserving transformation T^λ of the line $0 \le \alpha \le 1$ into itself, and, as before, it may be shown that this transformation is ergodic. Thus, if $f(x)$ belongs to L^2 and also to the class of Lebesgue integrable functions, we shall have for almost all sets $x_n(\alpha)$,

$$\lim_{T \to \infty} \frac{1}{2T} \int_{-T}^T \sum_n f[x_n(\alpha) + t + \tau] \overline{\sum_m f[x_m(\alpha) + t]} \, dt$$
$$= A \int_{-\infty}^\infty f(x + \tau) f(x) \, dx + A^2 \left| \int_{-\infty}^\infty f(x) \, dx \right|^2 \qquad (1.64)$$

The spectrum of $\sum_n f[x_n(\alpha) + t]$, as a function of t, will consist in a line of intensity $\sqrt{2\pi}A^2 \left| \int_{-\infty}^{\infty} f(x)\, dx \right|^2$ at $\omega = 0$, together with a continuous spectral distribution for which

$$\Lambda'(\omega) = A\sqrt{2\pi} \left| \frac{1}{\sqrt{2\pi}} \int_{-\infty}^{\infty} g(t) e^{-i\omega t}\, dt \right|^2 \tag{1.65}$$

Finally, let us consider the transformation of **the infinite product space**

$$\cdots, 0 \leq x_{-n} \leq 1, \cdots, 0 \leq x_0 \leq 1, \cdots, 0 \leq x_n \leq 1, \cdots \tag{1.66}$$

constituted by transforming x_k into x_{k+1}. This leaves invariant **the** infinite product measure, which is isomorphic with respect to Lebesgue measure. It is, furthermore, ergodic. Hence almost always, if

$$\sum_j |f(x_j)|^2 < \infty,$$

$$\lim_{N \to \infty} \frac{1}{2N+1} \sum_{m=-N}^{N} \sum_j f(x_{j+n+m})\overline{f(x_{j+m})} = \sum_j f(x_{j+n})\overline{f(x_j)}. \tag{1.67}$$

This gives us as the spectrum of

$$\sum_j f(x_{j+n}) \tag{1.68}$$

that determined by the function

$$\Lambda'(\omega) = \frac{1}{\sqrt{2\pi}} \left| \sum_j f(x_j) e^{-ij\omega} \right|^2. \tag{1.69}$$

1.7   Harmonic Analysis in the Complex Domain

Let us now turn from ergodic theory and the real aspects of harmonic analysis to the complex aspects of that theory. These are quite simple. If

$$\int_{-\infty}^{\infty} |f(t)|^2 e^{-2xt}\, dt < \text{const} \tag{1.70}$$

when x varies over the range $x_1 < x < x_2$, then the analytic function

$$G(x + iy) = \int_{-\infty}^{\infty} f(t) e^{-(x+iy)t}\, dt \tag{1.71}$$

is defined over the range $x_1 < x < x_2$, and uniformly over that range,

$$\int_{-\infty}^{\infty} |G(x + iy)|^2\, dy < \text{const}; \tag{1.72}$$

and, vice versa, if $G(x + iy)$ is any analytic function satisfying this last condition, we may represent it in terms of f as stated, while f will itself be subject to the condition first stated. If

$$\int_{-\infty}^{\infty} |f(t)|^2 e^{-2xt}\, dt < \text{const} \tag{1.73}$$

when x varies over the semi-infinite range $x_1 < x < \infty$ **then the analytic function**

$$G(x + iy) = \int_{-\infty}^{\infty} f(t) e^{-(x+iy)t}\, dt \tag{1.74}$$

is defined over the range $x_1 < x < \infty$ and uniformly over that range

$$\int_{-\infty}^{\infty} |f(t)|^2 e^{-2\omega t}\, dt < \text{const}. \tag{1.75}$$

This can be the case only if $f(t)$ vanishes for negative values of t. The transition from $G(x + iy)$ to an $f(t)$ of this sort is made as before. If the range of x is $-\infty < x < x_2$, $f(t)$ vanishes for positive values of t. In each case, $G(x + iy)$ is uniformly bounded for any range of x interior to that for which $\int_{-\infty}^{\infty} |f(t)|^2 e^{-2xt}$ is bounded.

Although we do not make explicit use of it in this book, the theorem that a bounded function of a complex variable is a constant plays a very important role in our researches. It is this theorem which permits a sufficient restriction on the behavior of a function in each half-plane separately, to determine the function completely. The technique of determining a function by subjecting it to separate restrictions in the two half-planes is the basis of our solution of the fundamental integral equation to which our predicting and filtering problems lead.

Finally, let us say a word about the factoring of a function (defined along the real axis) into the product of two analytic functions, each free from zeros and singularities in one half-plane. Let $\Phi(\omega)$ be a function of the real variable ω, and let

$$\int_{-\infty}^{\infty} \frac{|\log |\Phi(\omega)||}{1 + \omega^2}\, d\omega < \infty. \tag{1.76}$$

Let us put

$$\frac{1}{\pi} \int_{-\infty}^{\infty} \frac{\log |\Phi(\omega)|}{i[\omega - (u + iv)]}\, d\omega = \Xi(u + iv). \tag{1.765}$$

Then the function

$$\Xi(u + iv) \tag{1.77}$$

will be analytic in the half-plane $v > 0$, and its real part

$$\frac{1}{\pi} \int_{-\infty}^{\infty} \frac{\epsilon \log |\Phi(\omega)|}{(\omega - u)^2 + \epsilon^2}\, d\omega$$

on the line $v = \epsilon > 0$ will converge in the mean over every finite interval to $\log |\Phi(u)|$ as $\epsilon \to 0$. Let us put

$$\overline{\Psi(u + iv)} = e^{\frac{1}{2}\Xi(u+iv)}. \tag{1.775}$$

Then $\Psi(u + iv)$ will be free from zeros and singularities in the lower half-plane, as will be $\overline{\Psi(u + iv)}$ in the upper half-plane. If we put

$$\Psi(u) = \operatorname*{l.i.m.}_{\epsilon \to 0} \Psi(u - i\epsilon), \tag{1.78}$$

the limit-in-the-mean being taken over an arbitrary finite interval, then, for real ω, we shall have almost everywhere

$$\Phi(\omega) = |\Psi(\omega)|^2. \tag{1.785}$$

Clearly, if $\Phi(\omega)$ is an even rational function, real and positive on the axis of reals, we may factor it into the product

$$\Phi(\omega) = \Psi_1(\omega) \cdot \Psi_2(\omega), \tag{1.79}$$

where all the zeros and poles of $\Psi_1(\omega)$ lie above the axis of reals, and all the zeros and poles of $\Psi_2(\omega)$ lie below the axis of reals. It may be shown that if

$$\Psi_1(\omega) = c\Psi(\omega), \quad \Psi_2(\omega) = \frac{\overline{\Psi(\omega)}}{c}, \tag{1.793}$$

and also

$$\int_{-\infty}^{\infty} \frac{|\log |\Psi(\omega)||}{1 + \omega^2}\, d\omega = \infty, \tag{1.795}$$

then in fact no $\Psi(\omega)$ free from zeros and singularities in the lower half-plane exists, such that over every finite interval of the real axis $\Phi(\omega)$ is the limit-in-the-mean of

$$\Psi(\omega - i\epsilon) \cdot \overline{\Psi(\omega + i\epsilon)} \tag{1.799}$$

as $\epsilon \to 0$.

We shall see later that, when the function $\Phi(\omega)$ is not factorable as in (1.799) or, what is equivalent, when (1.795) holds, the future of the function f from which Φ is obtained is determinable completely in terms of its own past. A simple example of the sort is when f is analytic. In all practical cases the auto-correlation coefficient of a message is not completely determined by its own past. If it were so determined, then at no period in the message would it be possible to introduce new information. Thus the case of (1.795) is in a certain sense *singular* and is so described by Kolmogoroff in his paper Interpolation und Extrapolation von stationären zufälligen Folgen, *Bulletin de l'académie des sciences de U.S.S.R.*, Ser. Math. 5, 1941.

Chapter II

THE LINEAR PREDICTOR FOR A SINGLE TIME SERIES

2.01 Formulation of the Problem of the Linear Predictor

The present chapter will be devoted to the study of what is statistically the simplest case of prediction—that for the single time series. In general, the time series we study will be complex-valued. Certain formal advantages justify this generality; nevertheless, in all practical applications, we shall be concerned with the real-valued case. A similar situation obtains in the field of electrical engineering, where the classical theory treats alternating voltages and currents, for reason of formal simplicity, as real parts of fictitious complex voltages and currents.

In the first instance we shall discuss the continuous time series $f(t)$, and at a later stage the discrete series. The "norm" or absolute quadratic average of such a series will be the mean square of its absolute value or, in explicit form,

$$\lim_{T \to \infty} \frac{1}{2T} \int_{-T}^{T} |f(t)|^2 \, dt.$$

We have said that the methods of prediction contemplated are to be linear, invariant with respect to the choice of an origin in time, and dependent only on the past and present of the function under investigation. Examples of operators capable of making such predictions are:

The derivative $f'(t)$;

The ordinary integral $\int_{0}^{\infty} f(t - \tau) K(\tau) \, d\tau$;

The Stieltjes integral $\int_{0}^{\infty} f(t - \tau) \, dK(\tau)$;

The integral involving higher derivatives $\sum_{\nu=1}^{N} \int_{0}^{\infty} f^{(\nu)}(t - \tau) \, dK_{\nu}(\tau)$.

It will develop that the relevant statistical parameters of time series will (under these circumstances) be confined to the auto-correlation coefficient

$$\varphi(\tau) = \lim_{T \to \infty} \frac{1}{2T} \int_{-T}^{T} f(t + \tau)\overline{f(t)}\, dt. \qquad (2.011)$$

We concern ourselves only with the prediction of ensembles for which nearly all functions have the same auto-correlation coefficient.

Now let $f(t)$ denote a bounded time series for which $\varphi(\tau)$ exists, and let $\varphi(\tau)$ be continuous in the vicinity of $\tau = 0$. Let K be of finite total variation. The expression $f(t + \alpha)$ will denote the value of f at a period α units of time later than t, while $\int_{0}^{\infty} f(t - \tau)\, dK(\tau)$ will denote the result of applying to f an as yet imperfectly determined linear operator on its past. Thus, from the point of view of the theory of least squares, as has been indicated in paragraphs (0.7) and (1.1),

$$\lim_{T \to \infty} \frac{1}{2T} \int_{-T}^{T} \left| f(t + \alpha) - \int_{0}^{\infty} f(t - \tau)\, dK(\tau) \right|^2 dt$$

gives an estimate of the extent to which the operator fails to predict the future value of $f(t)$ after a lead of α units of time. By our lemmas. (1.161, 1.163), this may become

$$\lim_{T \to \infty} \frac{1}{2T} \int_{-T}^{T} \left| f(t + \alpha) - \int_{0}^{\infty} f(t - \tau)\, dK(\tau) \right|^2 dt$$

$$= \lim_{T \to \infty} \frac{1}{2T} \int_{-T}^{T} |f(t + \alpha)|^2\, dt -$$

$$2R\left\{ \lim_{T \to \infty} \frac{1}{2T} \int_{-T}^{T} f(t + \alpha)\, dt \int_{0}^{\infty} \overline{f(t - \tau)\, dK(\tau)} \right\} + \qquad (2.012)$$

$$\lim_{T \to \infty} \frac{1}{2T} \int_{-T}^{T} dt \int_{0}^{\infty} \overline{f(t - \tau)\, dK(\tau)} \int_{0}^{\infty} f(t - \sigma)\, dK(\sigma)$$

$$= \varphi(0) - 2R\left\{ \int_{0}^{\infty} \varphi(\alpha + \tau)\, d\overline{K(\tau)} \right\} + \int_{0}^{\infty} d\overline{K(\tau)} \int_{0}^{\infty} dK(\sigma)\varphi(\tau - \sigma).$$

2.02 The Minimization Problem

The formal minimization of expression (2.012) is obtained by adding to $K(\tau)$ the expression $\epsilon[\delta K(\tau)]$ differentiating (2.012), with respect to ϵ, equating this derivative to zero, and then allowing ϵ to approach zero. As a result we get

$$\int_{0}^{\infty} \left[\varphi(\alpha + \tau) - \int_{0}^{\infty} \varphi(\tau - \sigma)\, dK(\sigma) \right] d\delta K(\tau) = 0 \qquad (2.0205)$$

for all admissible $\delta K(\sigma)$. Formally this leads to

$$\varphi(\alpha + \tau) = \int_0^\infty \varphi(\tau - \sigma)\, dK(\sigma) \quad \text{for} \quad \tau > 0. \quad (2.0207)$$

However, in order to show that (2.0207) gives us a true minimum rather than a mere stationary solution, we proceed as follows: we put

$$\varphi(\alpha + \tau) = \int_0^\infty \varphi(\tau - \sigma)\, dQ(\sigma) \quad \text{for} \quad \tau > 0. \quad (2.021)$$

Then

$$\varphi(0) - 2R \left\{ \int_0^\infty \varphi(\alpha + \tau)\, d\overline{K(\tau)} \right\} + \int_0^\infty d\overline{K(\tau)} \int_0^\infty dK(\sigma)\varphi(\tau - \sigma)$$

$$= \varphi(0) - \int_0^\infty \varphi(\alpha + \tau)\, d\overline{Q(\tau)}$$

$$+ \int_0^\infty d[\overline{K(\tau)} - \overline{Q(\tau)}] \int_0^\infty d[K(\sigma) - Q(\sigma)]\varphi(\tau - \sigma)$$

$$= \varphi(0) - \int_0^\infty \varphi(\alpha + \tau)\, d\overline{Q(\tau)}$$

$$+ \lim_{T \to \infty} \frac{1}{2T} \int_{-T}^T dt \left| \int_0^\infty f(t - \tau)\, d[K(\tau) - Q(\tau)] \right|^2. \quad (2.022)$$

Since the last term is non-negative, the whole expression (2.022) is greater than or equal to

$$\varphi(0) - \int_0^\infty \varphi(\alpha + \tau)\, \overline{dQ(\tau)},$$

provided Q satisfies the conditions which we have already laid down for K.

Here, as throughout the paper, where a contrary assumption is not explicitly made, we shall assume that the integrated spectrum $\Lambda(\omega)$ is absolutely continuous, and shall write

$$\Phi(\omega) = \sqrt{2\pi}\Lambda'(\omega). \quad (2.023)$$

We may, in fact, confine ourselves for all practical purposes to the case in which $\Lambda(\omega)$ is absolutely continuous. The simplest exception to the absolute continuity of $\Lambda(\omega)$ is the case in which $\Lambda(\omega)$ has one or more jumps. In this case, $f(t)$ contains a part of the form $\sum_1^N A_n e^{i\Lambda_n \omega}$. For such a function, the phase relations between the different components at present or in the past determine with perfect strictness the phase relations into the indefinite future. The times at which $\sin (t)$ goes through zero are determined for all eternity by any one of them. This is not the behavior which we expect of a telephone message or of an economic time series. It is only such terms as depend on an external rigidly periodic influence, like the day or the year, which show even an approximation to such a behavior. A periodicity in which the phase relations gradually alter through the course of the ages is not in fact a true periodicity and does not correspond to a sharp jump of $\Lambda(\omega)$, but to a very rapid rise. It is a fact that the periods of the communications engineer are always more-or-less periods, never precise periods, and therefore have absolutely continuous spectra.

If the jump spectrum is an idealization, never perfectly realized in practice, this is even more the case with the continuous spectrum which is not absolutely continuous. In both cases, to establish the existence of such a spectrum presupposes an infinitely long run of observations. In both cases, according to the work of Kolmogoroff,* the past of a

---

* A. N. Kolmogoroff, Interpolation und Extrapolation, *Bulletin de l'académie des sciences de U.S.S.R.*, Ser. Math. 5, pp. 3–14, 1941. Kolmogoroff's work is of earlier origin than ours but is devoted to a slightly different question and consequently uses results which are more general but less specific. In both cases the object of study is the optimum prediction. In our case we actually obtain a function which we designate as the coefficient function $K(t)$ to be used directly in making such an optimum prediction. Incidentally, we develop an expression for the mean square error of the optimum prediction. Furthermore, we discuss the continuous as well as the discrete case in prediction. Kolmogoroff discusses only the discrete case of prediction and the mean square error in this case. In contrast to our approach, Kolmogoroff concerns himself with the more general case where $\Lambda(\omega)$ is not necessarily absolutely continuous. On the other hand, we discuss only absolutely continuous values of $\Lambda(\omega)$. Now, if $\Lambda(\omega)$ is not absolutely continuous, there is in general no unique optimum method of prediction based on non-singular integral or differential operators. The operators which furnish such an optimum prediction do not assume as convenient a form on Kolmogoroff's more general basis as on ours, but often appear as means or averages; so that it is only natural that Kolmogoroff proceeds only so far as the greatest lower bound of the mean square error of prediction, while we actually obtain the optimum predicting operators.

The author wishes to comment on the historical relation between the present work and that of Kolmogoroff. The present investigation was initiated in the early winter of 1940 as an attempt to solve an engineering problem. At that time and until the last week of 1941, by which time the paper was substantially complete, the author was not aware of the results of Kolmogoroff's work and scarcely aware of its existence; although Professor Feller of Brown University had mentioned Kolmogoroff's researches in casual conversation at an earlier period. Mr. I. E. Segal of the Princeton Graduate School brought Kolmogoroff's work to the author's attention at the Christmas meeting of the American Mathematical Society for 1941. Thus it would appear that the work of Kolmogoroff and that of the present writer represent two entirely separate attacks on the problem of time series, and that the parallelism between them may be attributed to the simple fact that the theory of the stochastic process had advanced to the point where the study of the prediction problem was the next thing on the agenda.

function with a spectrum crowded into a set of frequencies of zero measure determines its future for an infinite time. However, there are many well-known cases in physics and engineering where the discrete spectrum has been a useful approximation to the observed situation, while no case has yet been found in any such science where the non-absolutely continuous spectrum has proved a valuable tool. We say this without prejudice to the future.

Thus, on our assumptions,

$$
\int_0^\infty d[\overline{K(\tau)} - \overline{Q(\tau)}] \int_0^\infty d[K(\sigma) - Q(\sigma)]\varphi(\tau - \sigma)
$$

$$
= \frac{1}{2\pi} \int_0^\infty d[\overline{K(\tau)} - \overline{Q(\tau)}] \int_0^\infty d[K(\sigma) - Q(\sigma)] \int_{-\infty}^\infty \Phi(\omega)e^{i\omega(\tau-\sigma)}\, d\omega
$$

$$
= \frac{1}{2\pi} \int_{-\infty}^\infty \Phi(\omega)\, d\omega \left| \int_0^\infty e^{-i\omega\tau}\, d[K(\tau) - Q(\tau)] \right|^2 \qquad (2.026)
$$

if K and Q are of limited total variation. Thus, if $\Phi(\omega)$ has no interval over which it vanishes, we can have

$$
\int_0^\infty d[\overline{K(\tau)} - \overline{Q(\tau)}] \int_0^\infty d[K(\sigma) - Q(\sigma)]\varphi(\tau - \sigma) = 0
$$

when and only when K and Q are equivalent. In this case and in this case only,

$$
\lim_{T\to\infty} \frac{1}{2T} \int_{-T}^T \left| f(t + \alpha) - \int_0^\infty f(t - \tau)\, dK(\tau) \right|^2 dt
$$

$$
= \varphi(0) - \int_0^\infty \varphi(\alpha + \tau)\, d\overline{Q(\tau)}, \qquad (2.027)
$$

and as a consequence,

$$
\varphi(0) \geq \int_0^\infty \varphi(\alpha + \tau)\, d\overline{Q(\tau)}. \qquad (2.028)
$$

2.03 The Factorization Problem

We now wish to solve equation (2.0207), which we know to have not more than one admissible solution. As at the end of the last chapter, we factor $\Phi(u)$ into the product $|\Psi(u)|^2$, and, employing the same notation, over every finite range

$$
\Psi(u) = \text{l.i.m.}_{\epsilon\to 0} \exp\left\{ \frac{1}{2\pi} \int_{-\infty}^\infty \frac{\log|\Phi(\omega)|}{-i(\omega - u) - \epsilon}\, d\omega \right\}; \qquad (2.031)
$$

makes

this factoring possible,

$$\Psi(u + iv) = \exp\left\{\frac{1}{2\pi}\int_{-\infty}^{\infty}\frac{\log|\Phi(\omega)|}{-i[\omega - (u + iv)]}\,d\omega\right\}. \quad (2.032)$$

The function $\Psi(u + iv)$ will be free from singularities and zeros in the lower half-plane, while over any finite range of u,

$$\Psi(u + iv)e^{civ}$$

is bounded for $v \to \infty$. As we have already seen, if we can arrange $\Phi(u)$ as the quotient of the products

$$\Phi(u) = A^2\frac{\prod\limits_{1}^{n}(\omega - \omega_k)(\omega - \bar{\omega}_k)}{\prod\limits_{1}^{m}(\omega - \omega_j')(\omega - \bar{\omega}_j')} \quad (A \text{ real; } m > n), \quad (2.033)$$

where the imaginary parts of each ω_k and ω_j' are positive, then

$$\Psi(\omega) = A\frac{\prod\limits_{1}^{n}(\omega - \omega_k)}{\prod\limits_{1}^{m}(\omega - \omega_j')}, \quad (2.034)$$

and $\Psi(\omega)$ will belong to L^2 on the real axis, as it has a denominator at least one degree higher than the numerator. Of course, in the general case, since

$$\frac{1}{2\pi}\int_{-\infty}^{\infty}\Phi(\omega)\,d\omega = \varphi(0) < \infty, \quad (2.035)$$

$\Psi(\omega)$ will belong to L^2. The function

$$\psi(t) = \underset{B\to\infty}{\text{l.i.m.}}\frac{1}{2\pi}\int_{-B}^{B}\Psi(\omega)e^{i\omega t}\,d\omega \quad (2.036)$$

will accordingly exist; and since

$$\Psi(u + iv)$$

is of less than exponential growth as $v \to -\infty$, we must have

$$\psi(t) = 0, \quad t < 0$$

except at a set of points of zero measure. Certainly, $\psi(t)$ belongs to L^2. Thus we may conclude that for almost all values of β

$$F_\beta(t) = \int_{-\infty}^{t}\psi(t - \tau)\,dx(\tau, \beta) \quad (2.037)$$

will exist, and we shall have

$$\lim_{T \to \infty} \frac{1}{2T} \int_{-T}^{T} F_\beta(t + \sigma)\overline{F_\beta(t)} \, dt = \int_{0}^{1} d_\beta F_\beta(t + \sigma)\overline{F_\beta(t)}$$

$$= \int_{-\infty}^{\infty} \psi(t + \sigma)\overline{\psi(t)} \, dt \qquad (2.038)$$

$$= \frac{1}{2\pi} \int_{-\infty}^{\infty} |\Psi(\omega)|^2 \, e^{i\omega\sigma} \, d\omega = \varphi(\sigma).$$

Now,

$$F_\beta(t + \alpha) = \int_{-\infty}^{\infty} \psi(t + \alpha - \tau) \, dx(\tau, \beta)$$

$$+ \int_{t}^{t+\alpha} \psi(t + \alpha - \tau) \, dx(\tau, \beta) = P_\beta(t) + R_\beta(t),$$

where P_β involves only the past or present of $x(t, \beta)$, and R_β only its future. On the other hand,

$$\int_{0}^{\infty} F_\beta(t - \tau) \, dK(\tau) = \int_{0}^{\infty} dK(\sigma) \int_{-\infty}^{t-\sigma} \psi(t - \sigma - \tau) \, dx(\tau, \beta)$$

$$= \int_{-\infty}^{t} dx(\tau, \beta) \int_{-\infty}^{t-\tau} \psi(t - \sigma - \tau) \, dK(\sigma),$$

which last involves only the present and past of $x(t, \beta)$. Thus, because of the independence of different ranges of $x(t, \beta)$, then for almost all β,

$$\lim_{T \to \infty} \frac{1}{2T} \int_{-T}^{T} R_\beta(t) \int_{0}^{\infty} \overline{F_\beta(t - \tau) \, dK(\tau)} = 0. \qquad (2.0381)$$

If then we can solve the equation

$$\int_{-\infty}^{t} \psi(t - \sigma) \, dK(\sigma) = \psi(t + \alpha) \quad (t \geq 0), \qquad (2.0382)$$

the K we obtain will minimize

$$\lim_{T \to \infty} \frac{1}{2T} \int_{-T}^{T} \left| F_\beta(t + \alpha) - \int_{0}^{\infty} F_\beta(t - \tau) \, dK(\tau) \right|^2 dt; \qquad (2.0383)$$

and, since this minimization is unique, and $F_\beta(t)$ and $f(t)$ share the same $\varphi(t)$, we have solved

$$\varphi(\alpha + \tau) = \int_{0}^{\infty} \varphi(\tau - \sigma) \, dK(\sigma) \quad (\tau > 0). \qquad (2.039)$$

To solve equation (2.0382), let us put

$$\int_{0}^{\infty} e^{-i\omega t} \, dK(t) = k(\omega). \qquad (2.0391)$$

If we make a formal Fourier transformation of both sides, this yields

$$\int_0^\infty \psi(\alpha + t)e^{-i\omega t}\,dt = \Psi(\omega)k(\omega), \qquad (2.0392)$$

where α is a finite constant; with the formal solution

$$k(\omega) = \frac{\left[\int_0^\infty \psi(\alpha + t)e^{-i\omega t}\,dt\right]}{\Psi(\omega)}. \qquad (2.0393)$$

Clearly the function $k(\omega)$ will have no singularities in the half-plane below the real axis, nor can it grow exponentially there, so that one requirement for $k(\omega)$ is fulfilled. It remains to be ascertained whether $K(t)$ is of finite total variation. This will be the case if the numerator and the denominator of (2.0393) are rational functions, and if also the numerator is not of higher degree than the denominator.

Let us now investigate this numerator. If

$$\Psi(\omega) = \sum_{m,n} \frac{a_{m,n}}{(\omega - \omega_n)^m}, \qquad (2.0394)$$

then

$$\psi(t) = \underset{B\to\infty}{\text{l.i.m.}} \frac{1}{2\pi} \int_{-B}^{B} \sum_{m,n} \frac{a_{m,n}}{(\omega - \omega_n)^m} e^{i\omega t}\,d\omega$$

$$= \sum_{m,n} a_{m,n} \frac{i^m t^{m-1} e^{i\omega_n t}}{(m-1)!} \quad \text{if } t > 0; \text{ and } = 0 \text{ if } t < 0. \qquad (2.0395)$$

This may be proved by the use of Cauchy's theorem or by observing that

$$\int_0^\infty \frac{i^{\nu+1} t^\nu e^{i\omega_n t} e^{-i\omega t}}{\nu!}\,dt = \frac{1}{(\omega - \omega_n)^{\nu+1}}; \qquad (2.0396)$$

and that hence, by the Plancherel theorem,

$$\frac{1}{2\pi} \underset{B\to\infty}{\text{l.i.m.}} \int_{-B}^{B} \frac{e^{i\omega t}}{(\omega - \omega_n)^{\nu+1}}\,d\omega = \frac{i^{\nu+1} t^\nu e^{i\omega_n t}}{\nu!} \quad \text{if } t > 0$$

$$= 0 \text{ if } t < 0 \qquad (2.0397)$$

Then

$$\int_0^\infty \psi(\alpha + t)e^{-i\omega t}\,dt = \int_0^\infty e^{-i\omega t}\,dt \sum_{m,n} a_{m,n} \frac{i^m(\alpha + t)^{m-1}}{(m-1)!} e^{i\omega_n(\alpha + t)}$$

$$= \sum_{m,n} a_{m,n} \frac{e^{i\omega_n\alpha} i^m}{(m-1)!} \sum_{k=0}^{m-1} \frac{(m-1)!}{k!(m-1-k)!} \alpha^{m-1-k} \int_0^\infty t^k e^{i(\omega_n - \omega)t}\,dt$$

$$= \sum_{m,n} a_{m,n} e^{i\omega_n\alpha} \sum_{k=0}^{m-1} \frac{(i\alpha)^{(m-1-k)}}{(m-1-k)!(\omega - \omega_n)^{k+1}}. \qquad (2.0397)$$

Thus

$$k(\omega) = \frac{\sum\limits_{m,n} a_{m,n} e^{i\omega n\alpha} \sum\limits_{k=0}^{m-1} \dfrac{(i\alpha)^{(m-1-k)}}{(m-1-k)!(\omega-\omega_n)^{k+1}}}{\sum\limits_{m,n} \dfrac{a_{m,n}}{(\omega-\omega_n)^m}}. \qquad (2.0399)$$

That is, if $\Phi(\omega)$ is a rational function, with denominator of higher degree than the numerator, and has no real poles nor zeros, we have a method of determining the formal expression for $k(\omega)$ in which we do not depart from the ω-axis at all. The final $k(\omega)$ which we obtain may be transformed back into a $K(t)$, as will be the general procedure in statistical theory and practice; or we may use it directly for specifying the characteristic of an electrical network or mechanical structure to accomplish our work of prediction. Let it be noted that as the poles of $k(\omega)$ are all above the real axis, there will always exist a passive four-terminal network with a multiple of $k(\omega)$ as its voltage transfer ratio, and that the construction of such networks belongs to a branch of communication engineering having a well-established technique.

2.04   The Predictor Formula

It is possible to express all the processes leading up to (2.0393) within the compass of a single formula:

$$k(\omega) = \frac{1}{2\pi\Psi(\omega)} \int_0^\infty e^{-i\omega t}\, dt \int_{-\infty}^\infty \Psi(u) e^{iu(t+\alpha)}\, du. \qquad (2.041)$$

As will be seen, we first work with $\Psi(\omega)$, taking its Fourier transform, advance it an amount α, discard the part corresponding to negative values of t, transform back into a function of ω, and divide by $\Psi(\omega)$.

The mean square error of the prediction determined by $k(\omega)$ will be

$$\lim_{T\to\infty} \frac{1}{2T} \int_{-T}^T dt \left| \int_0^\infty f(t-\tau)\frac{d\tau}{2\pi} \int_{-\infty}^\infty \frac{e^{i\omega\tau}\, d\omega}{2\pi\Psi(\omega)} \left\{ \int_0^\alpha e^{-i\omega\sigma}\, d\sigma \right.\right.$$

$$\left.\left. \times \int_{-\infty}^\infty \Psi(u)e^{iu(\sigma+\alpha)}\, du - \int_{-\infty}^\infty e^{-i\omega\sigma}\, d\sigma \int_{-\infty}^\infty \Psi(u)e^{iu(\sigma+\alpha)}\, du \right\} \right|^2$$

$$= \lim_{T\to\infty} \frac{1}{2T} \int_{-T}^T dt \left| \int_0^\infty f(t-\tau)\frac{d\tau}{2\pi} \int_{-\infty}^\infty \frac{e^{-i\omega\tau}\, d\omega}{2\pi\Psi(\omega)} \int_0^\alpha e^{-i\omega\sigma}\, d\sigma \right.$$

$$\left. \times \int_{-\infty}^\infty \Psi(u)e^{iut}\, du \right|^2$$

$$= \int_0^\infty d\tau_1 \int_0^\infty \varphi(\tau_2 - \tau_1) \, d\tau_2 \int_{-\infty}^\infty \frac{e^{i\omega_1\tau_1}}{2\pi\Psi(\omega_1)} \, d\omega_1 \int_0^\alpha \psi(\sigma_1)e^{-i\omega_1\sigma_1} \, d\sigma_1$$

$$\times \int_{-\infty}^\infty \frac{e^{-i\omega_2\tau_2}}{2\pi\Psi(\overline{\omega_2})} \, d\omega_2 \int_0^\alpha \psi(\overline{\sigma_2})e^{i\omega_2\sigma_2} \, d\sigma_2$$

$$= \frac{1}{2\pi} \int_{-\infty}^\infty d\omega \left| \int_0^\alpha e^{-i\omega\sigma}\psi(\sigma) \, d\sigma \right|^2 = \int_0^\alpha |\psi(\sigma)|^2 \, d\sigma. \tag{2.042}$$

We shall denote this by the symbol $E(\alpha)$.

2.1 Examples of Prediction

Let us now turn back to the technical detail of prediction. A few examples will illustrate both the power of this method and some of the limitations and precautions which must be observed in applying it. Let our first case be

$$\Phi(\omega) = \frac{1}{1 + \omega^2}. \tag{2.10}$$

Here
$$\Psi(\omega) = \frac{1}{\omega - i}; \quad \overline{\Psi(\overline{\omega})} = \frac{1}{\omega + i}. \tag{2.11}$$

Accordingly,

$$k(\omega) = \frac{e^{-\alpha}}{\omega - i} \div \frac{1}{\omega - i} = e^{-\alpha}; \quad E(\alpha) = \frac{1}{2}(1 - e^{2\alpha}). \tag{2.12}$$

That is, the optimum prediction of $f(t + \alpha)$ is obtained by taking the product of $f(t)$ by a factor $e^{-\alpha}$ tending to zero as $\alpha \to \infty$. At first sight this seems surprising, for it looks as if this meant that $f(t)$ must tend to zero in some way or other. As a matter of fact, it says only that the predictable part of $f(t + \alpha)$ tends to zero, and that roughly the unpredictable part is as likely to be positive as negative. In other words, the values of $f(t + \alpha)$ will have a distribution centering about $e^{-\alpha}f(t)$. This is altogether reasonable. Again, let us consider the example

$$\Phi(\omega) = \frac{1}{1 + \omega^4} = \frac{1}{\left(\omega + \dfrac{1+i}{\sqrt{2}}\right)\left(\omega - \dfrac{1+i}{\sqrt{2}}\right)\left(\omega + \dfrac{1-i}{\sqrt{2}}\right)\left(\omega - \dfrac{1-i}{\sqrt{2}}\right)}. \tag{2.13}$$

Here

$$\Psi(\omega) = \frac{1}{\left(\omega - \dfrac{1+i}{\sqrt{2}}\right)\left(\omega + \dfrac{1-i}{\sqrt{2}}\right)} = \frac{\sqrt{2}/2}{\left(\omega - \dfrac{1+i}{\sqrt{2}}\right)} - \frac{\sqrt{2}/2}{\left(\omega + \dfrac{1-i}{\sqrt{2}}\right)}. \tag{2.14}$$

Accordingly

$$k(\omega) = \frac{e^{-\alpha\left(\frac{1-i}{\sqrt{2}}\right)}\left(\dfrac{\sqrt{2}/2}{\omega - \dfrac{1+i}{\sqrt{2}}}\right) - e^{-\alpha\left(\frac{1+i}{\sqrt{2}}\right)}\left(\dfrac{\sqrt{2}/2}{\omega + \dfrac{1-i}{\sqrt{2}}}\right)}{\left(\dfrac{\sqrt{2}/2}{\omega - \dfrac{1+i}{\sqrt{2}}}\right) - \left(\dfrac{\sqrt{2}/2}{\omega + \dfrac{1-i}{\sqrt{2}}}\right)}$$

$$= \omega \frac{\sqrt{2}}{2}\left(e^{-\alpha\left(\frac{1-i}{\sqrt{2}}\right)} - e^{-\alpha\left(\frac{1+i}{\sqrt{2}}\right)}\right) + \left(\frac{1-i}{2}\right) e^{-\alpha\left(\frac{1-i}{\sqrt{2}}\right)}$$

$$+ \left(\frac{1+i}{2}\right) e^{-\alpha\left(\frac{1+i}{\sqrt{2}}\right)}$$

$$= i\omega\sqrt{2}\, e^{-\alpha/\sqrt{2}} \sin\frac{\alpha}{\sqrt{2}} + e^{-\alpha/\sqrt{2}}\left(\cos\frac{\alpha}{\sqrt{2}} + \sin\frac{\alpha}{\sqrt{2}}\right). \tag{2.15}$$

What happens here is extremely interesting and suggestive. The $k(\omega)$ which we obtain is not the Fourier transform of any function of limited total variation, and the argument which we have given, interpreted strictly, breaks down. On the other hand, the operation of multiplication by $k(\omega)$ on the frequency scale corresponds to the operation

$$\left(\sqrt{2}\, e^{-\alpha/\sqrt{2}} \sin\frac{\alpha}{\sqrt{2}}\right)\frac{d}{dt} + e^{-\alpha/\sqrt{2}}\left(\cos\frac{\alpha}{\sqrt{2}} + \sin\frac{\alpha}{\sqrt{2}}\right) \tag{2.16}$$

on the time scale. This operator may well apply to all the functions $f(t)$ of the ensemble which we are predicting, and formally, at any rate, it represents a perfectly usable prediction of the future. There is no optimum prediction by means of functions $K(t)$ of limited total variation, although by such functions we may reduce the norm of the error of prediction as nearly as we wish to the greatest lower bound of its value. To attain the greatest lower bound, we must abandon the class of operators determined by $K(t)$ above and enter the class of differential operators. Without going into the argument by which it may be seen that this is really the rigorous situation, we may state that this is the fact, and that the theory of prediction is complete in this case as well as in the previous one. The essential point is that $\Psi(\omega)$, not $k(\omega)$, belongs to L^2.

Let

$$\Phi(\omega) = \frac{1}{(1 + \omega^2)^2}, \tag{2.17}$$

so that

$$\Psi(\omega) = \frac{1}{(\omega - i)^2}. \qquad (2.171)$$

Here

$$k(\omega) = e^{-\alpha} \frac{\left\{\dfrac{i\alpha}{(\omega - i)} + \dfrac{1}{(\omega - i)^2}\right\}}{\dfrac{1}{(\omega - i)^2}} = e^{-\alpha}[i\alpha(\omega - i) + 1] \qquad (2.172)$$

$$= \alpha e^{-\alpha} i\omega + e^{-\alpha}(1 + \alpha);$$
$$E(\alpha) = \tfrac{1}{4}\{1 - (1 + 2\alpha + 2\alpha^2)e^{-2\alpha}\}.$$

We thus again meet the situation in which the prediction operator is a differential operator.

Let

$$\Phi(\omega) = \frac{1 + \omega^2}{1 + \omega^4}. \qquad (2.18)$$

Here

$$\Psi(\omega) = \frac{\omega - i}{\left(\omega - \dfrac{1 + i}{\sqrt{2}}\right)\left(\omega + \dfrac{1 - i}{\sqrt{2}}\right)}$$

$$= \frac{\dfrac{1 + i(1 - \sqrt{2})}{2}}{\omega - \dfrac{1 + i}{\sqrt{2}}} + \frac{\dfrac{1 - i(1 - \sqrt{2})}{2}}{\omega + \dfrac{1 - i}{\sqrt{2}}}, \qquad (2.181)$$

$$k(\omega) = \frac{\dfrac{1 + i(1 - \sqrt{2})}{2} \dfrac{e^{\alpha\left(\frac{i-1}{\sqrt{2}}\right)}}{\omega - \dfrac{1 + i}{\sqrt{2}}} + \dfrac{1 - i(1 - \sqrt{2})}{2} \dfrac{e^{\alpha\left(\frac{-i-1}{\sqrt{2}}\right)}}{\omega + \dfrac{1 - i}{\sqrt{2}}}}{\dfrac{\omega - i}{\left(\omega - \dfrac{1 + i}{\sqrt{2}}\right)\left(\omega + \dfrac{1 - i}{\sqrt{2}}\right)}}$$

$$= \frac{1 + i(1 - \sqrt{2})}{2} e^{\alpha\left(\frac{i-1}{\sqrt{2}}\right)} \frac{\omega + \left(\dfrac{1 - i}{\sqrt{2}}\right)}{\omega - i}$$

$$+ \frac{1 - i(1 - \sqrt{2})}{2} e^{\alpha\left(\frac{-i-1}{\sqrt{2}}\right)} \frac{\omega - \dfrac{1 + i}{\sqrt{2}}}{\omega - i}$$

$$= \frac{A\omega + Bi}{\omega - i}, \qquad (2.182)$$

where

$$A = e^{-\alpha/\sqrt{2}} \left[\cos\left(\frac{\alpha}{\sqrt{2}}\right) + (\sqrt{2} - 1) \sin\left(\frac{\alpha}{\sqrt{2}}\right) \right];$$

$$B = e^{-\alpha/\sqrt{2}} \left[(\sqrt{2} - 1) \sin\left(\frac{\alpha}{\sqrt{2}}\right) - \cos\left(\frac{\alpha}{\sqrt{2}}\right) \right];$$

$$E(\alpha) = \frac{\sqrt{2}}{4} \{2 - A^2 - B^2\} = \frac{\sqrt{2}}{2} - e^{-\alpha\sqrt{2}} (\sqrt{2} - 1) \left(1 + \frac{\sqrt{2}}{2} \cos\alpha\sqrt{2}\right).$$

$$(2.19)$$

Here again the prediction operator does not involve differentiation. This will in general be the case when and only when the denominator of $\Phi(\omega)$ is two degrees higher than the numerator, although there may be particular values of α which give a prediction free from differentiation in other cases.

2.2 A Limiting Example of Prediction

The basis of our method of prediction is the separation of $\Phi(\omega)$ into two factors, one of which is bounded and free from zeros in every half-plane above a horizontal line above the real axis, while the other is similarly bounded and free from zeros in every half-plane below a horizontal line below the real axis. There are of course functions $\Phi(\omega)$ for which this factorization breaks down. It is very interesting to observe how the optimum prediction behaves in the neighborhood of a function $\Phi(\omega)$ for which it breaks down, and for which the factorization into $\Psi(\omega) \cdot \overline{\Psi(\omega)}$ is impossible. Such a $\Phi(\omega)$ is furnished by $e^{-\omega^2}$. An approximate $e^{-\omega^2}$, for which prediction is possible, is given by

$$\frac{1}{\left(1 + \dfrac{\omega^2}{n}\right)^n}. \qquad (2.20)$$

The corresponding $\Psi(\omega)$ is

$$\left(1 + \frac{i\omega}{\sqrt{n}}\right)^{-n}, \qquad (2.21)$$

which gives as a $\psi(t)$,

$$\frac{t^{n-1}\, e^{-t\sqrt{n}}}{n^{-n/2}\, (n-1)!}. \qquad (2.215)$$

The mean square error of prediction for lead α is

$$\int_0^\alpha \frac{t^{2n-2} e^{-2t\sqrt{n}}}{n^{-n}[(n-1)!]^2}\, dt. \qquad (2.22)$$

By differentiation, we see that the integrand is a maximum for a value of t given by the solution of

$$(2n - 2)t^{2n-3}e^{-2t\sqrt{n}} - 2\sqrt{n}t^{2n-2}e^{-2t\sqrt{n}} = 0. \qquad (2.225)$$

This will be

$$t = \frac{n-1}{\sqrt{n}}.$$

Let us put

$$t = \tau + \frac{n-1}{\sqrt{n}}.$$

Then the integrand becomes

$$\frac{t^{2n-2}e^{-2t\sqrt{n}}}{n^{-n}[(n-1)!]^2} = \frac{\left(\tau + \dfrac{n-1}{\sqrt{n}}\right)^{2n-2} e^{-2\tau\sqrt{n}}e^{-2(n-1)}}{n^{-n}[(n-1)!]^2}$$

$$= \frac{(n-1)^{2n-2}ne^{2-2n}}{[(n-1)!]^2}e^{-2\tau\sqrt{n}}\left(1 + \frac{\tau\sqrt{n}}{n-1}\right)^{2n-2}$$

$$= \frac{(n-1)^{2n-2}ne^{2-2n}}{[(n-1)!]^2}\left[1 - \frac{\tau^2 n}{(n-1)^2}\right]^{2n-2}$$

$$\times \left(1 + \begin{array}{c}\text{a term of order of magnitude}\\ \text{not exceeding } \left[\dfrac{\tau^3 n^{\frac{3}{2}}}{(n-1)^3}\right]\end{array}\right)^{2n-2}. \qquad (2.23)$$

Asymptotically

$$\frac{(n-1)^{2n-2}ne^{2-2n}}{[(n-1)!]^2} \sim \frac{(n-1)^{2n-2}ne^{2-2n}}{(n-1)^{2n-2}e^{2-2n}2\pi(n-1)} \sim \frac{1}{2\pi}. \qquad (2.24)$$

Thus

$$\int_0^\alpha \frac{1}{2\pi} e^{-2\left(t - \frac{n-1}{\sqrt{n}}\right)^2} dt \qquad (2.25)$$

will be a good representation of the error in prediction for large n. If α is substantially less than $\sqrt{n}$, prediction will be good, and if it is substantially greater than $\sqrt{n}$, prediction will be bad. Approximately, $\sqrt{n}$ is the period for which good prediction is possible.

Now

$$\left(1 + \frac{\omega^2}{n}\right)^{-n} = e^{-n\left(\frac{\omega^2}{n} - \frac{\omega^4}{2n^2} + \frac{\omega^6}{3n^3} - \cdots\right)}$$

$$= e^{-\omega^2 + \frac{\omega^4}{2n} - \frac{\omega^6}{3n^2} + \cdots} \qquad (2.26)$$

To a first approximation,

$$\left(1 + \frac{\omega^2}{n}\right)^{-n} = e^{-\omega^2}\left(1 + \frac{\omega^4}{2n}\right). \tag{2.27}$$

Here the error term in comparison with $e^{-\omega^2}$ is

$$\frac{\omega^4}{2n} e^{-\omega^2} \tag{2.28}$$

which has its maximum when

$$\omega = \sqrt{2}.$$

Approximately, the absolute maximum error is

$$\frac{4e^{-2}}{2n} = \frac{2e^{-2}}{n} = \frac{2e^{-2}}{(\text{time of good prediction})^2} \tag{2.29}$$

or

$$\frac{\text{time of good}}{\text{prediction}} = \frac{\sqrt{2}e^{-1}}{\sqrt{\text{allowable maximum error of } \Phi(\omega)}}. \tag{2.295}$$

Thus, if $\Phi(\omega)$ is allowed a tolerance of 10 per cent of $\Phi(\omega)$ maximum, the time of good prediction is about 1.6 seconds; if it is 1 per cent, the time is about 5 seconds. These should be compared with the root mean square of t taken with respect to $\varphi(t)$, which in this instance is $\sqrt{2}$. It will be seen that $\Phi(\omega)$ must be known quite accurately to make any sort of long-time prediction possible, and that this accuracy requirement increases as the square of the desired lead.

This point is made here because it arises in certain schemes of prediction proposed for use on the motion of airplanes, although it is not easy to handle them adequately in this direct manner. It has been proposed to predict the polar coordinates of the motion of an airplane, each on its own merits, by means of independent linear predictors. For a straight-line path, this would involve the prediction of an anti-tangent curve. The Fourier transform of such a curve is far richer in higher frequencies than the curve $e^{-\omega^2}$ and yields a correspondingly more unstable prediction. If we actually use the known velocities of planes and shells, we shall find that any prediction of the course of a plane which will be good enough to allow hitting the plane in the center part of its course, where its angular velocity is greatest, but where, on the other hand, the plane is nearest to the gun, will be so unstable elsewhere as to demand an accuracy in the rectilinearity of the path of the plane and in its tracking which is quite beyond reason. Important as is the method of prediction given in this paper, it has strict limitations in practice† and should never

† This is, in fact, true of any method of prediction.

be used to determine a curve which may be determined in a strictly geometrical manner. Statistical prediction is essentially a method of refining a prediction which would be perfect by itself in an idealized case but which is corrupted by statistical errors, either in the observed quantity itself or in the observation. Geometrical facts must be predicted geometrically and analytical facts analytically, leaving only statistical facts to be predicted statistically.

2.3 The Prediction of Functions Whose Derivatives Possess Auto-correlation Coefficients

Up to the present, we have been predicting functions which themselves possess an auto-correlation coefficient. Let us now investigate the prediction problem for functions whose first derivative possesses an auto-correlation coefficient. Let $f(t)$ be a function with a derivative $f'(t)$, with an auto-correlation coefficient φ_d, and let

$$\Phi_d(\omega) = \int_{-\infty}^{\infty} \varphi_d(t)e^{-i\omega t}\, dt; \quad \varphi_d(t) = \frac{1}{2\pi}\int_{-\infty}^{\infty} \Phi_d(\omega)e^{i\omega t}\, d\omega. \quad (2.30)$$

Just as we have factored $\Phi(\omega)$ into $\Psi(\omega) \cdot \overline{\Psi(\overline{\omega})}$, let us factor

$$\Phi_d(\omega) = \Psi_d(\omega) \cdot \overline{\Psi_d(\overline{\omega})}, \quad (2.305)$$

where $\Psi_d(\omega)$ is free from singularities and zeros in the lower half-plane. Then the predicted value of $f'(t + \alpha)$ will be the result of applying to $f'(t)$ the operator

$$\frac{1}{2\pi\Psi_d(\omega)}\int_0^{\infty} e^{-i\omega t}\, dt \int_{-\infty}^{\infty} \Psi_d(u)e^{iu(t+\alpha)}\, du. \quad (2.31)$$

It is natural to regard the best value of $f(t + \beta) - f(t)$ as the result of integrating the best value of $f'(t + \alpha)$ from 0 to β; and indeed, if we are looking for an optimum prediction in the least square sense, an application of our method of minimization will give exactly this result. That is, the best estimate of $f(t + \beta)$ will be obtained by adding $f(t)$ to the result of applying the operator

$$\frac{1}{2\pi\Psi_d(\omega)}\int_0^{\infty} e^{-i\omega t}\, dt \int_{-\infty}^{\infty} \Psi_d(u)\frac{e^{iu(t+\beta)} - e^{iut}}{iu}\, du \quad (2.315)$$

to $f'(t)$, or the operator

$$\frac{i\omega}{2\pi\Psi_d(\omega)}\int_0^{\infty} e^{-i\omega t}\, dt \int_{-\infty}^{\infty} \Psi_d(u)\frac{e^{iu(t+\beta)} - e^{iut}}{iu}\, du \quad (2.32)$$

to $f(t)$. This yields the predicting operator

$$k(\omega) = 1 + \frac{\omega}{2\pi\Psi_d(\omega)} \int_0^\infty e^{-i\omega t}\, dt \int_{-\infty}^\infty \Psi_d(u) \frac{e^{iu(t+\beta)} - e^{iut}}{u}\, du. \quad (2.325)$$

If $\Psi_d(u)$ behaves like $k(u)$ at 0 (since it has no singularities in the lower half-plane), this becomes

$$\frac{\omega}{2\pi\Psi_d(\omega)} \int_0^\infty e^{-i\omega t}\, dt \int_{-\infty}^\infty \frac{\Psi_d(u)}{u} e^{iu(t+\beta)}\, du \quad (2.33)$$

so that, if we put

$$\Phi(u) = \frac{\Phi_d(u)}{u^2}; \quad \Psi(u) = \frac{\Psi_d(u)}{u}, \quad (2.335)$$

the form we have already established in (2.325) for the prediction of operator $k(\omega)$ remains valid.

Let us generalize this. Let $f^{(n)}(t)$ have the auto-correlation coefficient $\varphi_n(t)$, yielding $\Phi_n(\omega)$ and $\Psi_n(\omega)$, as $f(t)$ has yielded $\Phi(\omega)$ and $\Psi(\omega)$ in the original case. Let

$$\Phi(\omega) = \omega^{-2n}\Phi_n(\omega); \quad \Psi(\omega) = \omega^{-n}\Psi_n(\omega). \quad (2.34)$$

Then the predicting operator for lead β will be

$$k(\omega) = 1 + i\omega\beta + \cdots + \frac{(i\omega\beta)^{n-1}}{(n-1)!} + \frac{1}{2\pi\Psi(\omega)} \int_0^\infty e^{-i\omega t}\, dt$$

$$\times \int_{-\infty}^\infty \Psi(u)e^{iut}\left[(e^{iu\beta} - 1) - (iu\beta) - \cdots - \frac{(iu\beta)^{n-1}}{(n-1)!} \right] du, \quad (2.345)$$

which will be a form in which we may write the predicting operator for the case where $f(t)$ itself possesses an auto-correlation coefficient. To establish this, we follow exactly the same lines as before, noting that Taylor's theorem with remainder asserts that

$$f(t + \beta) = f(t) + \beta f'(t) + \cdots + \frac{\beta^{n-1}}{(n-1)!} f^{(n-1)}(t)$$

$$+ \int_0^\beta dx_1 \int_0^{x_1} dx_2 \cdots \int_0^{x_{n-1}} dx_n f^{(n)}(t + x_n); \quad (2.35)$$

and that

$$\int_0^\beta dx_1 \int_0^{x_1} dx_2 \cdots \int_0^{x_{n-1}} dx_n\, e^{iux_n}$$

$$= \frac{1}{(iu)^n}\left[e^{iu\beta} - 1 - iu\beta - \cdots - \frac{(iu\beta)^{n-1}}{(n-1)!} \right]. \quad (2.355)$$

There are many cases in which these formulas are useful in practice. For example, we may wish to predict the time of flight of a shell from an anti-aircraft gun to an airplane moving in a straight path. This is certainly not a function with a finite mean, but for a considerable portion of the path it is a function with a second derivative not changing size very rapidly, and is not altogether unsuitable as a basis of a prediction.

The mean square error of the prediction established by our last $k(\omega)$ will be

$$\lim_{T \to \infty} \frac{1}{2T} \int_{-T}^{T} dt \left| \int_{0}^{\infty} f(t - \tau) \frac{d\tau}{2\pi} \right.$$

$$\times \int_{-\infty}^{\infty} e^{i\omega\tau} d\omega \left\{ 1 + i\omega\beta + \cdots + \frac{(i\omega\beta)^{n-1}}{(n-1)!} + \frac{1}{2\pi\Psi(\omega)} \int_{0}^{\infty} e^{-i\omega\sigma} d\sigma \right\}$$

$$\times \int_{-\infty}^{\infty} \Psi(u)e^{iu\sigma} \left[(e^{iu\beta} - 1) - \cdots - \frac{(iu\beta)^{n-1}}{(n-1)!} \right.$$

$$\left. - (1 + iu\beta) - \cdots - \frac{(iu\beta)^{n-1}}{(n-1)!} \right] du -$$

$$\frac{1}{2\pi\Psi(\omega)} \int_{-\infty}^{\infty} e^{-i\omega\sigma} d\sigma \int_{-\infty}^{\infty} \Psi(u)e^{iu\sigma} \left[(e^{iu\beta} - 1) - \cdots - \frac{(iu\beta)^{n-1}}{(n-1)!} \right] du \Bigg|^2$$

$$\lim_{T \to \infty} \frac{1}{2T} \int_{-T}^{T} dt \left| \int_{0}^{\infty} f(t - \tau) \frac{d\tau}{2\pi} \int_{-\infty}^{\infty} \frac{e^{i\omega\tau}}{2\pi\Psi(\omega)} d\omega \int_{-\infty}^{0} e^{-i\omega\sigma} d\sigma \right.$$

$$\times \int_{-\infty}^{\infty} \Psi(u)e^{iu\sigma} \left[e^{iu\beta} - 1 - \cdots - \frac{(iu\beta)^{n-1}}{(n-1)!} \right] du \Bigg|^2$$

$$\lim_{T \to \infty} \frac{1}{2T} \int_{-T}^{T} dt \left| \int_{0}^{\infty} f^{(n)}(t - \tau) \frac{d\tau}{2\pi} \int_{-\infty}^{\infty} \frac{e^{i\omega\tau}}{2\pi\Psi_n(\omega)} d\omega \int_{-\infty}^{\infty} e^{-i\omega\sigma} d\sigma \right.$$

$$\times \int_{-\infty}^{\infty} \Psi_n(u) \frac{e^{iu\sigma}}{u^n} \left[e^{iu\beta} - 1 - \cdots - \frac{(iu\beta)^{n-1}}{(n-1)!} \right] du \Bigg|^2,$$

$$\tag{2.36}$$

as an n-fold integration by parts shows. Let us simplify this expression by putting

$$\psi_n(t) = \frac{1}{2\pi} \int_{-\infty}^{\infty} \Psi_n(u)e^{iut} dt \tag{2.365}$$

and

$$\psi(\beta, t) = \int_{0}^{\beta} d\sigma_1 \int_{0}^{\sigma_1} d\sigma_2 \cdots \int_{0}^{\sigma_{n-1}} \psi_n(t + \sigma_n) d\sigma_n. \tag{2.37}$$

Then the mean square error of prediction becomes

$$\lim_{T \to \infty} \frac{1}{2T} \int_{-T}^{T} \left| \int_{0}^{\infty} f^{(n)}(t-\tau) \, d\tau \int_{-\infty}^{\infty} \frac{e^{i\omega\tau}}{2\pi \Psi_n(\omega)} \int_{-\infty}^{0} e^{-i\omega\sigma} \psi(\beta, \sigma) \, d\sigma \right|^2 dt$$

$$= \int_{0}^{\infty} d\tau_1 \int_{0}^{\infty} \varphi_n(\tau_2 - \tau_1) \, d\tau_2 \int_{-\infty}^{\infty} \frac{e^{i\omega_1\tau_1}}{2\pi \Psi_n(\omega_1)}$$

$$\times \int_{-\infty}^{0} e^{-i\omega_1\sigma_1} \psi(\beta, \sigma_1) \, d\sigma_1 \int_{-\infty}^{\infty} \frac{e^{-i\omega_2\tau_2}}{2\pi \Psi_n(\omega_2)} \int_{-\infty}^{0} e^{i\omega_2\sigma_2} \overline{\psi(\beta, \sigma_2)} \, d\sigma_2$$

$$= \frac{1}{2\pi} \int_{-\infty}^{\infty} d\omega \left| \int_{-\infty}^{0} e^{-i\omega\sigma} \psi(\beta, \sigma) \, d\sigma \right|^2$$

$$= \int_{-\beta}^{0} |\psi(\beta, \sigma)|^2 \, d\sigma. \tag{2.375}$$

Since $\psi_n(t)$ vanishes for negative arguments, let us notice that, if $\sigma < 0$,

$$\psi(\beta, \sigma) = \int_{0}^{\beta} d\sigma_1 \int_{0}^{\sigma_1} d\sigma_2 \cdots \int_{\sigma}^{\sigma_{n-1}+\sigma} \psi_n(\sigma_n) \, d\sigma_n$$

$$= \int_{0}^{\beta} d\sigma_1 \cdots \int_{0}^{\sigma_{n-1}+\sigma} \psi_n(\sigma_n) \, d\sigma_n$$

$$= \int_{0}^{\beta} d\sigma_1 \cdots \int_{0}^{\sigma_{n-2}+\sigma} d\sigma_{n-1} \int_{0}^{\sigma_{n-1}} \psi_n(\sigma_n) \, d\sigma_n$$

$$= \cdots \cdots$$

$$= \int_{0}^{\beta+\sigma} d\sigma_1 \cdots \int_{0}^{\sigma_{n-1}} \psi_n(\sigma_n) \, d\sigma_n. \tag{2.38}$$

Thus the mean square error of prediction becomes

$$\int_{0}^{\beta} \left| \int_{0}^{\sigma_1} d\sigma_1 \int_{0}^{\sigma_1} d\sigma_2 \cdots \int_{0}^{\sigma_{n-1}} \psi_n(\sigma_n) \, d\sigma_n \right|^2 d\sigma. \tag{2.39}$$

2.4 Spectrum Lines and Non-absolutely Continuous Spectra

In all our prediction up to the present, we have confined our attention to the practical case of functions $f(t)$ generating absolutely continuous spectral functions $\Lambda(\omega)$. In the more general case of discrete or non-absolutely continuous spectra this theory of prediction has not yet been as completely closed as in the specific case where $\Lambda(\omega)$ is absolutely continuous, although the ground work for this has been laid by André Kolmogoroff (*loc. cit.*). The main point in the generalization is that, if $\Phi(\omega)$ is defined in terms of $\Lambda'(\omega)$ wherever the latter exists, two cases must be considered, the first where

$$\int_{-\infty}^{\infty} \frac{|\log |\Phi(\omega)||}{1 + \omega^2} \, d\omega \tag{2.40}$$

diverges, and the second where it converges. The first case is singular, and methods may be found to predict $f(t)$ to any desired degree of accuracy on the basis of its past alone. If (2.40) converges, and $\Psi(\omega)$ is defined as in (1.775), and

$$\psi(t) = \frac{1}{2\pi} \int_{-\infty}^{\infty} \Psi(\omega) e^{i\omega t}\, d\omega, \tag{2.401}$$

then the greatest lower bound of the mean square error of prediction for lead α is

$$\int_{0}^{\alpha} |\psi(\sigma)|^2\, d\sigma. \tag{2.402}$$

Let us now proceed from the norm of the error of the optimum prediction to the technique of obtaining such an optimum prediction. In the case of discrete spectra, the technique to be followed is perhaps best illustrated by the following example. Let $\varphi(t) = [e^{i\lambda t} + \varphi_1(t)]$, where

$$\varphi_1(t) = \frac{1}{2\pi} \int_{-\infty}^{\infty} \Phi(\omega) e^{i\omega t}\, d\omega. \tag{2.404}$$

Let

$$g(t) = f(t) - \frac{1}{T} \int_{A}^{A+T} f(t - \tau) e^{i\lambda \tau}\, d\tau. \tag{2.41}$$

Then

$$\lim_{B \to \infty} \frac{1}{2B} \int_{-B}^{B} g(t + \sigma)\overline{g(\sigma)}\, d\sigma$$

$$= \varphi(t) - \frac{1}{T} \int_{A}^{A+T} \varphi(t + \tau) e^{-i\lambda \tau}\, d\tau - \frac{1}{T} \int_{A}^{A+T} \varphi(t - \tau) e^{+i\lambda \tau}\, d\tau$$

$$+ \frac{1}{T^2} \int_{A}^{A+T} e^{i\lambda \sigma}\, d\sigma \int_{A}^{A+T} \phi(t + \tau - \sigma) e^{-i\lambda \tau}\, d\tau$$

$$= \varphi_1(t) + \text{(an expression vanishing as } T \to \infty). \tag{2.42}$$

While it is true that the expression described verbally does not vanish uniformly, the following procedure will give a prediction arbitrarily near the optimum: we predict $g(t)$ (for a large T) as though $\varphi_1(t)$ were its auto-correlation coefficient, and then add the "cancelling" term

$$\frac{1}{T} \int_{A}^{A+T} f(t - \tau) e^{i\lambda \tau}\, dt.$$

If $\varphi(t)$ contains several spectrum lines, we may remove them one by one in this fashion. This procedure may be used to give approximate results even in case of an infinity of spectrum lines.

2.5 Prediction by the Linear Combination of Given Operators

Let us now discuss the problem of prediction by means of a linear combination of given operators. We have seen that the mean square error of prediction for the operator with the time characteristic $K(t)$ and the frequency characteristic $k(\omega)$ will be

$$\lim_{T \to \infty} \frac{1}{2T} \int_{-T}^{T} \left| f(t + \alpha) - \int_{0}^{\infty} f(t - \tau)\, dK(\tau) \right|^2 dt$$

$$= \varphi(0) - 2\mathrm{R}\left\{ \int_{0}^{\infty} \varphi(\tau + \alpha)\, d\overline{K(\tau)} \right\} +$$

$$\int_{0}^{\alpha} dK(\sigma) \int_{0}^{\infty} d\overline{K(\tau)} \varphi(\tau - \sigma)$$

$$= \frac{1}{2\pi} \int_{-\infty}^{\infty} \Phi(\omega)\, |\, e^{i\alpha\omega} - k(\omega)\, |^2\, d\omega. \tag{2.50}$$

Thus, if

$$k(\omega) = \sum_{1}^{N} a_n k_n(\omega), \tag{2.51}$$

the problem of prediction consists in approximating in the mean to $\sqrt{\Phi(\omega)}e^{i\alpha\omega}$ by a sum $\sum_{1}^{n} a_n k_n(\omega)\sqrt{\Phi(\omega)}$. In the case in which $\Psi(\omega)$ exists, it may be convenient to replace $\sqrt{\Phi(\omega)}$ by $\Psi(\omega)$, which will make no difference in the result. The important restriction on this problem is that the admissible functions $k_n(\omega)$ are transforms of functions vanishing for negative arguments, and themselves have no singularities or large infinities of growth in the lower half-plane. If $\Phi(\omega)$ is factorable and $\Psi(\omega)$ exists, this will also be true of the functions $k_n(\omega)\Psi(\omega)$, while, in general, it will not be true of $e^{i\alpha\omega}\Psi(\omega)$, so that in this case a perfect solution of the prediction problem is impossible. If, on the other hand, $\Phi(\omega)$ is not factorable, the set of functions $k(\omega)\sqrt{\Phi(\omega)}$, where $k(\omega)$ has the desired behavior in the lower half-plane and $k(\omega)\sqrt{\Phi(\omega)}$ belongs to L^2, is closed. Otherwise there will exist a non-null function $l(\omega)$ of L^2 such that always

$$\int_{-\infty}^{\infty} l(\omega)\sqrt{\Phi(\omega)}k(\omega)\, d\omega = 0, \tag{2.515}$$

and in particular

$$\int_{-\infty}^{\infty} \frac{l(\omega)\sqrt{\Phi(\omega)}}{\omega - \omega_1}\, d\omega = 0, \tag{2.52}$$

for all ω_1 above the axis of reals. It will follow that $l(\omega)\sqrt{\Phi(\omega)}$ is a possible set of boundary values for a function analytic above the axis of reals, and that hence

$$\int_{-\infty}^{\infty} \frac{\left| \log \left| l(\omega) \sqrt{\Phi(\omega)} \right| \right|}{1 + \omega^2} d\omega < \infty, \qquad (2.525)$$

which gives rise to

$$-\int_{-\infty}^{\infty} \frac{\left| \log_{-} \left| l(\omega) \sqrt{\Phi(\omega)} \right| \right|}{1 + \omega^2} d\omega < \infty. \qquad (2.53)$$

Since $l(\omega)$ belongs to L^2,

$$\int_{-\infty}^{\infty} \frac{\log \left| l(\omega) \right|}{1 + \omega^2} d\omega < \infty. \qquad (2.535)$$

Because

$$-\int_{-\infty}^{\infty} \frac{1}{2} \frac{\log_{-} \left| \Phi(\omega) \right|}{1 + \omega^2} d\omega - \int_{-\infty}^{\infty} \frac{\log \left| l(\omega) \right|}{1 + \omega^2} d\omega < \infty, \qquad (2.54)$$

we arrive at

$$-\int_{-\infty}^{\infty} \frac{\log_{-} \left| \Phi(\omega) \right|}{1 + \omega^2} d\omega < \infty. \qquad (2.545)$$

As, however, $\Phi(\omega)$ is absolutely integrable,

$$\int_{-\infty}^{\infty} \frac{\log_{+} \left| \Phi(\omega) \right|}{1 + \omega^2} d\omega; \qquad (2.55)$$

and on combining these, we get

$$\int_{-\infty}^{\infty} \frac{\left| \log \left| \Phi(\omega) \right| \right|}{1 + \omega^2} d\omega < \infty, \qquad (2.555)$$

which is known to contradict our assumption that $\Phi(\omega)$ is not factorable.

In this case, a perfect prediction is possible, and we may obtain as good a prediction as we wish by orthogonalizing a closed set such as

$$\frac{\sqrt{\Phi(\omega)}}{(1 + i\omega)^n} \qquad (2.56)$$

and expressing $\sqrt{\Phi(\omega)} e^{-ia\omega}$ in terms of these orthogonalized functions. In the factorable case, we orthogonalize a set of functions $\Psi(\omega) \cdot k_n(\omega)$. For example, if

$$\Phi(\omega) = \frac{1}{1 + \omega^2}, \qquad (2.565)$$

a possible set of functions $\Psi(\omega)k_n(\omega)$ is the orthogonal set

$$\frac{(1 - i\omega)^n}{\sqrt{\pi}(1 + i\omega)^{n+1}}. \tag{2.57}$$

Here we solve the prediction problem by expanding $\Psi(\omega)e^{-i\alpha\omega}$ in terms of this set; and since

$$\int_{-\infty}^{\infty} \frac{e^{i\alpha\omega}}{1 + i\omega} \frac{(1 + i\omega)^n}{(1 - i\omega)^{n+1}} d\omega = \begin{cases} e^{-\alpha}\pi & \text{if } n = 1; \\ 0 & \text{if } n > 1; \end{cases} \tag{2.575}$$

we obtain as our prediction operator $e^{-\alpha}$, as before.

2.6   The Linear Predictor for a Discrete Time Series

The problem of prediction is of interest in the two closely related fields of communication engineering and of time series in statistics. In the latter field, while continuous time series do occur and are important, the numerical data will generally be placed in the form of discrete time series. In such a case the function $f(t)$ of the continuous parameter t is replaced by the function f_ν of the parameter ν, which varies by discrete steps. Similarly the function $\varphi(\tau)$ will be replaced by the discrete set of autocorrelation coefficients

$$\varphi_\nu = \lim_{N \to \infty} \frac{1}{2N + 1} \sum_{\mu = -N}^{N} f_{\mu+\nu} f_\mu. \tag{2.600}$$

The analogue of our previous function $\Phi(\omega)$ will be the periodic function

$$\Phi(\omega) = \sum_{-\infty}^{\infty} \varphi_\nu e^{-i\nu\omega} \tag{2.605}$$

of period 2π. As may readily be proved, this periodic function will always be non-negative.

The problem of factoring $\Phi(\omega)$ occurs in the same way in the discrete case as in the continuous case. One way of accomplishing this is to first form $\log \Phi(\omega)$, which will have the Fourier series

$$\sum_{-\infty}^{\infty} a_\nu e^{-i\nu\omega}. \tag{2.610}$$

Under these conditions, let us put

$$L(\omega) = -\sum_{-\infty}^{-1} a_\nu e^{-i\nu\omega} + \sum_{1}^{\infty} a_\nu e^{-i\nu\omega} \tag{2.615}$$

and

$$\Psi(\omega) = \sqrt{\Phi(\omega)} \exp\left[\frac{i}{2} L(\omega)\right]. \tag{2.620}$$

Then we have

$$\Psi(\omega) = \sum_0^\infty b_\nu e^{-i\nu\omega}. \qquad (2.625)$$

It will be clear that the function $\Psi(\omega)$ will have no singularities or zeros below the axis of reals and that its logarithm in that half-plane will be as small as possible at infinity. Let it be observed that the computation of $\Psi(\omega)$ can be carried through with the aid of the harmonic analyzer and elementary arithmetical tools.

Now the formula for $k(\omega)$ which we have already obtained in the continuous case has, as an analogue, the formula

$$k(\omega) = \frac{1}{2\pi\Psi(\omega)} \sum_0^\infty e^{-i\nu\omega} \int_{-\pi}^{\pi} \Psi(u) e^{iu\nu} \, du \qquad (2.630)$$

in the discrete case. If we now write

$$K_\nu = \frac{1}{2\pi} \int_{-\pi}^{\pi} e^{i\nu\omega} k(\omega) \, d\omega, \qquad (2.635)$$

then by the use of these K_ν's we minimize the expression

$$\lim_{N \to \infty} \frac{1}{2N+1} \sum_{-N}^{N} \left| f_{\nu+\alpha} - \sum_{\mu=0}^{\infty} f_{\nu-\mu} K_\mu \right|^2. \qquad (2.640)$$

The minimum of this expression will be

$$\sum_0^{\alpha-1} |b_\nu|^2. \qquad (2.645)$$

This checks precisely with Kolmogoroff's results for the non-absolutely continuous case, although, as said before, he extends his result to include more general spectra.

This is a completely satisfactory method for obtaining an optimum prediction by means of the φ_ν of a discrete set of data. There is, however, another method of factoring $\Phi(\omega)$ into the product $\Psi(\omega) \cdot \overline{\Psi(\overline{\omega})}$ which may be applied on occasion. Let us consider the case where $\Phi(\omega)$ is the polynomial

$$\sum_{-N}^{N} \varphi_\nu e^{-i\nu\omega}. \qquad (2.650)$$

Let us solve the algebraic equation

$$\sum_0^{2N} \varphi_{\nu-N} e^{-i\nu\omega} = 0. \qquad (2.655)$$

Then the roots

$$e^{-i\omega} = A + Bi \quad (A^2 + B^2 > 1) \qquad (2.660)$$

will correspond to values of ω in the upper half-plane. Similarly the roots

$$e^{i\omega} = A - Bi \quad (A^2 + B^2 > 1) \tag{2.665}$$

will correspond to values of ω in the lower half-plane. Let us next form the partial product

$$\prod[e^{-i\omega} - (A + Bi)][e^{i\omega} - (A - Bi)]. \tag{2.670}$$

It will be seen without difficulty that this must be $\Phi(\omega)$ itself, except for a constant factor, and that the partial product

$$\prod[e^{-i\omega} - (A + Bi)], \quad \text{for all roots for which } A^2 + B^2 > 1 \tag{2.675}$$

must be $\Psi(\omega)$, except for a constant factor. In this case we have replaced the combination of logarithmic transformation and Fourier analysis by the solution of an algebraic equation which may be of a high order. The choice of methods depends on the degree of the equation and on the instruments or other mathematical computation facilities available. In either case the computation may eventually be carried out and always gives us valid and reasonable method for the handling of economic, meteorological, geophysical, and other statistics.

CHAPTER III

THE LINEAR FILTER FOR A SINGLE TIME SERIES

3.0 Formulation of the General Filter Problem

Let $f(t)$ and $g(t)$ be two complex time series. Let $f(t)$ represent a message and $g(t)$ a disturbance. We wish to determine that linear operator which, when applied to $f(t) + g(t)$, will give us the best approximation to $f(t + \alpha)$. In order to do this, we need statistical information concerning $f(t)$ and $g(t)$, which will be given by their auto-correlation and cross-correlation coefficients. We shall suppose that sufficient auxiliary conditions are satisfied to permit the free shifting of the time origin of the series as justified by the lemmas of the last chapter. Of course, the results of this chapter will include those of the last in the particular case in which $g(t)$ vanishes. In order to avoid as far as possible the duplication of arguments already given, we shall use a slightly different approach to the solution of the integral equation both of this chapter and of the last, although the methods of both chapters are applicable to either case.

Formally, the problem of this chapter exhibits certain differences according as the sign of α is positive or negative. If it is positive, we again have a prediction problem before us, albeit a prediction problem from perturbed data. If we start from correlation coefficients with rational Fourier transforms, the prediction operator on the frequency scale will likewise be rational. On the other hand, if α is negative, we arrive in the first instance at an operator which will be realizable, in that it will be a function of a complex variable with the desired behavior in one half-plane, but which will not be rational and will require another stage of approximation before it can be realized in an electric or mechanical network of a finite number of meshes. Offsetting this disadvantage, it will perform its filtering function as between the message $f(t)$ and the noise or disturbance $g(t)$ more perfectly and with increasing perfection as $\alpha \to -\infty$. In general the spectra of $f(t)$ and $g(t)$ will overlap, and when this is the case, not even an infinite lag in filtering will give perfect discrimination. The degree by which this discrimination fails to be perfect will determine the lag which may advantageously be designed into the filter and indirectly establish the number of network meshes justified.

The significance of lag in a filter may be seen from the following consideration: we shall find that, even though we approach the problem from the standpoint of time characteristic, we eventually arrive at a filter which is essentially an instrument for the separation of different frequency ranges. However, to determine the spectrum of an impulse with perfect sharpness, we must know the history of that impulse over all time. This we can never do, but the longer we wait before operating with the impulse, the more of that impulse has had an opportunity to come through and the more completely is its spectrum determined.

While our treatment of the filter, like all treatments, ultimately involves the spectra of the message and the noise or perturbations which it is supposed to separate, our criterion of performance is the mean square distortion of the message over the time and involves transient behavior as well as steady-state behavior. It is quite as critical of distortion of phase as of distortion of amplitude. In this it differs from methods more familiar in communication engineering theory, which have been devised for the most part with reference to voice-transmission and ultimately with reference to the human ear—an organ of unusually fine frequency discrimination, fair amplitude discrimination, and very bad phase discrimination. However, in television work and in other related techniques, the final receiving instrument is highly sensitive to phase, and existing filter techniques have proved distinctly inadequate. This has also been experienced in the case of mechanical filters, designed to smooth out irregularities in the input of accurate servo-mechanisms. It is hoped that the methods of this chapter may prove useful in these fields.

3.1 Minimization Problem for Filters

Let us consider the expression

$$\lim_{T \to \infty} \frac{1}{2T} \int_{-T}^{T} \left| f(t + \alpha) - \int_{0}^{\infty} [f(t - \tau) + g(t - \tau)] \, dK(\tau) \right|^2 dt.$$
(3.10)

Under very general conditions, this expression may be written

$$\varphi_{11}(0) - 2R \left\{ \int_{0}^{\infty} [\varphi_{11}(\alpha + \tau) + \varphi_{12}(\alpha + \tau)] \, d\overline{K(\tau)} \right\} +$$

$$\int_{0}^{\infty} dK(\sigma) \int_{0}^{\infty} d\overline{K(\tau)} \{ \varphi_{11}(\tau - \sigma) + \varphi_{12}(\tau - \sigma) + \overline{\varphi_{12}(\sigma - \tau)} + \varphi_{22}(\tau - \sigma) \},$$
(3.105)

where

$$\varphi_{11}(\tau) = \lim_{T \to \infty} \frac{1}{2T} \int_{-T}^{T} f(t + \tau) \overline{f(t)} \, dt,$$
(3.11)

$$\varphi_{12}(\tau) = \lim_{T \to \infty} \frac{1}{2T} \int_{-T}^{T} f(t + \tau)\overline{g(t)}\, dt, \tag{3.111}$$

$$\varphi_{22}(\tau) = \lim_{T \to \infty} \frac{1}{2T} \int_{-T}^{T} g(t + \tau)\overline{g(t)}\, dt. \tag{3.112}$$

Let us put

$$\varphi_{11}(\tau) + \varphi_{12}(\tau) + \overline{\varphi_{12}(-\tau)} + \varphi_{22}(\tau) = \varphi(\tau). \tag{3.12}$$

Then clearly

$$\varphi(\tau) = \overline{\varphi(-\tau)}, \tag{3.125}$$

and the expression which we wish to minimize will be

$$\varphi_{11}(0) - 2\mathrm{R}\left\{ \int_0^\infty \left[\varphi_{11}(\alpha + \tau) + \varphi_{12}(\alpha + \tau)\right] d\overline{K(\tau)} \right\}$$

$$+ \int_0^\infty dK(\sigma) \int_0^\infty d\overline{K(\tau)}\varphi(\tau - \sigma). \tag{3.13}$$

If we write

$$\varphi_{11}(\alpha + \tau) + \varphi_{12}(\alpha + \tau) = h(\tau), \tag{3.135}$$

this minimization is reduced to that of the general real expression

$$-2\mathrm{R}\left\{ \int_0^\infty h(\tau)\, d\overline{K(\tau)} \right\} + \int_0^\infty dK(\sigma) \int_0^\infty d\overline{K(\tau)}\varphi(\tau - \sigma). \tag{3.14}$$

Let us suppose that

$$h(\tau) = \int_0^\infty \varphi(\tau - \sigma)\, dQ(\sigma). \tag{3.145}$$

Then (3.14) becomes

$$- \int_0^\infty dQ(\sigma) \int_0^\infty \varphi(\tau - \sigma)\, d\overline{K(\tau)}$$

$$- \int_0^\infty d\overline{Q(\sigma)} \int_0^\infty \varphi(\sigma - \tau)\, dK(\tau)$$

$$+ \int_0^\infty dK(\sigma) \int_0^\infty d\overline{K(\tau)}\varphi(\tau - \sigma)$$

$$= - \int_0^\infty dQ(\sigma) \int_0^\infty \varphi(\tau - \sigma)\, d\overline{Q(\tau)}$$

$$+ \int_0^\infty d[K(\sigma) - Q(\sigma)] \int_0^\infty d[\overline{K(\tau)} - \overline{Q(\tau)}]\varphi(\tau - \sigma).$$

Let us now suppose that

$$\int_0^\infty e^{-i\omega t}\, dK(t) = k(\omega); \tag{3.15}$$

$$\int_0^\infty e^{-i\omega t}\, dQ(t) = q(\omega); \tag{3.16}$$

$$\varphi(t) = \frac{1}{2\pi} \int_{-\infty}^\infty \Phi(\omega) e^{i\omega t}\, d\omega. \tag{3.165}$$

Then the expression to be minimized becomes

$$-\frac{1}{2\pi} \int_{-\infty}^\infty |q(\omega)|^2 \Phi(\omega)\, d\omega + \frac{1}{2\pi} \int_{-\infty}^\infty |k(\omega) - q(\omega)|^2 \Phi(\omega)\, d\omega, \tag{3.17}$$

which will attain its minimum when

$$q(\omega) = k(\omega), \tag{3.175}$$

which minimum will be

$$-\frac{1}{2\pi} \int_{-\infty}^\infty \Phi(\omega)\, |q(\omega)|^2\, d\omega. \tag{3.18}$$

3.2 The Factorization of the Spectrum

In general, let us consider the integral equation

$$h(t) = \int_0^\infty \varphi(t - \tau)\, dK(\tau) \quad (t > 0), \tag{3.20}$$

where

$$h(t) = \frac{1}{2\pi} \int_{-\infty}^\infty H(\omega) e^{i\omega t}\, d\omega, \tag{3.205}$$

$$\varphi(t) = \frac{1}{2\pi} \int_{-\infty}^\infty \Phi(\omega) e^{i\omega t}\, d\omega, \tag{3.21}$$

and $\varphi(t) = \overline{\varphi(-t)}$, so that $\Phi(\omega)$ is real. We shall suppose that

$$\int_0^\infty e^{-i\omega t}\, dK(t) = k(\omega). \tag{3.215}$$

For the present, let us confine our attention to the case in which $\Phi(\omega)$ is rational. Here we shall limit ourselves to the case in which $\Phi(\omega)$ has no real zeros. We may then write

$$\Phi(\omega) = |\Psi(\omega)|^2, \tag{3.22}$$

where $\Psi(\omega)$ is a rational function free from zeros and poles in the lower half-plane. If we put

$$\psi(t) = \frac{1}{2\pi} \int_{-\infty}^{\infty} \Psi(\omega) e^{i\omega t} \, d\omega = 0 \quad \text{if} \quad t < 0, \qquad (3.225)$$

we shall have

$$\varphi(\tau) = \begin{cases} \int_{0}^{\infty} \psi(t+\tau)\overline{\psi(t)} \, dt & (\tau > 0); \\ \int_{-\tau}^{\infty} \psi(t+\tau)\overline{\psi(t)} \, dt & (\tau < 0). \end{cases} \qquad (3.23)$$

Then (3.20) becomes

$$\begin{aligned} h(t) &= \int_{0}^{t} dK(\tau) \int_{0}^{\infty} \psi(t-\tau+\sigma)\overline{\psi(\sigma)} \, d\sigma \\ &\quad + \int_{t}^{\infty} dK(\tau) \int_{\tau-t}^{\infty} \psi(t-\tau+\sigma)\overline{\psi(\sigma)} \, d\sigma \\ &= \int_{0}^{\infty} \overline{\psi(\sigma)} \, d\sigma \int_{0}^{\sigma+t} \psi(t-\tau+\sigma) \, dK(\tau) \quad (t > 0). \quad (3.24) \end{aligned}$$

Now let us put

$$h(t) = \int_{0}^{\infty} \overline{\psi(\sigma)} \, L(\sigma+t) \, d\sigma \quad (-\infty < t < \infty). \qquad (3.245)$$

We see that, if we extend φ and dK to cover negative arguments, for which dK is to vanish,

$$\int_{-\infty}^{\infty} \psi(t-\tau) \, dK(\tau) = \begin{cases} L(t) & (t > 0); \\ 0 & (t < 0). \end{cases} \qquad (3.25)$$

If

$$l(\omega) = \int_{-\infty}^{\infty} L(t) e^{-i\omega t} \, dt, \qquad (3.255)$$

equation (3.245) becomes

$$H(\omega) = l(\omega) \cdot \overline{\Psi(\omega)}, \qquad (3.26)$$

[where $H(\omega)$ is the Fourier transform of $h(t)$] which leads to

$$l(\omega) = \frac{H(\omega)}{\overline{\Psi(\omega)}}, \qquad (3.265)$$

or

$$L(t) = \frac{1}{2\pi} \int_{-\infty}^{\infty} \frac{H(\omega)}{\overline{\Psi(\omega)}} e^{i\omega t} \, d\omega. \qquad (3.27)$$

Then (3.25) becomes

$$\Psi(\omega)k(\omega) = \int_0^\infty L(t)e^{-i\omega t}\, dt, \tag{3.275}$$

which again leads to

$$k(\omega) = \frac{1}{2\pi\Psi(\omega)} \int_0^\infty e^{-i\omega t}\, dt \int_{-\infty}^\infty \frac{H(u)}{\Psi(u)} e^{iut}\, du. \tag{3.28}$$

The denominator of this expression is a rational function free from zeros in the lower half-plane, while the numerator is free from singularities in the lower half-plane, and if $L(t)$ satisfies the condition

$$\int_0^\infty |L(t)|\, dt < \infty, \tag{3.285}$$

it will be bounded in that half-plane. Thus $k(\omega)$ is of at most rational growth in the lower half-plane, in which it is free of singularities. If

$$k(\omega) = \int_{-\infty}^\infty e^{-i\omega t}\, dK_1(t), \tag{3.29}$$

then $K_1(t)$ is constant for negative arguments and is a possible $K(t)$.

3.3 Prediction and Filtering

Let us consider two cases in particular. To begin with, let

$$h(t) = \varphi(t + \alpha). \tag{3.30}$$

In this case,

$$\frac{1}{2\pi} \int_{-\infty}^\infty \frac{H(u)}{\Psi(u)} e^{iut}\, du = \frac{1}{2\pi} \int_{-\infty}^\infty \frac{\Phi(u)}{\Psi(u)} e^{iu\alpha}e^{iut}\, du$$

$$= \begin{cases} \psi(t + \alpha) & (t > -\alpha), \\ 0 & (t < -\alpha). \end{cases} \tag{3.305}$$

This will yield us

$$k(\omega) = \frac{\displaystyle\int_0^\infty \psi(t + \alpha)e^{-i\omega t}\, dt}{\Psi(\omega)}. \tag{3.31}$$

If $\Phi(\omega)$ is rational, this will be a rational expression. In fact, if

$$\Psi(\omega) = \sum_{m,n} A_{m,n} \frac{1}{(\omega - \omega_n)^m}, \tag{3.315}$$

we shall have

$$\psi(t) = \frac{1}{2\pi} \int_{-\infty}^\infty e^{i\omega t}\, d\omega \sum_{m,n} A_{m,n} \frac{1}{(\omega - \omega_n)^m}. \tag{3.32}$$

Now,

$$\frac{i^m}{(m-n)!} \int_0^\infty e^{-i\omega t} e^{i\omega_n t} t^{m-1}\, dt = \frac{1}{(\omega - \omega_n)^m} \quad (I\{\omega_n\} > 0), \quad (3.325)$$

and hence

$$\frac{1}{2\pi} \int_{-\infty}^\infty \frac{e^{i\omega t}\, d\omega}{(\omega - \omega_n)^m} = \frac{i^m}{(m-1)!} t^{m-1} e^{i\omega_n t} \quad (t > 0). \quad (3.33)$$

Therefore

$$\psi(t) = \sum_{m,n} A_{m,n} \frac{i^m}{(m-1)!} t^{m-1} e^{i\omega_n t}, \quad (3.335)$$

and

$$\psi(t + \alpha) = \sum_{m,n} A_{m,n} \frac{i^m}{(m-1)!} (t+\alpha)^{m-1} e^{i\omega_n(t+\alpha)}$$

$$= \sum_{m,n} A_{m,n} \frac{e^{i\omega_n \alpha} i^m}{(m-1)!} \sum_{k=0}^{m-1} \frac{(m-1)! \alpha^k t^{m-1-k}}{k!(m-1-k)!} e^{i\omega_n t}$$

$$= \sum_{m,n} A_{m,n} e^{i\omega_n \alpha} \sum_{k=0}^{m-1} \frac{(i\alpha)^k}{k!} \frac{i^{m-k} t^{m-1-k}}{(m-1-k)!} e^{i\omega_n t}. \quad (3.34)$$

As a consequence of this,

$$\int_0^\infty \psi(t+\alpha) e^{-i\omega t}\, dt = \sum_{m,n} A_{m,n} e^{i\omega_n \alpha} \sum_{k=0}^{m-1} \frac{(i\alpha)^k}{k!} \frac{1}{(\omega - \omega_n)^{m-k}}. \quad (3.345)$$

This gives us

$$k(\omega) = \frac{\displaystyle\sum_{m,n} \frac{1}{(\omega - \omega_n)^m} \sum_{\mu=m} A_{\mu,n} e^{i\omega_n \alpha} \frac{(i\alpha)^{\mu-m}}{(\mu-m)!}}{\displaystyle\sum_{m,n} A_{m,n} \frac{1}{(\omega - \omega_n)^m}}. \quad (3.35)$$

Again, let $H(\omega)$ be of the form $M(\omega) e^{i\alpha\omega}$, where $M(\omega)$ is rational and has no real zeros or singularities and has a denominator of higher degree than the numerator. Then we may write

$$\frac{M(\omega)}{\Psi(\omega)} = \sum_{m,n} \frac{\alpha_{m,n}}{(\omega - \omega_n)^m} + \sum_{m,n} \frac{\beta_{m,n}}{(\omega - \omega_n')^m} \quad (I\{\omega_n\} > 0, I\{\omega_n'\} < 0);$$

$$(3.355)$$

then

$$\frac{1}{2\pi} \int_{-\infty}^\infty \frac{M(\omega)}{\Psi(\omega)} e^{i\omega t}\, d\omega = \begin{cases} \displaystyle\sum_{m,n} \alpha_{m,n} \frac{i^m}{(m-1)!} t^{m-1} e^{i\omega_n t} & (t > 0); \\[2mm] \displaystyle\sum_{m,n} \beta_{m,n} \frac{i^m}{(m-1)!} t^{m-1} e^{i\omega_n' t} & (t < 0). \end{cases} \quad (3.36)$$

Let us call this function $w(t)$. Then, if α is positive,

$$\frac{1}{2\pi} \int_{-\infty}^{\infty} \frac{H(u)}{\Psi(u)} e^{iut} \, du$$

$$= \sum_{m,n} \alpha_{m,n} \frac{i^n}{(m-1)!} (t+\alpha)^{m-1} e^{i\omega_n(t+\alpha)} \quad (t > 0). \quad (3.365)$$

If, on the other hand, α is negative,

$$\frac{1}{2\pi} \int_{-\infty}^{\infty} \frac{H(u)}{\Psi(u)} e^{iut} \, du$$

$$= \begin{cases} \sum\limits_{m,n} \alpha_{m,n} \dfrac{i^n}{(m-1)!} (t+\alpha)^{m-1} e^{i\omega_n(t+\alpha)} & (t > -\alpha); \\[2mm] \sum\limits_{m,n} \beta_{m,n} \dfrac{i^m}{(m-1)!} (t+\alpha)^{m-1} e^{i\omega_{n'}(t+\alpha)} & (0 < t < -\alpha). \end{cases} \quad (3.37)$$

Thus the cases of lead and of lag must be treated **differe**ntly. In the first case,

$$k(\omega) = \frac{\sum\limits_{m,n} \dfrac{1}{(\omega - \omega_n)^m} \sum\limits_{\mu=m+1}^{\infty} \alpha_{\mu,n} e^{i\omega_n\alpha} \dfrac{(i\alpha)^{\mu-m}}{(\mu-m)!}}{\Psi(\omega)}, \quad (3.375)$$

which is rational if $\Phi(\omega)$ is rational. In the second case, $k(\omega)$ will not be rational; and, if the function $k(\omega)$ is to be approximated as the voltage ratio of an electric circuit, a further investigation is needed.

3.4   The Error of Performance of a Filter; Long-lag Filters

In any case, the minimum of

$$-2\mathrm{R}\left\{ \int_0^{\infty} h(\tau) \, d\overline{K(\tau)} \right\} + \int_0^{\infty} dK(\sigma) \int_0^{\infty} d\overline{K(\tau)} \varphi(\tau - \sigma) \quad (3.40)$$

will be given by

$$\frac{1}{2\pi} \int_{-\infty}^{\infty} \Phi(\omega) \left\{ - \left| \frac{1}{2\pi\Psi(\omega)} \int_0^{\infty} e^{-i\omega t} \, dt \int_{-\infty}^{\infty} \frac{H(u)}{\Psi(u)} e^{iut} \, du \right|^2 \right\} d\omega$$

$$= \int_0^{\infty} \left\{ - \left| \frac{1}{2\pi} \int_{-\infty}^{\infty} \frac{H(u)}{\Psi(u)} e^{iut} \, du \right|^2 \right\} dt. \quad (3.405)$$

If we put

$$\varphi_{ij}(\tau) = \frac{1}{2\pi} \int_{-\infty}^{\infty} \Phi_{ij}(\omega) e^{i\omega\tau} \, d\omega \quad (i, j = 1, 2), \quad (3.41)$$

the minimum of

$$\lim_{T \to \infty} \frac{1}{2T} \int_{-T}^{T} \left| f(t + \alpha) - \int_{0}^{\infty} [f(t - \tau) + g(t - \tau)] \, dK(\tau) \right|^2 dt$$

(3.415)

will be given by

$$= \frac{1}{2\pi} \int_{0}^{\infty} \left\{ \varphi_{11}(t) - \left| \frac{1}{2\pi} \int_{-\infty}^{\infty} \frac{H(u)}{\overline{\Psi(u)}} e^{iut} \, du \right|^2 \right\} dt.$$

(3.42)

If $g(t)$ vanishes, this will be

$$= \frac{1}{2\pi} \int_{0}^{\alpha} |\psi(t)|^2 \, dt.$$

(3.425)

In general

$$\int_{0}^{\infty} \left| \sum_{m,n} A_{m,n} \frac{i^m}{(m-1)!} t^{m-1} e^{i\omega n t} \right|^2 dt$$

$$= \sum_{m,n} \sum_{\mu,\nu} A_{m,n} A_{\mu,\nu} \frac{(-1)^\mu i^{(m+\mu-2)}}{(m-1)!(\mu-1)!} \left[\frac{1}{(\omega_n - \overline{\omega}_\nu)^{m+\mu-1}} \right],$$

(3.43)

and this may be used to determine the minimum of

$$\lim_{T \to \infty} \frac{1}{2T} \int_{-T}^{T} \left| f(t + \alpha) - \int_{0}^{\infty} [f(t - \tau) + g(t - \tau)] \, dK(\tau) \right|^2 dt$$

(3.435)

whenever $\alpha > 0$ and all the functions $\Phi_{ij}(\omega)$ are rational. If, on the other hand, $\alpha \to -\infty$, we shall have for the limit of the minimum

$$\lim_{\alpha \to -\infty} \frac{1}{2\pi} \int_{-\infty}^{\infty} \left\{ \Phi_{11}(\omega) \right.$$

$$\left. - \Phi(\omega) \left| \frac{1}{2\pi\Psi(\omega)} \int_{0}^{\infty} e^{-i\omega t} \, dt \int_{-\infty}^{\infty} \frac{M(u)e^{iu(t+\alpha)}}{\overline{\Psi(u)}} \, du \right|^2 \right\} d\omega$$

$$= \frac{1}{2\pi} \int_{-\infty}^{\infty} \left\{ \Phi_{11}(\omega) - \frac{\Phi(\omega) |M(\omega)|^2}{|\Psi(\omega) \cdot \overline{\Psi(\omega)}|^2} \right\} d\omega$$

$$= \frac{1}{2\pi} \int_{-\infty}^{\infty} \left\{ \Phi_{11}(\omega) - \frac{|\Phi_{11}(\omega) + \Phi_{12}(\omega)|^2}{\Phi_{11}(\omega) + \Phi_{12}(\omega) + \overline{\Phi_{12}(\omega)} + \Phi_{22}(\omega)} \right\} d\omega$$

$$= \frac{1}{2\pi} \int_{-\infty}^{\infty} \frac{\Phi_{11}(\omega)\Phi_{22}(\omega) - |\Phi_{12}(\omega)|^2}{\Phi_{11}(\omega) + \Phi_{12}(\omega) + \overline{\Phi_{12}(\omega)} + \Phi_{22}(\omega)} \, d\omega.$$

(3.44)

In the particular case where $f(t)$ and $g(t)$ have zero cross-correlation under any finite lag, $\Phi_{12}(\omega)$ is identically zero, and the minimum value of (3.415) will tend to approach

$$\frac{1}{2\pi} \int_{-\infty}^{\infty} \frac{\Phi_{11}(\omega)\Phi_{22}(\omega)}{\Phi_{11}(\omega) + \Phi_{22}(\omega)} \, d\omega \qquad (3.445)$$

as the lag $-\alpha$ becomes infinite. Whether the cross-correlation is zero or not, let it be noted that $f(t)$ and $g(t)$ occur symmetrically in these expressions.

We have now considered the performance of long-lag filters from the point of view of their "norm" or figure of merit. It is appropriate to consider the asymptotic form of their $k(\omega)$. This will be

$$k(\omega) = \frac{e^{i\omega\alpha}}{2\pi\Psi(\omega)} \int_{\alpha}^{\infty} e^{-i\omega t} \int_{-\infty}^{\infty} \frac{M(u)}{\Psi(u)} e^{iut} \, du; \qquad (3.45)$$

and if we consider only the asymptotic value of $k(\omega)e^{-i\omega\alpha}$, this will be

$$\frac{M(\omega)}{\Phi(\omega)} = \frac{\Phi_{11}(\omega) + \Phi_{12}(\omega)}{\Phi(\omega)}. \qquad (3.46)$$

3.5 Filters and Ergodic Theory

A fundamental theorem in the theory of the Brownian motion asserts that, if the responses of two linear resonators to Brownian inputs, whether the same, different, or partly the same and partly different, have a zero cross-correlation coefficient with respect to the parameter of distribution of the Brownian motion, then they are not merely linearly independent, but (as the parameters of the Brownian distributions vary) they have entirely independent distributions. Now the problem of optimum prediction is solved by reducing $f(t + \alpha)$ to a part linearly dependent on the past of $f(t)$ and a part uncorrelated with the past of $f(t)$. If the first part is

$$\int_{0}^{\infty} f(t - \tau) \, dK(\tau), \qquad (3.50)$$

then the second will be

$$f(t + \alpha) - \int_{0}^{\infty} f(t - \tau) \, dK(\tau); \qquad (3.505)$$

and by the ergodic theorem, the cross-correlation of the latter and $f(t + \alpha)$ with respect to the Brownian parameters of distribution will almost always be the average in time, or

$$\qquad (3.51)$$

which accordingly must vanish for positive s. This is the integral equation of prediction. The integral equation of filtering, or

$$\varphi_{11}(s + \alpha) - \int_0^\infty [\varphi_{11}(s - \tau) + \varphi_{22}(s - \tau)] \, dK(\tau) = 0 \quad (s > 0),$$

$$(3.52)$$

may be regarded similarly as the statement of the vanishing of a cross-correlation, and in the Brownian case will be found to assert that the error of performance of our optimum filter is wholly independent of known data and thus wholly unpredictable. Of course, its distribution will be known, but this will be a Gaussian distribution about zero determined exclusively by the functions $\varphi_{ij}(t)$ and will have nothing further to do with the function $f(t)$.

3.6 Computation of Specific Filter Characteristics

It may be of interest to work out several filter characteristics both for lead and for lag. We shall assume that $\varphi_{12}(t)$ is identically zero. As for $\varphi_{22}(t)$, we shall take a case which, although not formally contained in the theory we have given, constitutes a limiting case of it, and one of the greatest importance in practice. This is the case in which the noise input is due to a shot effect and has an equipartition of power in frequency. Theoretically, of course, this is not strictly realizable, as it would demand an infinite power; practically, as in the case of Planck's law in optics, it may hold within the limits of observation up to frequencies of a magnitude so great that they are no longer of interest for our particular problem. Thus we shall put $\Phi_{22}(\omega) = \epsilon^2$. As to $\Phi_{11}(\omega)$, it will depend on the particular problem considered. For an example, let us consider the case $\Phi_{11}(\omega) = 1/(1 + \omega^2)$. Then

$$H(\omega) = \frac{e^{i\alpha\omega}}{1 + \omega^2} ; \tag{3.60}$$

$$\Phi(\omega) = \frac{1}{1 + \omega^2} + \epsilon^2 = \frac{1 + \epsilon^2 + \epsilon^2\omega^2}{1 + \omega^2} ; \tag{3.601}$$

$$\Psi(\omega) = \frac{\sqrt{1 + \epsilon^2} + \epsilon i\omega}{1 + i\omega} ; \tag{3.602}$$

$$\frac{H(\omega)}{\Psi(\omega)} = \frac{e^{i\alpha\omega}}{(1 + i\omega)(\sqrt{1 + \epsilon^2} - \epsilon i\omega)} ; \tag{3.603}$$

$$\frac{1}{2\pi} \int_{-\infty}^\infty \frac{H(u)}{\Psi(u)} e^{iut} \, du = \frac{1}{2\pi} \int_{-\infty}^\infty \frac{e^{iu(t+\alpha)}}{(1 + iu)(\sqrt{1 + \epsilon^2} - \epsilon iu)} \, du$$

$$= \frac{1}{2\pi} \int_{-\infty}^{\infty} \frac{e^{iu(t+\alpha)}}{\epsilon + \sqrt{1+\epsilon^2}} \left(\frac{1}{1+iu} + \frac{\epsilon}{\sqrt{1+\epsilon^2} - \epsilon iu} \right) du$$

$$= \begin{cases} \dfrac{e^{-(t+\alpha)}}{(\epsilon + \sqrt{1+\epsilon^2})} & (t > -\alpha) \\ \\ e^{\dfrac{\sqrt{1+\epsilon^2}(t+\alpha)}{\epsilon(\epsilon + \sqrt{1+\epsilon^2})}} & (t < -\alpha). \end{cases} \qquad (3.604)$$

If α is positive, this gives us

$$k(\omega) = \frac{1+i\omega}{\sqrt{1+\epsilon^2} + \epsilon i\omega} \int_0^{\infty} \frac{e^{-(t+\alpha)} e^{-i\omega t}}{\epsilon + \sqrt{1+\epsilon^2}} dt$$

$$= \frac{1+i\omega}{\sqrt{1+\epsilon^2} + \epsilon i\omega} \cdot \frac{e^{-\alpha}}{\epsilon + \sqrt{1+\epsilon^2}} \cdot \frac{1}{1+i\omega}$$

$$= \frac{e^{-\alpha}}{\epsilon + \sqrt{1+\epsilon^2}} \cdot \frac{1}{\sqrt{1+\epsilon^2} + \epsilon i\omega}. \qquad (3.605)$$

3.7 Lagging Filters

If α is negative, we must have recourse to approximations. For example, let us notice that

$$e^{i\alpha\omega} \cong \left(\frac{1 + (\alpha i\omega/2\nu)}{1 - (\alpha i\omega/2\nu)} \right)^{\nu} \qquad (3.70)$$

Thus

$$\frac{H(\omega)}{\Psi(\omega)} \cong \left(\frac{1 + (\alpha i\omega/2\nu)}{1 - (\alpha i\omega/2\nu)} \right)^{\nu} \frac{1}{(1+i\omega)(\sqrt{1+\epsilon^2} - \epsilon i\omega)}$$

$$= \sum_1^N \frac{A_k}{[1 - (\alpha i\omega/2\nu)]^k} + \frac{B}{1+i\omega} + \frac{C}{\sqrt{1+\epsilon^2} - \epsilon i\omega}, \qquad (3.705)$$

where simultaneous equations for the A_k, B, and C may be obtained, for example, by substituting different values for ω in either the equation given or in its derivatives. Thus if ν is 1 and $\alpha \neq -2$, we have

$$(A_1 + B)\sqrt{1+\epsilon^2} + C = 1; \qquad (3.71)$$

$$A_1(\sqrt{1+\epsilon^2} - \epsilon) + B\left(-\epsilon - \frac{\alpha}{2}\sqrt{1+\epsilon^2} \right) + C\left(1 - \frac{\alpha}{2} \right) = \frac{\alpha}{2}; \qquad (3.715)$$

$$-A_1\epsilon + \frac{B\alpha\epsilon}{2} - \frac{C}{2} = 0; \qquad (3.72)$$

$$= \frac{\alpha^2/2}{\left(1 + \frac{\alpha}{2}\right)\left(\frac{\alpha}{2}\sqrt{1 + \epsilon^2} - \epsilon\right)} \; ; \quad B = \frac{1 - (\alpha/2)}{\left(1 + \frac{\alpha}{2}\right)(\epsilon + \sqrt{1 + \epsilon^2})} .$$

$$(3.73)$$

$$k(\omega) = \frac{1 + i\omega}{\sqrt{1 + \epsilon^2} + \epsilon i\omega} \left(\sum_1^{\cdot} \frac{A_k}{(1 - \alpha i\omega/2\nu)^k} + \frac{B}{1 + i\omega} \right), \quad (3.74)$$

and in this special case

$$k(\omega) = \frac{\alpha^2/2}{\left(1 + \frac{\alpha}{2}\right)\left(\frac{\alpha}{2}\sqrt{1 + \epsilon^2} - \epsilon\right)} \cdot \frac{1 + i\omega}{(\sqrt{1 + \epsilon^2} + \epsilon i\omega)\left(1 - \frac{\alpha i\omega}{2}\right)}$$

$$+ \frac{1 - (\alpha/2)}{\left(1 + \frac{\alpha}{2}\right)(\epsilon + \sqrt{1 + \epsilon^2})(\sqrt{1 + \epsilon^2} + \epsilon i\omega)} . \quad (3.75)$$

In this work, there is room for a considerable amount of freedom in selecting the rational operator which is taken to approximate $e^{i\alpha\omega}$. The problem of determining such an operator is the well-known one of designing pure delay networks and has been discussed at length in the *Bell System Technical Journal* and elsewhere. Given $\Phi(\omega)$, each such design leads to the determination of a rational filter characteristic with no singularities below the real axis. The realization of such real functions as the voltage-transfer-ratio characteristics of networks is also, at least in large measure, established engineering practice and may be found in such books as Guillemin's *Communication Networks*.

An alternative approach to filter design may be found in the use of Laguerre functions or similar combinations of algebraic and exponential functions to approximate to

$$\int_{-\infty}^{\infty} \frac{H(u)}{\Psi(u)} e^{iut} \, du \quad (0 \le t \le \infty). \quad (3.76)$$

Such a method will probably have no significant advantages over methods depending on an approximation to $e^{i\alpha\omega}$.

The detailed design of a filter involves certain choices of constants which must be justified economically. In general, it does not pay to eliminate a small error from a quantity when there is a large irremovable error in it. The irremovable error in the mean square of the performance of a filter, as we have seen, is

$$\frac{1}{2\pi} \int_{-\infty}^{\infty} \frac{\Phi_{11}(\omega)\Phi_{22}(\omega)}{\Phi_{11}(\omega) + \Phi_{22}(\omega)} \, d\omega. \tag{3.77}$$

This minimum error is attainable only in a filter having an infinite time of delay. There is manifestly no use in increasing the delay time of a filter if the part of the error

$$\frac{1}{2\pi} \int_{0}^{\infty} \left\{ \Phi_{11}(\omega) - \Phi(\omega) \left| \frac{1}{2\pi\Psi(\omega)} \int_{0}^{\infty} e^{i\omega t} \, dt \int_{-\infty}^{\infty} \frac{H(u)}{\overline{\Psi(\omega)}} e^{i\omega t} \, du \right|^2 \right\} d\omega \tag{3.78}$$

due to the finiteness of this delay is already small compared with the intrinsic error.

3.8 The Determination of Lag and Number of Meshes in a Filter

If we thus fix on the reasonable delay for a filter, there is still another error dependent on the fact that the theoretically optimum design is not, in fact, realizable with a finite network of resistances, capacities, and inductances. This is the error implicit in our approximation to $e^{i\alpha\omega}$. Again, such an error may be estimated, and there is no point in reducing this part of the error to a level substantially below that of the error implicit in the delay already chosen. It is this last error which determines the number of meshes and parts appropriate to the complete filter network. Once this final error is decided upon, the rational voltage ratio characteristic of the network is determined, and its design is a matter of known technique.

The filter theory here presented, like our prediction theory, though it is adapted to the use of electrical circuits, may be carried out as a purely numerical computation, as may be indicated in certain studies of meteorological or geophysical time series, or may be applied to mechanical structures, as in the smoothing of the performance of hand-cranks and servo-mechanisms. In the latter cases, the large time scale of the process may put the use of purely passive electrical networks out of question, as really large inductances are not practical. On the other hand, such filters may be realized mechanically; or they may be realized electrically by the use of active networks, in which vacuum tubes or other amplifying devices appear, but in which inductances do not appear; or they may be realized by a combination of mechanical and electrical devices. In all cases, for a shot-effect noise, the information required for filter design consists in the spectrum of the message to be transmitted, the noise level, and the permissible delay.

3.9 Detecting Filters for High Noise Level

An especially interesting and important type of filter is that employed in the observation of very faint messages when the noise level is very high. Here certain simplifying assumptions may be made. We shall have

$$\Phi_{22}(\omega) = 1; \quad \Phi_{11}(\omega) = \epsilon F(\omega); \quad \Phi(\omega) = 1 + \epsilon F(\omega) \quad (3.900)$$

if the noise is suitably normalized. To factor $\Phi(\omega)$, we introduce the function

$$G(\omega) = \frac{1}{2\pi} \int_0^\infty e^{-i\omega t} dt \int_{-\infty}^\infty F(u)e^{iut} du. \quad (3.901)$$

Then approximately

$$\Phi(\omega) = | 1 + \epsilon G(\omega) |^2 ; \quad (3.9015)$$

and if we put

$$1 + \epsilon G(\omega) = \Psi(\omega), \quad (3.902)$$

we shall have approximately

$$\frac{H(\omega)}{\Psi(\omega)} = \frac{\epsilon F(\omega)e^{i\omega a}}{1 + \epsilon \overline{G(\omega)}} = \epsilon F(\omega)e^{i\omega a}[1 - \epsilon\overline{G(\omega)}]. \quad (3.9025)$$

To a first degree of approximation,

$$k(\omega) = \frac{\epsilon}{2\pi} \int_0^\infty e^{-i\omega t} dt \int_{-\infty}^\infty F(u)e^{iu(t+a)} du$$

$$= e^{i\omega a} \frac{\epsilon}{2\pi} \int_\alpha^\infty e^{-i\omega t} dt \int_{-\infty}^\infty F(u)e^{iut} du. \quad (3.903)$$

This means that, if we allow a long delay and neglect the effect of this delay, the frequency character of the desired filter will be $\epsilon F(\omega)$ itself.

The next degree of approximation is

$$k(\omega)e^{-i\omega a} \cong \frac{\Phi_{11}(\omega)}{\Phi(\omega)} \cong \frac{\epsilon F(\omega)}{1 + \epsilon F(\omega)}. \quad (3.9035)$$

It will be seen that this function is qualitatively very similar to $F(u)$, and that, except for a numerical factor, a filter with frequency characteristic $F(\omega)$ will not perform too badly for a considerable range of large noise intensities. Of course, the criterion which we have used for the performance of a filter is perhaps not so obviously natural at high noise levels as at low. Nevertheless, it is still not a valueless one.

3.91 Filters for Pulses

The problem of filtering at high noise levels arises chiefly in connection with the detection of extremely faint messages, at the threshold of detectability. A closely related problem is that of the proper pulse form for such messages. For many purposes, a message to be detected by such means must be accurately localizable in time and, for the avoidance of incoming and outgoing interference, must also be accurately localizable in frequency. Let the time form of such a pulse be $f(t)$, and its Fourier transform (the frequency form of the pulse) be $g(u)$. Here

$$g(u) = \frac{1}{\sqrt{2\pi}} \lim_{A \to \infty} \int_{-A}^{A} f(t)e^{-iut}\, dt. \tag{3.910}$$

measure of the time spread of such a pulse will be

$$\frac{\int_{-\infty}^{\infty} t^2\, |f(t)|^2\, dt}{\int_{-\infty}^{\infty} |f(t)|^2\, dt}. \tag{3.9105}$$

Thus a reasonable measure of the combined time and frequency spread will be

$$\frac{\int_{-\infty}^{\infty} t^2\, |f(t)|^2\, dt}{\int_{-\infty}^{\infty} |f(t)|^2\, dt} + \frac{\lambda^2 \int_{-\infty}^{\infty} u^2\, |g(u)|^2\, du}{\int_{-\infty}^{\infty} |g(u)|^2\, du}$$

$$= \frac{\int_{-\infty}^{\infty} \left[t^2\, |f(t)|^2 + \lambda^2 \left| \frac{df(t)}{dt} \right|^2 \right] dt}{\int_{-\infty}^{\infty} |f(t)|^2\, dt}. \tag{3.911}$$

Assuming the total energy of the pulse to be fixed, the problem minimizing the combined time and frequency spreads reduces to that of minimizing

$$\int_{-\infty}^{\infty} \left([t^2 f(t)]^2 + \lambda^2 \left[\frac{df(t)}{dt} \right]^2 \right) dt, \tag{3.9115}$$

while $\int_{-\infty}^{\infty} [f(t)]^2\, dt$ is constant. If we now vary $f(t)$ by adding to it $\delta f(t)$, we see that we should have

$$0 = \int_{-\infty}^{\infty} t^2 f(t)\delta f(t)\, dt + \lambda^2 \int_{-\infty}^{\infty} \frac{df(t)}{dt} \frac{d}{dt} [\delta f(t)]\, dt$$

$$= \int_{-\infty}^{\infty} \left[t^2 f(t) - \lambda^2 \frac{d^2 f(t)}{dt^2} \right] \delta f(t)\, dt \tag{3.912}$$

whenever

$$\int_{-\infty}^{\infty} f(t)\delta f(t)\ dt = 0. \tag{3.9125}$$

This leads to the Euler-Lagrange equation,

$$t^2 f(t) - \lambda^2 \frac{d^2 f(t)}{dt^2} = \mu f(t), \tag{3.913}$$

and the L^2 solution of this, with smallest characteristic value, will be

$$f(t) = \exp\left(\frac{-t^2}{2\lambda}\right). \tag{3.9135}$$

This is accordingly the desired pulse shape, and the desired $k(\omega)e^{-i\omega a}$ will be

$$F(\omega) = \text{const}\ \exp\ (-\lambda\omega^2). \tag{3.914}$$

For detection of faint pulses of this form, we accordingly wish a filter with characteristic approximating $e^{-\lambda\omega^2}$. Fortunately, the time characteristic of such a filter will be nearly

$$(\text{const})\ \exp\left[\frac{-(t - \tau)^2}{4\lambda}\right], \tag{3.9145}$$

and this may be approximated by taking

$$t^n \exp\left(-t \sqrt{\frac{n}{2\lambda}}\right) \cong (\text{const})\ \exp\left[-\frac{(t - \text{const})^2}{4\lambda}\right]. \tag{3.915}$$

On the frequency scale this yields us

$$(\text{const})\ \frac{1}{\left(\sqrt{\dfrac{n}{2\lambda}} + i\omega\right)^n}, \tag{3.9155}$$

and our problem is completely solved.

3.92 Filters Having Characteristics Linearly Dependent on Given Characteristics

Let us now explore the problem of the filter consisting in a linear combination of fixed operators with variable coefficients. Let us seek to minimize

$$M = \lim_{T \to \infty} \frac{1}{2T} \int_{-T}^{T} \left| f(t + \alpha) \right.$$
$$\left. - \sum_{1}^{n} a_k \int_{0}^{\infty} [f(t - \tau) + g(t - \tau)]\ dK_k(\tau) \right|^2 dt$$

$$= \varphi_{11}(0) - 2R\left\{ \int_0^\infty [\varphi_{11}(\alpha + \tau) + \varphi_{12}(\alpha + \tau)] \sum_1^n \bar{a}_k \, d\overline{K_k(t)} \right\}$$

$$+ \int_0^\infty \sum_1^n a_k \, dK_k(\sigma) \int_0^\infty \sum_1^n \bar{a}_k \, d\overline{K_k(\tau)} \varphi(\tau - \sigma). \qquad (3.920)$$

Let us use the notation

$$\int_0^\infty e^{-i\omega t} \, dK_k(t) = k_k(\omega) \quad (k = 1, \cdots, n). \qquad (3.9205)$$

Then, using reductions now familiar to us, we may write

$$M = \frac{1}{2\pi} \int_{-\infty}^\infty \Phi_{11}(\omega) \, d\omega$$

$$- 2R\left\{ \sum_1^n \bar{a}_k \frac{1}{2\pi} \int_{-\infty}^\infty [\Phi_{11}(\omega) + \Phi_{12}(\omega)]e^{i\alpha\omega}\overline{k_k(\omega)} \, d\omega \right\}$$

$$+ \frac{1}{2\pi} \sum_1^n a_j \sum_1^n \bar{a}_k \int_{-\infty}^\infty \Phi(\omega) k_j(\omega)\overline{k_k(\omega)} \, d\omega. \qquad (3.921)$$

If our $k_k(\omega)$ are so normalized that

$$\frac{1}{2\pi} \int_{-\infty}^\infty \Phi(\omega) k_j(\omega)\overline{k_k(\omega)} \, d\omega = \begin{cases} 0 \text{ if } j \neq k; \\ 1 \text{ if } j = k; \end{cases} \qquad (3.9215)$$

this gives us

$$M = \frac{1}{2\pi} \int_{-\infty}^\infty \Phi_{11}(\omega) \, d\omega -$$

$$2R\left\{ \sum_1^n \bar{a}_k \frac{1}{2\pi} \int_{-\infty}^\infty [\Phi_{11}(\omega) + \Phi_{12}(\omega)]e^{i\alpha\omega}\overline{k_k(\omega)} \, d\omega \right\} + \sum_1^n |a_k|^2$$

$$= \frac{1}{2\pi} \int_{-\infty}^\infty \Phi_{11}(\omega) \, d\omega - \sum_1^n \left| \frac{1}{2\pi} \int_{-\infty}^\infty [\Phi_{11}(\omega) + \Phi_{12}(\omega)]e^{i\alpha\omega}\overline{k_k(\omega)} \, d\omega \right|^2$$

$$+ \sum_1^n \left| a_k - \frac{1}{2\pi} \int_{-\infty}^\infty [\Phi_{11}(\omega) + \Phi_{12}(\omega)]e^{i\alpha\omega}\overline{k_k(\omega)} \, d\omega \right|^2. \qquad (3.922)$$

This will be a minimum when and only when

$$a_k = \frac{1}{2\pi} \int_{-\infty}^\infty [\Phi_{11}(\omega) + \Phi_{12}(\omega)]e^{i\alpha\omega}\overline{k_k(\omega)} \, d\omega, \qquad (3.9225)$$

and the minimum will be

$$\frac{1}{2\pi} \int_{-\infty}^\infty \Phi_{11}(\omega) \, d\omega - \sum_1^n \left| \frac{1}{2\pi} \int_{-\infty}^\infty [\Phi_{11}(\omega) + \Phi_{12}(\omega)]e^{i\alpha\omega}\overline{k_k(\omega)} \, d\alpha \right|^2$$

$$(3.$$

Under these conditions,

$$\sum_1^n a_k k_k(\omega) = \tag{3.9235}$$

$$\frac{1}{\Psi(\omega)}\left[\sum_1^n k_k(\omega)\Psi(\omega)\frac{1}{2\pi}\int_{-\infty}^{\infty}\frac{\Phi_{11}(\omega)+\Phi_{22}(\omega)}{\Psi(\omega)}e^{ia\omega}\overline{k_k(\omega)\Psi(\omega)}\,d\omega\right]$$

which is the formal development of $\dfrac{\Phi_{11}(\omega)+\Phi_{22}(\omega)}{\Psi(\omega)}e^{ia\omega}$ in the functions $k_k(\omega)\cdot\Psi(\omega)$, multiplied by $1/\Psi(\omega)$. If the set of functions $k_k(\omega)\cdot\Psi(\omega)$, all of which are free from singularities in the half-plane below the real axis, is complete in the set of such functions [and if it is not, it may be made so by adjoining other functions $k_k(\omega)\cdot\Psi(\omega)$, which may be taken so as to satisfy (3.9215)], we obtain as the formal limit for $\sum_1^n a_k k_k(\omega)$ the expression

$$\frac{1}{2\pi\Psi(\omega)}\int_0^{\infty}e^{-i\omega t}\,dt\int_{-\infty}^{\infty}\frac{\Phi_{11}(u)+\Phi_{12}(u)}{\Psi(u)}e^{iau}\,du,\tag{3.924}$$

which we have already seen to solve the filter problem as stated, without any reference to a specific set of functions $k_k(\omega)$.

Let it be noted that we have here assumed the factorability of $\Phi(\omega)$ into $|\Psi(\omega)|^2$, where $\Psi(\omega)$ is free from singularities in the lower half-plane. If this is not the case, as we have seen,

$$\int_{-\infty}^{\infty}\frac{\log|\Phi(\omega)|}{1+\omega^2}\,d\omega = -\infty.\tag{3.9245}$$

Under these circumstances the set of functions $\sqrt{\Phi(\omega)}k(\omega)$, where $k(\omega)$ is free from singularities in the lower half-plane, is closed L^2. Otherwise there will exist a function $\Phi(\omega)l(\omega)$ of class L^2, not equivalent to zero, such that

$$\int_{-\infty}^{\infty}\Phi(\omega)k(\omega)l(\omega)\,d\omega = 0\tag{3.925}$$

for every $k(\omega)$ for which

$$\int_{-\infty}^{\infty}\Phi(\omega)|k(\omega)|^2\,d\omega < \infty\tag{3.9255}$$

and which has no singularity in the lower half-plane. This will certainly be the case for every function $k(\omega)$ of class L^2 having no singularity in the lower half-plane. It will follow at once that

$$\Phi(\omega)\cdot l(\omega)\tag{3.926}$$

will be orthogonal to every function of class L^2 vanishing for negative arguments, and will itself vanish for positive arguments. Thus

$$\int_{-\infty}^{\infty} \frac{\log |\Phi(\omega)| + \log |l(\omega)|}{1 + \omega^2} d\omega > -\infty. \qquad (3.9265)$$

This would mean, by (3.9245), that

$$\int_{-\infty}^{\infty} \frac{\log |\sqrt{\Phi(\omega)}l(\omega)|}{1 + \omega^2} d\omega = \infty, \qquad (3.927)$$

which is manifestly false, as the function $\sqrt{\Phi(\omega)}l(\omega)$ belongs to L^2. Thus no such $l(\omega)$ exists, and the set of functions $\sqrt{\Phi(\omega)}k(\omega)$ is closed. In other words, we may choose the functions $\sqrt{\Phi(\omega)}k_n(\omega)$ in such a way that

$$\sqrt{\Phi(\omega)} \sum_{1}^{\infty} a_k k_k(\omega) = \frac{\Phi_{11}(\omega) + \Phi_{12}(\omega)}{\sqrt{\Phi(\omega)}} e^{i\alpha\omega}, \qquad (3.9275)$$

and that formally

$$\sum_{1}^{\infty} a_k k_k(\omega) = \frac{\Phi_{11}(\omega) + \Phi_{12}(\omega)}{\Phi(\omega)} e^{i\alpha\omega}. \qquad (3.928)$$

This means that in such a case the performance of a filter for a finite delay may be made to approximate as nearly as we wish the performance of a filter for an infinite delay. This is quite reasonable, since for such messages and noises the entire future of the message-plus-noise is determined by its past, and nothing new ever happens.

Let it be noted that the situation depends on the factorability or non-factorability of $\Phi(\omega)$, which involves both the message and the noise, and not on the factorability or non-factorability of a term containing the message alone. Even with a perfectly predictable message, the presence of an imperfectly predictable noise makes the filtering problem a significant one.

The problem which we have just solved is that of the design of a filter having a character which is the sum of fixed operators with adjustable coefficients. The functions $k_k(\omega)$ may be any functions obtained by normalizing in the proper sense the functions $(1 + ai\omega)^n$ $(n = 0, 1, 2, \cdots)$, for then they themselves [and a fortiori the functions $k_k(\omega)$] will be closed in the set of all functions of L^2 which are free from singularities in the half-plane below the real axis. Since we have an algorithm for obtaining the coefficients, the filter-design problem is solved. Such adjustable filters are of the greatest value in experimental installations, in which the adjustability may actually be realized by the turning of rheostats or potentiometers, or even in permanent installations in which the variety of work to be undertaken is very great. Of course, they will ordinarily be more complicated than the fixed-constant sets having the minimum number of elements for the same performance.

3.93 Computation of Filter: Résumé

Let us then sum up the mathematical stages in the design of a filter of fixed or variable characteristic. The first stage is the computation of the even function $\Phi_{11}(\omega)$. On the basis of this, with a proper choice of the scale constant P, the coefficients

$$\int_{-\infty}^{\infty} \Phi_{11}(\omega) e^{2ni \tan^{-1}\omega P} \frac{2P}{1 + \omega^2 P^2} \, d\omega \qquad (3.930)$$

are then computed. Then the Cesaro sum

$$\frac{1}{2\pi} \sum_{\nu=-N}^{N} \left(1 - \frac{|\nu|}{N}\right) e^{-2\nu i \tan^{-1}\omega P} \int_{-\infty}^{\infty} \Phi_{11}(u) e^{2\nu i \tan^{-1}u P} \, du \qquad (3.9305)$$

is computed as an approximate value for $\Phi_{11}(\omega)$. This is then written in the quotient form

$$\frac{\text{(polynomial in } \omega^2 P^2)}{(1 + \omega^2 P^2)^{N-1}} \qquad (3.931)$$

and the numerator and denominator are factored into linear factors. In factoring the numerator, algebraic equations of high order may have to be solved for their complex roots, and the use of a device such as the Isograph* of the Bell Telephone Laboratories is indicated. Then, by selecting in both numerator and denominator only those roots with positive imaginary part, the function $\Psi(\omega)$ is determined. In the case of a lead filter, all is plain sailing from here on. In the case of a lag filter, through considerations such as those we have already indicated; the proper lag is determined, as well as the degree to which it is worth while to imitate $e^{i\alpha\omega}$ in determining the proper approximation to this lag. Then we call on the existing technique of delay-mechanism design to realize this approximation in terms of the simplest rational characteristic possible. When this approximation is known, we have already given the formulae which determine the final filter characteristic. Finally, whether for lead or for lag, we have to realize the (now determined) characteristic by a network, which is then subject to the many known tricks of network transformation.

* See Industrial Mathematics, by T. C. Fry, *Bell System Technical Journal*, Vol. 20, No. 3, July, 1941, p. 276. There are also well-known computational-algebraic methods of achieving the same result.

So much for the fixed filter. For the variable filter, we are faced instead with the choice of a suitable closed set of functions $1/(i\omega + a)^k$ and of their orthogonalization with respect to the function $\Phi(\omega)$. This alone determines the structure of the filter, while the determination of the numbers a_k in terms of α gives the setting of the apparatus for a desired lead or lag.

Much less important, though of real interest, is the problem of the numerical filter for statistical work, as contrasted with the filter as a physically active piece of engineering apparatus. In the case of continuous data, there is little new to say of this, except that the $k(\omega)$ already obtained must be translated into a $K(t)$ from which we may evaluate $\int_0^\infty f(t - \tau)\, dK(\tau)$. In that particular subcase of the discrete case in which f and g are independent, we follow the lines of the prediction theory of the previous chapter and define the function $\Phi(\omega)$ in terms of the auto-correlation coefficient

$$\varphi_{11\nu} = \lim_{N \to \infty} \frac{1}{2N + 1} \sum_{\mu = -N}^{N} f_{\nu+\mu} \bar{f}_\mu, \tag{3.9315}$$

where the f_ν constitute the time series with which we are working. We further put

$$\Phi_{11}(\omega) = \sum_{-\infty}^{\infty} \varphi_{11\nu} e^{-i\nu\omega}. \tag{3.932}$$

This will be a periodic function of period 2π. Similarly,

$$\varphi_{22\nu} = \lim_{N \to \infty} \frac{1}{2N + 1} \sum_{\mu = -N}^{N} g_{\nu+\mu} \bar{g}_\mu; \quad \Phi_{22}(\omega) = \sum_{-\infty}^{\infty} \varphi_{22\nu} e^{-i\nu\omega}. \tag{3.9325}$$

As an approximation, we may use Cesaro methods as before and may put

$$\sum_{-N}^{N} \left(1 - \frac{|\nu|}{N}\right) (\varphi_{11\nu} + \varphi_{22\nu}) e^{-i\nu\omega} = \left| \sum_{0}^{N} \psi_\nu e^{i\nu\omega} \right|^2, \tag{3.933}$$

where the factoring is so carried out that

$$\Psi(\omega) = \sum_{0}^{N} \psi_\nu e^{i\nu\omega} \neq 0 \quad (\mathrm{I}\{\omega\} < 0). \tag{3.9335}$$

Here again the isograph may be used. We then put

$$k(\omega) = \frac{1}{2\pi\Psi(\omega)} \sum_{0}^{\infty} e^{-i\nu\omega} \int_{-\pi}^{\pi} \frac{\Phi_{11}(u) e^{i\alpha u}}{\overline{\Psi(u)}} e^{iu\nu}\, du$$

$$\tag{3.934}$$

If now we write

$$K_\nu = \frac{1}{2\pi} \int_{-\pi}^{\pi} e^{i\nu\omega} k(\omega)\, d\omega, \tag{3.935}$$

we shall minimize

$$\lim_{N \to \infty} \frac{1}{2N+1} \sum_{-N}^{N} \left| f_{\nu+\alpha} - \sum_{\mu=0}^{\infty} (f_{\nu-\mu} + g_{\nu-\mu}) K_\mu \right|^2. \tag{3.936}$$

_ of this expression will be

$$\frac{1}{2\pi} \int_{-\pi}^{\pi} \left\{ \Phi_{11}(\omega) - [\Phi_{11}(\omega) + \Phi(\omega)] \,|\, k(\omega) \,|^2 \right\} d\omega. \tag{3.937}$$

CHAPTER IV

THE LINEAR PREDICTOR AND FILTER FOR MULTIPLE TIME SERIES

4.0 Symbolism and Definitions for Multiple Time Series

The difficulties of the present chapter are rendered much more considerable by the sheer bulk of notation required to deal effectively with multiple time series. Let us then agree on the following points:

The symbols $f_k(t)\,(1 \leq k \leq n)$ shall signify *messages*.

The symbols $g_k(t)\,(1 \leq k \leq n)$ shall signify *disturbances*.

The symbols $\varphi_{jk}{}^{mm}(t)$ shall signify *correlation coefficients of messages*, or symbolically

$$\varphi_{jk}{}^{mm}(t) = \lim_{T \to \infty} \frac{1}{2T} \int_{-T}^{T} f_j(t+\tau)\overline{f_k(\tau)}\, d\tau \qquad (4.00)$$

The symbols $\varphi_{jk}{}^{dd}(t)$ shall signify *correlation coefficients of disturbances*, or symbolically

$$\varphi_{jk}{}^{dd}(t) = \lim_{T \to \infty} \frac{1}{2T} \int_{-T}^{T} g_j(t+\tau)\overline{g_k(\tau)}\, d\tau. \qquad (4.003)$$

The symbols $\varphi_{jk}{}^{md}(t)$ shall signify *correlation coefficients between messages and disturbances*, or symbolically

$$\varphi_{jk}{}^{md}(t) = \lim_{T \to \infty} \frac{1}{2T} \int_{-T}^{T} f_j(t+\tau)\overline{g_k(\tau)}\, d\tau. \qquad (4.005)$$

Let us put

$$\varphi_{jk}(t) = \varphi_{jk}{}^{mm}(t) + \varphi_{jk}{}^{md}(t) + \varphi_{kj}{}^{md}(-t) + \varphi_{jk}{}^{dd}(t); \qquad (4.01)$$

$$\chi_k(t) = \varphi_{1k}{}^{mm}(t) + \varphi_{1k}{}^{md}(t). \qquad (4.015)$$

We shall write

$$\frac{1}{2\pi} \int_{-\infty}^{\infty} \Phi_{jk}(\omega)e^{i\omega t}\, d\omega = \varphi_{jk}(t); \qquad (4.02)$$

$$\frac{1}{2\pi} \int_{-\infty}^{\infty} \mathrm{X}_j(\omega)e^{i\omega t}\, d\omega = \chi_j(t). \qquad (4.025)$$

Here

$$\Phi_{jk}(\omega) = \overline{\Phi_{kj}(\omega)}. \tag{4.03}$$

We shall put

$$\Phi(\omega) = |\Phi_{jk}(\omega)|. \tag{4.035}$$

Where it can be done, we shall put on the real axis

$$\Phi_{jj}(\omega) = |\Psi_j(\omega)|^2, \quad \Phi(\omega) = |\Psi(\omega)|^2, \tag{4.04}$$

where $\Psi_j(\omega)$ and $\Psi(\omega)$ are free from zeros and singularities in the lower half-plane and are bounded at infinity in that half-plane.

4.1 Minimization Problem for Multiple Time Series

The problem which we now wish to solve is that of the best approximation in the least square sense to $f_1(t + \alpha)$, by the sum of a set of linear operators on the pasts of $f_1(t) + g_1(t), \cdots, f_n(t) + g_n(t)$. In symbols, we wish to minimize

$$\begin{aligned}
M &= \lim_{T \to \infty} \frac{1}{2T} \int_{-T}^{T} \left| f_1(t + \alpha) - \sum_{k=1}^{n} \int_{0}^{\infty} \{f_k(t - \tau)\} \, dK_k(\tau) \right|^2 dt \\
&= \varphi_{11}{}^{mm}(0) - 2R \left\{ \sum_{k=1}^{n} \int_{0}^{\infty} \{\varphi_{1k}{}^{mm}(\alpha + \tau) + \varphi_{1k}{}^{md}(\alpha + \tau)\} \, d\overline{K_k(\tau)} \right\} \\
&\quad + \sum_{j=1}^{n} \sum_{k=1}^{n} \int_{0}^{\infty} dK_j(\sigma) \int_{0}^{\infty} d\overline{K_k(\tau)} \{\varphi_{jk}{}^{mm}(\tau - \sigma) \\
&\quad + \varphi_{jk}{}^{md}(\tau - \sigma) + \varphi_{kj}{}^{md}(\sigma - \tau) + \varphi_{jk}{}^{dd}(\tau - \sigma)\} \\
&= \varphi_{11}{}^{mm}(0) - 2R \left\{ \sum_{k=1}^{n} \int_{0}^{\infty} \chi_k(\alpha + \tau) \, d\overline{K_k(\tau)} \right\} \\
&\quad + \sum_{j=1}^{n} \sum_{k=1}^{n} \int_{0}^{\infty} dK_j(\sigma) \int_{0}^{\infty} d\overline{K_k(\tau)} \varphi_{jk}(\tau - \sigma). \tag{4.10}
\end{aligned}$$

If now we let

$$\chi_k(\alpha + \tau) = \sum_{j=1}^{n} \int_{0}^{\infty} \varphi_{jk}(\tau - \sigma) \, dQ_j(\sigma) \quad (\tau > 0), \tag{4.105}$$

we get

$$\begin{aligned}
M &= \varphi_{11}{}^{mm}(0) - 2R \left\{ \sum_{j=1}^{n} \sum_{k=1}^{n} \int_{0}^{\infty} dQ_j(\sigma) \int_{0}^{\infty} \varphi_{jk}(\tau - \sigma) \, d\overline{K_k(\tau)} \right\} \\
&\quad + \sum_{j=1}^{n} \sum_{k=1}^{n} \int_{0}^{\infty} dK_j(\sigma) \int_{0}^{\infty} \varphi_{jk}(\tau - \sigma) \, d\overline{K_k(\tau)} \\
&= \varphi_{11}{}^{mm}(0) - \sum_{j=1}^{n} \sum_{k=1}^{n} \int_{0}^{\infty} dQ_j(\sigma) \int_{0}^{\infty} \varphi_{jk}(\tau - \sigma) \, d\overline{Q_k(\tau)} \\
&\quad + \sum_{j=1}^{n} \sum_{k=1}^{n} \int_{0}^{\infty} d[Q_j(\sigma) - K_j(\sigma)] \int_{0}^{\infty} \varphi_{jk}(\tau - \sigma) \, d[\overline{Q_k(\tau)} - \overline{K_k(\tau)}]
\end{aligned}$$

$$= \varphi_{11}^{mm}(0) - \sum_{j=1}^{n} \sum_{k=1}^{n} \int_{0}^{\infty} dQ_j(\sigma) \int_{0}^{\infty} \varphi_{jk}(\tau - \sigma) \, d\overline{Q_k(\tau)}$$

$$+ \lim_{T \to \infty} \frac{1}{2T} \int_{-T}^{T} \left| \sum_{j=1}^{n} \int_{0}^{\infty} [f_j(t - \tau) + g_j(t - \tau)] \, d[Q_j(\tau) - K_j(\tau)] \right|^2 dt$$

$$\geq \varphi_{11}^{mm}(0) - \sum_{j=1}^{n} \sum_{k=1}^{n} \int_{0}^{\infty} dQ_j(\sigma) \int_{0}^{\infty} \varphi_{jk}(\tau - \sigma) \, d\overline{Q_k(\tau)}. \quad (4.11)$$

To minimize this expression, we may obviously put

$$K_j(\tau) = Q_j(\tau) \quad (j = 1, \cdots, n) \quad (4.115)$$

and we have reduced our problem to that of the solution of the system of equations (4.105).

Let us now put

$$q_j(\omega) = \int_{0}^{\infty} e^{-i\omega t} \, dQ_j(t); \quad k_j(\omega) = \int_{0}^{\infty} e^{i\omega t} \, dK_j(t). \quad (4.12)$$

$$\sum_{j=1}^{n} \sum_{k=1}^{n} \int_{0}^{\infty} d[Q_j(\sigma) - K_j(\sigma)] \int_{0}^{\infty} \varphi_{jk}(\tau - \sigma) \, d[\overline{Q_k(\tau)} - \overline{K_k(\tau)}]$$

$$= \sum_{j=1}^{n} \sum_{k=1}^{n} \frac{1}{2\pi} \int_{-\infty}^{\infty} \Phi_{jk}(\omega)[q_j(\omega) - k_j(\omega)][\overline{q_k(\omega)} - \overline{k_k(\omega)}] \, d\omega. \quad (4.125)$$

If then the Hermitian form

$$\sum_{j=1}^{n} \sum_{k=1}^{n} \Phi_{jk}(\omega) a_j \bar{a}_k \quad (4.13)$$

is positively defined for every value of ω, M cannot be minimized *unless* $K_j(\tau) = Q_j(\tau)$, and this gives us a unique solution of our minimization problem. We suppose, of course, that the Hermitian expression

$$\sum_{j=1}^{n} \sum_{k=1}^{n} \int_{-\infty}^{\infty} \Phi_{jk}(\omega) q_j(\omega) \overline{q_k(\omega)} \, d\omega \quad (4.135)$$

4.2 Method of Undetermined Coefficients

The functions $q_j(\omega)$ will be free from singularities in the lower half-plane and will there fulfill some condition akin to boundedness. On the other hand, the functions

$$X_k(\omega) e^{i\alpha\omega} - \sum_{j=1}^{n} \Phi_{jk}(\omega) q_j(\omega) = H_k(\omega) \quad (4.20)$$

will be free from singularities in the upper half-plane and will fulfill some boundedness condition there. We shall have

$$\Phi(\omega)q_1(\omega) = \begin{vmatrix} X_1(\omega)e^{ia\omega} - H_1(\omega) & \Phi_{21}(\omega) & \cdots & \Phi_{n1}(\omega) \\ X_2(\omega)e^{ia\omega} - H_2(\omega) & \Phi_{22}(\omega) & \cdots & \Phi_{n2}(\omega) \\ \cdots\cdots\cdots\cdots\cdots\cdots\cdots\cdots\cdots\cdots\cdots\cdots \\ X_n(\omega)e^{ia\omega} - H_n(\omega) & \Phi_{2n}(\omega) & \cdots & \Phi_{nn}(\omega) \end{vmatrix}. \qquad (4.205)$$

Let the cofactor of $\Phi_{ij}(\omega)$ in $\| \Phi_{ij}(\omega) \|$ be $F_{ij}(\omega)$. Then we may put

$$\Phi(\omega)q_1(\omega) = \sum_1^n [X_j(\omega)e^{ia\omega} - H_j(\omega)]F_{1j}(\omega); \qquad (4.21)$$

as a consequence,

$$\Phi(\omega)q_1(\omega) = \sum_1^n X_j(\omega)e^{-ia\omega}F_{1j}(\omega) + \sum \frac{A_{\mu\nu}}{(\omega - \omega_\nu)^\mu} + H(\omega), \qquad (4.215)$$

where $H(\omega)$ is of algebraic growth and free from singularities in the upper half-plane, and ω_ν is a singularity of some $F_{1j}(\omega)$ in the lower half-plane, which never has a multiplicity greater than μ in any $F_{1j}(\omega)$. Moreover, it must be possible for (4.135) to be finite. To find such a $q_1(\omega)$, as in the last chapter, we reduce our last equation to

$$\Psi(\omega)q_1(\omega) = \sum_1^n \frac{X_j(\omega)e^{ia\omega}F_{1j}(\omega)}{\overline{\Psi(\bar{\omega})}} + \sum \frac{B_{\mu\nu}}{(\omega - \omega_\nu)^\mu} + H_1(\omega) \qquad (4.22)$$

where $H_1(\omega)$ is of algebraic growth and free from singularities in the upper half-plane. Here we have used the fact that

$$\frac{1}{(\omega - \omega_\nu)^\mu \overline{\Psi(\bar{\omega})}} \qquad (4.225)$$

has only singularities of the form

$$\frac{B_{\mu_1\nu}}{(\omega - \omega_\nu)^{\mu_1}} \quad (\mu_1 \leq \mu) \qquad (4.23)$$

above the real axis, while

$$\frac{H(\omega)}{\overline{\Psi(\bar{\omega})}} \qquad (4.235)$$

has no such singularities. Thus, by the technique of our last chapter,

$$q_1(\omega) = r_1(\omega) + \frac{\sum B_{\mu\nu}}{[\overline{\Psi(\bar{\omega})}(\omega - \omega_\nu)^\mu]}, \qquad (4.24)$$

where

$$r_1(\omega) = \frac{1}{2\pi\Psi(\omega)} \int_0^\infty e^{-i\omega t}\, dt \int_{-\infty}^\infty \left[\frac{\sum\limits_1^n X_j(u)e^{i\alpha u}F_{1j}(u)e^{iut}}{\overline{\Psi(u)}} \right] du.$$

(4.245)

In other words, $r_1(\omega)$ represents that part of

$$\frac{\sum\limits_1^n X_j(\omega)e^{i\alpha\omega}F_{1j}(\omega)}{\overline{\Psi(\omega)}}$$

(4.25)

having singularities only above the real axis, multiplied by $1/\Psi(\omega)$. In determining this part in practice, it will be convenient for $\alpha < 0$, or the case of a lagging filter, to approximate $e^{i\alpha\omega}$ by some rational approximate lag characteristic, such as

$$\left(\frac{1 + (i\alpha\omega/2n)}{1 - (i\alpha\omega/2n)} \right)^n.$$

(4.255)

It will be understood that the same approximation is used consistently throughout the problem.

We have thus determined $q_1(\omega)$, except that the parameters $B_{\mu\nu}$ are still indeterminate. We may proceed to determine $q_2(\omega)$ in a similar way, and so on. We thus reduce the final solution of our problem to the solution of a finite set of linear algebraic equations in a finite number of parameters. Since we know that our entire problem has a unique solution, the result is that solution.

Let us now confine ourselves to the case $n = 2$. Here (4.20) becomes

$$\begin{cases} X_1(\omega)e^{i\alpha\omega} - \Phi_{11}(\omega)q_1(\omega) - \Phi_{21}(\omega)q_2(\omega) = H_1(\omega); \\ X_2(\omega)e^{i\alpha\omega} - \Phi_{12}(\omega)q_1(\omega) - \Phi_{22}(\omega)q_2(\omega) = H_2(\omega). \end{cases}$$

(4.26)

Then

$$X_2(\omega)e^{i\alpha\omega} - \Phi_{12}(\omega)r_1(\omega) - \sum \frac{\Phi_{12}(\omega)B_{\mu\nu}}{\Psi(\omega)(\omega - \omega_\nu)^\mu} - \Phi_{22}(\omega)q_2(\omega) = H_2(\omega).$$

This gives us

$$q_2(\omega) = \frac{1}{2\pi\Psi_2(\omega)} \int_0^\infty e^{-i\omega t}\, dt$$

(4.265)

$$\times \int_{-\infty}^\infty \left[\frac{X_2(u)e^{i\alpha u} - \Phi_{12}(u)r_1(u) - \sum \dfrac{B_{\mu\nu}}{(u-\omega_\nu)^\mu}\dfrac{\Phi_{12}(u)}{\Psi(u)}}{\overline{\Psi_2(u)}} \right] e^{iut}\, du.$$

Thus the first of equations (4.26) becomes

$$X_1(\omega) - \Phi_{11}(\omega)\left[r_1(\omega) + \sum \frac{B_{\mu\nu}}{(\omega - \omega_\nu)^\mu \Psi(\omega)}\right] + \frac{\Phi_{21}(\omega)}{2\pi\Psi_2(\omega)}\int_0^\infty e^{-i\omega t}\,dt$$

$$\times \int_{-\alpha}^\infty \left[\frac{X_2(u)e^{i\alpha u} - \Phi_{12}(u)r_1(u) - \sum \dfrac{B_{\mu\nu}}{(u - \omega_\nu)^u}\dfrac{\Phi_{12}(u)}{\Psi(u)}}{\Psi_2(\omega)}\right]e^{iut}\,du$$

$$= H_1(u), \quad (4.27)$$

where $H_1(\omega)$ is free from singularities above the real axis. If we take this equation exactly as it stands for $\alpha > 0$, or use the same approximation (4.255) to $e^{i\alpha\omega}$ as we used in determining $r_1(\omega)$ if $\alpha < 0$, we obtain from the partial fraction development of the left side a set of linear equations in the quantities $B_{\mu\nu}$, which we may solve for the value of $B_{\mu\nu}$. Similar methods may be used for n greater than 2.

4.3 Multiple Prediction

In the special case of the prediction problem as contrasted with the filter problem,

$$X_i(\omega) = \Phi_{ii}(\omega) \quad (i = 1, 2, \cdots). \quad (4.31)$$

Here

$$r_1(\omega) = \frac{1}{2\pi\Psi(\omega)}\int_0^\infty e^{-i\omega t}\,dt\int_{-\infty}^\infty \Psi(u)e^{iu(\alpha+t)}\,du, \quad (4.32)$$

so that

$$q_1(\omega) = \frac{1}{2\pi\Psi(\omega)}\int_0^\infty e^{-i\omega t}\,dt\int_{-\infty}^\infty \Psi(u)e^{iu(\alpha+t)}\,du$$

$$+ \sum_1^n \frac{B_{\mu\nu}}{(\omega - \omega_\nu)^\mu \Psi(\omega)}, \quad (4.33)$$

where the ω_ν are the poles of $\Phi_{12}(\omega)$ and $\Phi_{22}(\omega)$ in the upper half-plane. Thus

$$q_2(\omega) = \frac{1}{2\pi\Psi_2(\omega)}\int_0^\infty e^{i\omega t}\,dt\int_{-\infty}^\infty \frac{\Phi_{12}(u)[e^{i\alpha u} - q_1(\omega)]}{\Psi_2(u)}e^{iut}\,du, \quad (4.34)$$

and

$$\Phi_{11}(\omega)[e^{i\alpha\omega} - q_1(\omega)] - \Phi_{21}(\omega)q_2(\omega) = H_1(\omega) \quad (4.35)$$

is free from singularities above the real axis.

4.4 Special Cases of Prediction

Let us try this method in a particular example of prediction. Let

$$\Phi_{11}(\omega) = \Phi_{22}(\omega) = \frac{1}{1 + \omega^2} ;$$

$$\Phi_{21}(\omega) = \frac{\epsilon}{(1 + i\omega)^2} ; \quad \Phi_{12}(\omega) = \frac{\epsilon}{(1 - i\omega)^2} \quad (\epsilon < 1). \quad (4.41)$$

Here

$$\Psi_1(\omega) = \Psi_2(\omega) = \frac{1}{1 + i\omega} ; \quad \Psi(\omega) = \frac{\sqrt{1 - \epsilon^2}}{(1 + i\omega)^2} ; \quad (4.42)$$

and

$$r_1(\omega) = e^{-\alpha}[1 + \alpha(1 + i\omega)]. \quad (4.43)$$

The only possible ω_ν is i, with a multiplicity never greater than 2. Thus

$$q_1(\omega) = A + B(1 + i\omega). \quad (4.44)$$

The only values of $q_1(\omega)$ for which our Hermitian form will be bounded will be

$$q_1(\omega) = A. \quad (4.45)$$

It may readily be seen that this will yield

$$q_2(\omega) = \frac{\epsilon(1 + i\omega)}{2\pi} \int_0^\infty e^{-i\omega t} dt \int_{-\infty}^\infty \frac{e^{i\alpha u} - A}{1 - iu} e^{iut} du = 0. \quad (4.46)$$

Thus the prediction of $f_1(t)$ in this instance depends on its own past alone, and not at all on that of $f_2(t)$. The prediction problem reduces to that of an earlier section (2.1), and we have $A = e^{-\alpha}$.

Let us interchange the roles of $f_1(t)$ and $f_2(t)$ in this same example. Let

$$\Phi_{11}(\omega) = \Phi_{22}(\omega) = \frac{1}{1 + \omega^2} ; \quad \Phi_{21}(\omega) = \frac{\epsilon}{(1 - i\omega)^2} ;$$

$$\Phi_{12}(\omega) = \frac{\epsilon}{(1 + i\omega)^2} \quad (\epsilon < 1). \quad (4.465)$$

Again,

$$\Psi_1(\omega) = \Psi_2(\omega) = \frac{1}{1 + i\omega} ; \quad \Psi(\omega) = \frac{\sqrt{1 - \epsilon^2}}{(1 + i\omega)^2} ; \quad (4.47)$$

and

$$r_1(\omega) = e^{-\alpha}[1 + \alpha(1 + i\omega)]. \quad (4.475)$$

The only possible ω_ν is i, with a multiplicity never greater than 1. Thus

$$q_1(\omega) = e^{-\alpha} + B(1 + i\omega). \quad (4.48)$$

The only value of $q_1(\omega)$ for which our Hermitian form will be bounded will be

$$q_1(\omega) = e^{-\alpha}. \qquad (4.485)$$

This in turn yields

$$q_2(\omega) = \frac{\epsilon(1 + i\omega)}{2\pi} \int_0^\infty e^{-i\omega t}\, dt \int_{-\infty}^\infty \frac{1 - iu}{(1 + iu)^2}(e^{i\alpha u} - e^{-\alpha})e^{iut}\, du$$

$$= \frac{\epsilon(1 + i\omega)}{2\pi} \int_0^\infty e^{-i\omega t}\, dt \int_{-\infty}^\infty \left\{\frac{2}{(1 + iu)^2} - \frac{1}{1 + iu}\right\}(e^{i\alpha u} - e^{-\alpha})e^{iut}\, du$$

$$= \epsilon(1 + i\omega)\frac{2\alpha e^{-\alpha}}{1 + i\omega}$$

$$= 2\alpha\epsilon e^{-\alpha}. \qquad (4.49)$$

The formulae (4.26) now become

$$\frac{1}{1 + \omega^2}(e^{i\alpha\omega} - e^{-\alpha}) - \frac{\epsilon}{(1 - i\omega)^2}2\alpha\epsilon e^{-\alpha} = H_1(\omega); \qquad (4.491)$$

$$\frac{\epsilon}{(1 + i\omega)^2}(e^{i\alpha\omega} - e^{-\alpha}) - \frac{1}{1 + \omega^2}2\alpha\epsilon e^{-\alpha} = H_2(\omega); \qquad (4.492)$$

and it may readily be seen that the $H_1(\omega)$ and $H_2(\omega)$ thus defined are free from singularities above the axis of reals.

4.5   A Discrete Case of Prediction

It may be as well to choose our third example as a case in the prediction of discrete time series. Accordingly, let

$$\alpha = 1; \quad \Phi_{11}(\omega) = \Phi_{22}(\omega) = 1;$$

$$\Phi_{21}(\omega) = \epsilon e^{i\omega}; \quad \Phi_{12}(\omega) = \epsilon e^{-i\omega} \quad (\epsilon < 1). \quad (4.50)$$

Here

$$\Psi(\omega) = \sqrt{1 - \epsilon^2}; \quad \Psi_{11}(\omega) = \Phi_{22}(\omega) = 1. \qquad (4.505)$$

In a discrete case such as this, we get

$$r_1(\omega) = \frac{1}{2\pi\Psi(\omega)} \sum_{n=0}^\infty e^{-i\omega n} \int_{-\pi}^\pi \Psi(u)e^{iu(n+1)}\, du$$

$$= \frac{1}{2\pi} \sum_{n=0}^\infty e^{-i\omega n} \int_{-\pi}^\pi e^{iu(n+1)}\, du$$

$$= 0. \qquad (4.51)$$

Furthermore, $\Psi_{12}(\omega)$ and $\Psi_{22}(\omega)$ are bounded above the real axis. Thus

$$q_1(\omega) = 0. \qquad (4.515)$$

This leads to

$$q_2(\omega) = \frac{1}{2\pi} \sum_{n=0}^{\infty} e^{-i\omega n} \int_{-\pi}^{\pi} \epsilon e^{-iu} (e^{iu}) e^{inu} \, du = \epsilon. \qquad (4.52)$$

On the other hand, let

$$\alpha = 1; \quad \Phi_{11}(\omega) = \Phi_{22}(\omega) = 1;$$
$$\Phi_{21}(\omega) = \epsilon e^{-i\omega}; \quad \Phi_{12}(\omega) = \epsilon e^{i\omega} \quad (\epsilon < 1). \qquad (4.525)$$

Here again

$$\Psi(\omega) = \sqrt{1 - \epsilon^2}; \quad \Psi_1(\omega) = \Psi_2(\omega) = 1. \qquad (4.53)$$

As before,

$$r_1(\omega) = 0. \qquad (4.535)$$

On the other hand, $\Phi_{12}(\omega)$ behaves like a constant multiple of $e^{-i\omega}$ above the real axis. Thus we put

$$q_1(\omega) = r_1(\omega) + A + Be^{-i\omega} = A + Be^{-i\omega}. \qquad (4.54)$$

Then

$$q_2(\omega) = \frac{1}{2\pi} \sum_{n=0}^{\infty} e^{-i\omega n} \int_{-\pi}^{\pi} \epsilon e^{iu} (e^{iu} - A - Be^{-iu}) e^{inu} \, du$$
$$= -B\epsilon. \qquad (4.545)$$

Thus

$$\Phi_{11}(\omega)[e^{i\omega} - q_1(\omega)] - \Phi_{12}(\omega) q_2(\omega) = e^{i\omega} - A - Be^{-i\omega} + B\epsilon^2 e^{-i\omega}; \qquad (4.55)$$

and if this is to be a possible $H_1(\omega)$,

$$B = 0.$$

Since $f(t)$ now must be predicted on its own merits,

$$q_1(\omega) = \frac{1}{2\pi\Psi_1(\omega)} \sum_{n=0}^{\infty} e^{-i\omega n} \int_{-\pi}^{\pi} \Psi_1(u) e^{iu} e^{iun} \, du = 0, \qquad (4.555)$$

so that, in this case, no prediction whatever is possible.

4.6   General Technique of Discrete Prediction

These trivial cases are yet enough to illustrate the technique of multiple prediction in the discrete case, which will be the typical case of the business statistician, the meteorologist, and the geophysicist. As always, the first step to be taken is the determination of the φ_{ij}'s and all related functions. Here there is a technical point worth consideration. We define $\varphi_{ij}{}^{mm}(\nu)$ as

$$\lim_{T \to \infty} \frac{1}{2T} \sum_{-T}^{T} f(n + \nu) \overline{f(n)}. \qquad (4.60)$$

However, an infinite process like this cannot be carried out in completeness; besides, there is a great convenience in regarding $\Phi_{ij}{}^{mm}(\omega)$ as a terminating series in positive and negative powers of $e^{i\omega}$. Is it then advisable to take

$$\frac{1}{2N+1} \sum_{-N}^{N} f(n+\nu)\overline{f(n)} \tag{4.605}$$

as an approximate representation of $\varphi_{ij}{}^{mm}(\nu)$? The answer is no. The most essential property of a single $\varphi_{ij}{}^{mm}(\nu)$ is that it may be written in the form

$$\int_{-\pi}^{\pi} e^{i\nu\omega}\, d\Lambda(\omega) \tag{4.61}$$

where $\Lambda(\omega)$ is monotonically increasing. Similarly, the quadratic form

$$\sum_{i,j} \sum_{\mu,\nu} \varphi_{ij}{}^{mm}(\mu - \nu) a_{\mu}\bar{a}_{\nu} \tag{4.615}$$

must be non-negative for every ω. This is not true if we replace $\varphi_{ij}{}^{mm}(\mu - \nu)$ by

$$\frac{1}{2N+1} \sum_{-N}^{N} f_i(n+\mu-\nu)\overline{f_j(n)}. \tag{4.62}$$

On the other hand, this is true if we replace $\varphi_{ij}{}^{mm}(\mu - \nu)$ by the approximating function

$$\frac{1}{2N+1} \sum_{\substack{-N \le n \le N \\ -N \le n+\mu-\nu \le N}} f_i(n+\mu-\nu)\overline{f_j(n)}. \tag{4.625}$$

To take the simplest case,

$$\sum_{\mu,\nu} a_{\mu}\bar{a}_{\nu} \frac{1}{2N+1} \sum_{\substack{-N \le n \le N \\ -N \le n+\mu-\nu \le N}} f(n+\mu-\nu)\overline{f(n)}$$

$$= \frac{1}{2N+1} \sum_{n} \left| \sum_{-N-n \le \mu \le N-n} a_{\mu}f(n+\mu) \right|^2 \ge 0.$$

In the discrete case, the fundamental equations we have to solve are the system

$$\chi_k(\alpha + \nu) = \sum_{j=1}^{n} \sum_{\mu=0}^{\infty} \varphi_{jk}(\nu - \mu)Q_j(\mu) \quad (\nu \ge 0) \tag{4.635}$$

corresponding to (4.105). If we put

$$\sum_{\nu=-\infty}^{\infty} \chi_k(\nu)e^{-i\nu\omega} = X_k(\omega); \quad \sum_{\nu=-\infty}^{\infty} \varphi_{jk}(\nu)e^{-i\nu\omega} = \Phi_{jk}(\omega);$$

$$\sum_{0}^{\infty} Q_j(\mu)e^{-i\mu\omega} = q_j(\omega); \tag{4.64}$$

this leads us to

$$X_k(\omega)e^{i\omega\alpha} - \sum_{j=1}^{n} \Phi_{jk}(\omega)q_j(\omega) = \sum_{1}^{\infty} b_{\nu k}e^{i\omega\nu}. \qquad (4.645)$$

We proceed from this to the analogue of (4.26), namely

$$\begin{cases} [e^{i\alpha\omega} - q_1(\omega)]\Phi_{11}(\omega) - \Phi_{21}(\omega)q_2(\omega) = \sum_{1}^{\infty} b_{\nu}e^{i\omega\nu}; \\ [e^{i\alpha\omega} - q_1(\omega)]\Phi_{12}(\omega) - \Phi_{22}(\omega)q_2(\omega) = \sum_{1}^{\infty} c_{\nu}e^{i\omega\nu}. \end{cases} \qquad (4.65)$$

Forming the determinant of these two equations, we get

$$[e^{i\alpha\omega} - q_1(\omega)]\Phi(\omega) = -\sum_{1}^{\infty} b_{\nu}e^{i\omega\nu}\Phi_{22}(\omega) + \sum c_{\nu}e^{i\omega\nu}\Phi_{21}(\omega). \qquad (4.655)$$

Now let us put

$$\Phi(\omega) = \Psi(\omega) \cdot \overline{\Psi(\bar{\omega})}, \qquad (4.66)$$

where

$$\Psi(\omega) = d_0 + \sum_{1}^{n} d_{\nu}e^{-i\nu\omega} \qquad (4.665)$$

has no poles below the real axis. Then

$$[e^{i\alpha\omega} - q_1(\omega)]\Psi(\omega) = \sum_{1}^{\infty} e_{\nu}e^{i\omega\nu}\Phi_{22}(\omega) + \sum_{1}^{\infty} f_{\nu}e^{i\omega\nu}\Phi_{21}(\omega). \qquad (4.67)$$

Hence

$$q_1(\omega)\Psi(\omega) = \qquad (4.675)$$

$$\frac{1}{2\pi}\sum_{0}^{\infty} e^{-i\nu\omega}\int_{-\pi}^{\pi}\left\{\Psi(u)e^{i\alpha u} - \sum_{1}^{\infty} e_{\nu}e^{iu\nu}\Phi_{22}(u) - \sum_{1}^{\infty} f_{\nu}e^{iu\nu}\Phi_{21}(u)\right\}e^{iu\nu} du.$$

That is, $q_1(\omega)\Psi(\omega)$ is the summation of

$$\frac{1}{2\pi}\sum_{0}^{\infty} e^{-i\nu\omega}\int_{-\pi}^{\pi}\Psi(u)e^{iu(\alpha+\nu)} du \qquad (4.68)$$

and terms of the form

$$A_k e^{-ik\omega} \quad (0 \leq k \leq \rho) \qquad (4.685)$$

where ρ is smaller by one than the degree of the highest term (containing a positive power of $e^{-i\omega}$) in either $\Phi_{22}(\omega)$ or $\Phi_{21}(\omega)$.

We then have

$$\Phi_{12}(\omega)\left\{e^{i\alpha\omega} - \frac{1}{2\pi\Psi(u)}\sum_0^\infty e^{-i\nu u}\int_{-\pi}^\pi \Psi(u)e^{iu(\alpha+\nu)}\,du - \sum_0^n \frac{A_k e^{ik\omega}}{\Psi(\omega)}\right\}$$

$$- \Phi_{22}(\omega)q_2(\omega) = \sum_1^\infty c_\nu e^{i\omega\nu}, \quad (4.69)$$

which we solve in a similar manner, obtaining

$$q_2(\omega) = \frac{1}{2\pi\Psi_2(\omega)}\sum_0^\infty e^{-i\nu\omega}\int_{-\pi}^\pi \frac{\Phi_{12}(u)}{\Psi_2(u)}\left\{e^{i\alpha u}\right.$$

$$\left.- \frac{1}{2\pi\Psi(u)}\sum_0^\infty e^{-i\mu u}\int_{-\pi}^\pi \Psi(v)e^{iv(\alpha+\mu)}\,dv - \sum_0^\infty \frac{A_k e^{iku}}{\Psi(u)}\right\}e^{iu\nu}\,du. \quad (4.691)$$

Finally,

$$\Phi_{11}(\omega)\{e^{-i\alpha\omega} - q_1(\omega)\} - \Phi_{21}(\omega)q_2(\omega) = \sum_1^\infty b_\nu e^{i\omega\nu}, \quad (4.692)$$

which gives us a set of simultaneous linear equations in the A_k, adequate to determine their values.

Once we have the functions $q_1(\omega)$ and $q_2(\omega)$, we develop them into Fourier series, the coefficients of which will be respectively $Q_1(\nu)$ and $Q_2(\nu)$. Then the best prediction of $f_1(t)$ will be

$$\sum_{\mu=0}^\infty f_1(t+\nu)Q_1(\nu) + \sum_{\mu=0}^\infty f_2(t-\nu)Q_2(\nu). \quad (4.693)$$

In essence, our methods for the treatment of time series are very closely related to the conventional methods which develop the ellipsoid determined by the correlation coefficients of the several quantities $f_j(t - \nu)$. The existing methods, however, do not take adequate consideration of the time structure of the data correlated. The fact that they show a statistical invariance under the translation group is a certain indication that the Fourier methods are desirable. Consequently no use is generally made of the simplifications which result from the consideration of the entire past of a function as the basis of prediction, rather than of two or three fixed epochs in the pasts, and such a technique grows unmanageably complicated as a larger and larger number of epochs are taken as the basis for prediction. To determine a reasonable distribution of the past epochs capable of serving as the basis of prediction is also practically impossible by methods of previous techniques. On the other hand, our methods really do make use of the structure of the translation group, which dominates all time series and gives an intelligible asymptotic theory when prediction on the basis of the entire past is considered.

The methods which we have here given for the case of a double time series are extensible, without difficulty of principle, to time series of any multiplicity. We have given clear indications, moreover, as to how the filter problem is to be handled as well as the predictor problem.

CHAPTER V

MISCELLANEOUS PROBLEMS ENCOMPASSED BY THE TECHNIQUE OF THIS BOOK

5.0 The Problem of Approximate Differentiation

It will have become obvious to the thoughtful reader that the methods of this book may be extended considerably beyond the prediction and filtering problems to which they have been already applied. The indication for their use is: the existence of a linear problem, invariant under the translation group, which is not capable of an exact solution, but in which a measure of the failure of an approximate solution may be given as the mean of the square of the modulus of an expression known to be linear in terms of the function upon which we are operating.

A very important practical problem is that of the determination of the derivative of a message function which is corrupted by a noise. This is a problem of vital importance to all designers of servo-mechanisms. If a set of low-frequency data is disturbed by a high-frequency noise, then, if we take the rigorous theory of differentiation and actually seek to determine

$$\frac{f(t + \Delta t) - f(t)}{\Delta t} \tag{5.00}$$

for a very short Δt, the result will have more to do with the disturbance than with the message. If, on the other hand, we take an excessively large Δt, we shall obviously have thrown away valid information concerning the derivative. The whole question turns on the proper definition of the word "excessive."

As before, let $f(t)$ be a message and $g(t)$ a noise. Let

$$\begin{cases} \varphi_1(\tau) = \lim_{T \to \infty} \frac{1}{2T} \int_{-T}^{T} f(t + \tau)\overline{f(t)}\, dt; \\[2mm] \varphi_2(\tau) = \lim_{T \to \infty} \frac{1}{2T} \int_{-T}^{T} g(t + \tau)\overline{g(t)}\, dt; \\[2mm] 0 = \lim_{T \to \infty} \frac{1}{2T} \int_{-T}^{T} f(t + \tau)\overline{g(t)}\, dt; \\[2mm] \varphi(t) = \varphi_1(t) + \varphi_2(t). \end{cases} \tag{5.005}$$

Let us seek to determine $k(t)$ so as to minimize

$$M = \lim_{T \to \infty} \frac{1}{2T} \int_{-T}^{T} \left| f'(t) - \int_{0}^{\infty} [f(t-\tau) + g(t-\tau)] \, dK(\tau) \right|^2 dt.$$

(5.01)

At least formally,

$$M = \lim_{T \to \infty} \frac{1}{2T} \int_{-T}^{T} |f'(t)|^2 \, dt -$$

$$2\mathrm{R} \left\{ \int_{0}^{\infty} \left[\lim_{T \to \infty} \frac{1}{2T} \int_{-T}^{T} f'(t) \overline{f(t-\tau)} \, dt \right] d\overline{K(\tau)} \right\}$$

$$+ \int_{0}^{\infty} dK(\sigma) \int_{0}^{\infty} d\overline{K(\tau)} \varphi(\tau - \sigma)$$

$$= -\varphi_1''(0) - 2\mathrm{R} \left\{ \int_{0}^{\infty} \varphi_1'(\tau) \, d\overline{K(\tau)} \right\}$$

$$+ \int_{0}^{\infty} dK(\sigma) \int_{0}^{\infty} d\overline{K(\tau)} \varphi(\tau - \sigma). \qquad (5.015)$$

Let us assume a $Q(t)$ satisfying

$$\varphi_1'(\tau) = \int_{0}^{\infty} \varphi(\tau - \sigma) \, dQ(\sigma) \quad (\tau > 0). \qquad (5.02)$$

Then

$$M = \varphi''(0) - \int_{0}^{\infty} dQ(\sigma) \int_{0}^{\infty} d\overline{Q(\tau)} \varphi(\tau - \sigma) +$$

$$\int_{0}^{\infty} d[K(\sigma) - Q(\sigma)] \int_{0}^{\infty} d[\overline{K(\tau)} - \overline{Q(\tau)}] \varphi(\tau - \sigma). \quad (5.025)$$

We shall use the notation of Chapter III and shall assume that $\Phi(\omega)$ has no real zeros. Then, as in Chapter III, M is minimized when and only when

$$K(\sigma) = Q(\sigma). \qquad (5.03)$$

We solve (5.02) as in Chapter III. Using the notation of that chapter,

$$\Phi_1(\omega) i\omega - \Phi(\omega) q(\omega) = H(\omega), \qquad (5.035)$$

where $H(\omega)$ is free from singularities in the upper half-plane. Then, by a reasoning now familiar,

$$e^{-i\omega t} \, dt \qquad \frac{i u \Phi_1(u) e^{iut}}{\Psi(u)} \, du. \qquad (5.04)$$

5.1 An Example of Approximate Differentiation

Let us turn to particular cases. Let

$$\Phi_1(\omega) = \frac{1}{1 + \omega^4} \; ; \quad \Phi_2(\omega) = \epsilon^4. \tag{5.10}$$

Then

$$\Phi(\omega) = \frac{1 + \epsilon^4 + \epsilon^4\omega^4}{1 + \omega^4}, \tag{5.105}$$

and

$$\Psi(\omega) - \frac{\sqrt{1 + \epsilon^4} + \epsilon\sqrt{2}\sqrt[4]{1 + \epsilon^4}i\omega - \epsilon^2\omega^2}{1 + \sqrt{2}i\omega - \omega^2}. \tag{5.11}$$

Thus we see that

$$\frac{i\omega\Phi(\omega)}{\Psi(\omega)} = \frac{i\omega}{(1 + \sqrt{2}i\omega - \omega^2)(\sqrt{1 + \epsilon^4} - \epsilon\sqrt{2}\sqrt[4]{1 + \epsilon^4}i\omega - \epsilon^2\omega^2)}$$

$$= \frac{Ai\omega + B}{1 + \sqrt{2}i\omega - \omega^2} + \frac{Ci\omega + D}{\sqrt{1 + \epsilon} - \epsilon\sqrt{2}\sqrt[4]{1 + \epsilon^4}i\omega - \epsilon^2\omega^2}. \tag{5.115}$$

We determine the unknown coefficients by the equations

$$\begin{cases} B\sqrt{1 + \epsilon^4} + D = 0; \\ A\sqrt{1 + \epsilon^4} - B\epsilon\sqrt{2}\sqrt[4]{1 + \epsilon^4} + C + D\sqrt{2} = 1; \\ -A\epsilon\sqrt{2}\sqrt[4]{1 + \epsilon^4} + B\epsilon^2 + \sqrt{2}C + D = 0; \\ A\epsilon^2 + C = 0. \end{cases} \tag{5.12}$$

Eliminating C and D,

$$\begin{cases} A(\sqrt{1 + \epsilon^4} - \epsilon^2) - B(\epsilon\sqrt{2}\sqrt[4]{1 + \epsilon^4} + \sqrt{2}\sqrt{1 + \epsilon^4}) = 1; \\ -A(\epsilon\sqrt{2}\sqrt[4]{1 + \epsilon^4} + \epsilon^2\sqrt{2}) + B(\epsilon^2 - \sqrt{1 + \epsilon^4}) = 0. \end{cases} \tag{5.13}$$

This gives us

$$A\left\{\sqrt{1 + \epsilon^4} - \epsilon^2 + \frac{(\epsilon\sqrt{2}\sqrt[4]{1 + \epsilon^4} + \epsilon^2\sqrt{2})(\epsilon\sqrt{2}\sqrt[4]{1 + \epsilon^4} + \sqrt{2}\sqrt{1 + 2^4})}{\sqrt{1 + \epsilon^4} - \epsilon^2}\right\} = 1. \tag{5.14}$$

$$A = \frac{\sqrt{1 + \epsilon^4} - \epsilon^2}{1 + 2\epsilon^4 - 2\epsilon^2\sqrt{1 + \epsilon^4} + 2\epsilon^2\sqrt{1 + \epsilon^4} + 2\epsilon^3\sqrt[4]{1 + \epsilon^4} + 2\epsilon\sqrt[4]{(1 + \epsilon^4)^3} + 2\epsilon^2\sqrt{1 + \epsilon^4}}$$

$$= \frac{\sqrt{1+\epsilon^4} - \epsilon^2}{1 + 2\epsilon^4 + 2\epsilon^2\sqrt{1+\epsilon^4} + 2\epsilon^3\sqrt[4]{1+\epsilon^4} + 2\epsilon\sqrt[4]{(1+\epsilon^4)^3}}$$

$$= \frac{\sqrt{1+\epsilon^4} - \epsilon^2}{(\epsilon^2 + \sqrt{1+\epsilon^4})(\epsilon^2 + \sqrt{1+\epsilon^4} + 2\epsilon\sqrt[4]{1+\epsilon^4})}$$

$$= \frac{\sqrt[4]{1+\epsilon^4} - \epsilon}{(\epsilon^2 + \sqrt{1+\epsilon^4})(\epsilon + \sqrt[4]{1+\epsilon^4})} ; \tag{5.15}$$

and

$$B = \frac{A\epsilon\sqrt{2}(\epsilon + \sqrt[4]{1+\epsilon^4})}{\epsilon^2 - \sqrt{1+\epsilon^4}} = \frac{-\epsilon\sqrt{2}}{(\epsilon^2 + \sqrt{1+\epsilon^4})(\epsilon + \sqrt[4]{1+\epsilon^4})}. \tag{5.16}$$

Hence

$$q(\omega) = \frac{1}{(\epsilon^2 + \sqrt{1+\epsilon^4})(\epsilon + \sqrt[4]{1+\epsilon^4})} \cdot \frac{(\sqrt{1+\epsilon^4} - \epsilon^2)i\omega - \epsilon\sqrt{2}}{\sqrt{1+\epsilon^4} + \epsilon\sqrt{2}\sqrt[4]{1+\epsilon^4}i\omega - \epsilon^2\omega^2}. \tag{5.17}$$

It will be seen at once that this tends to $i\omega$ as ϵ tends to 0. This is precisely as it should be.

5.2　A Misleading Example of Approximate Differentiation

A case which presents certain difficulties is that in which

$$\Phi_1(\omega) = \frac{1}{1+\omega^2} ; \quad \Phi_2(\omega) = \epsilon^2. \tag{5.20}$$

Here

$$\Phi(\omega) = \frac{1 + \epsilon^2 + \epsilon^2\omega^2}{1+\omega^2}, \tag{5.21}$$

and

$$\Psi(\omega) - \frac{\sqrt{1+\epsilon^2} + \epsilon i\omega}{1 + i\omega}. \tag{5.22}$$

This leads to

$$\frac{i\omega\Phi_1(\omega)}{\overline{\Psi(\overline{\omega})}} = \frac{i\omega}{(1 + i\omega)(\sqrt{1+\epsilon^2} - \epsilon i\omega)}$$

$$= \frac{A}{1 + i\omega} + \frac{B}{\sqrt{1+\epsilon^2} - \epsilon i\omega}. \tag{5.23}$$

We determine the unknown coefficients by the equations

$$\begin{cases} A\sqrt{1+\epsilon^2} + B = 0; \\ -A\epsilon + B = 1. \end{cases} \tag{5.24}$$

Eliminating B,

$$A = \frac{-1}{\epsilon + \sqrt{1 + \epsilon^2}}. \tag{5.25}$$

Thus

$$q(\omega) = \frac{-1}{(\epsilon + \sqrt{1 + \epsilon^2})(\sqrt{1 + \epsilon^2} + \epsilon i \omega)}. \tag{5.26}$$

It will be seen that, as $\epsilon \to 0$, this tends to -1 and not to $i\omega$, so that the operator $q(\omega)$ has nothing to do with differentiation. The reason is that the assumed function $f(t)$ with the given $\Phi_1(\omega)$ is almost never differentiable. The expression M to be minimized is infinite, and its minimization cannot lead to a significant problem.

5.3 Interpolation and Extrapolation

Another problem which may be attacked by our methods is that of interpolation. Here we shall explicitly confine ourselves to the formal theory and avoid considerations of convergence. If $f(t)$ is of such a nature that $\Phi(\omega)$ vanishes outside $(-\pi, \pi)$, it is a known fact* that

$$f(t) = \sum_{-\infty}^{\infty} f(2n\pi) \frac{\sin \pi(n - t)}{\pi(n - t)}. \tag{5.30}$$

As will be seen, this involves the knowledge of every $f(2n\pi)$ for $-\infty < n < \infty$. It is thus a matter of interest to see what becomes of the best approximation to this expression in terms of the present and past of $f(2n\pi)$ only.

Let us put

$$\lim_{N \to \infty} \frac{1}{2N + 1} \sum_{n=-N}^{N} f[2\pi(m + n)]\overline{f(2\pi n)} = \varphi_m. \tag{5.31}$$

$$M = \lim_{N \to \infty} \frac{1}{2N + 1} \sum_{n=-N}^{N} \left| \sum_{m=-\infty}^{\infty} f[2\pi(n + m)] \frac{\sin \pi(m - t)}{\pi(m - t)} \right.$$
$$\left. - \sum_{k=0}^{\infty} f[2\pi(n - k)]Q_k \right|^2$$

$$= \sum_{m=-\infty}^{\infty} \sum_{n=-\infty}^{\infty} \varphi_{m-n} \frac{\sin \pi(m - t)}{\pi(m - t)} \cdot \frac{\sin \pi(n - t)}{\pi(n - t)}$$

$$- 2\mathrm{R} \left\{ \sum_{m=-\infty}^{\infty} \sum_{k=0}^{\infty} \varphi_{m+k} \overline{Q}_k \frac{\sin \pi(m - t)}{\pi(m - t)} \right\} + \sum_{j=0}^{\infty} \sum_{k=0}^{\infty} \varphi_{k-j} \overline{Q}_k Q_j. \tag{5.32}$$

---

*See Paley and Wiener, *Fourier Transform in the Complex Domain*, American Mathematical Society Colloquium Publication, Vol. 19, 1934.

By exactly the same reasoning by which we have obtained (3.145) or (5.02), the minimization of this expression leads to the integral equation

$$\sum_{k=-\infty}^{\infty} \varphi_{m+k} \frac{\sin \pi(m-t)}{\pi(m-t)} = \sum_{j=0}^{\infty} \varphi_{k-j} Q_j \quad (k \geq 0). \qquad (5.33)$$

As a consequence of this,

$$\sum_{k=-\infty}^{\infty} e^{-ik\omega} \sum_{m=-\infty}^{\infty} \varphi_{m+k} \frac{\sin \pi(m-t)}{\pi(m-t)} - \sum_{k=-\infty}^{\infty} e^{-ik\omega} \sum_{j=0}^{\infty} \varphi_{k-j} Q_j$$
$$= \sum_{1}^{\infty} A_\nu e^{i\nu\omega}, \qquad (5.34)$$

which we may write

$$\sum_{k=-\infty}^{\infty} \varphi_k e^{-ik\omega} \left\{ \sum_{m=-\infty}^{\infty} e^{im\omega} \frac{\sin \pi(m-t)}{\pi(m-t)} - \sum_{j=0}^{\infty} Q_j e^{ij\omega} \right\} = \sum_{1}^{\infty} A_\nu e^{i\nu\omega}. \qquad (5.35)$$

Now let us define

$$\Phi(\omega) = \sum_{-\infty}^{\infty} \varphi_k e^{-ik\omega}, \qquad (5.355)$$

and let us notice that

$$\sum_{-\infty}^{\infty} e^{im\omega} \frac{\sin (m-t)\pi}{(m-t)\pi} = \frac{1}{2\pi} \sum_{m=-\infty}^{\infty} e^{im\omega}$$
$$\times \int_{-\pi}^{\pi} e^{i(t-m)u} \, du = \begin{cases} e^{it\omega} (-\pi \leq \omega \leq \pi); \\ 0 \text{ otherwise.} \end{cases} \qquad (5.36)$$

We get

$$\Phi(\omega) \left\{ e^{it\omega} - \sum_{j=0}^{\infty} Q_j e^{-ij\omega} \right\} = \sum_{1}^{\infty} A_n e^{in\omega}. \qquad (5.37)$$

If we factor $\Phi(\omega)$ as before, we get

$$\Psi(\omega) \left\{ e^{it\omega} - \sum_{j=0}^{\infty} Q_j e^{-ij\omega} \right\} = \sum_{1}^{\infty} B_n e^{in\omega}, \qquad (5.38)$$

or finally

$$q(\omega) = \sum_{j=0}^{\infty} Q_j e^{-ij\omega} = \frac{1}{\Psi(\omega)} \sum_{0}^{\infty} e^{-in\omega} \int_{-\pi}^{\pi} e^{it\omega} \Psi(u) e^{inu} \, du, \qquad (5.39)$$

which is our interpolation formula. It will be seen that it contains our extrapolation formula, with which it formally agrees.

Similar formulae may be obtained which are related to the interpolation formula as the filter formula is related to the prediction formula. Modifications may be made in the techniques of this book in an almost unlimited number of ways. For example, what we have done for the simple differentiator may be repeated without difficulty in the case of higher derivatives. It is scarcely worth while to go into details, for these details will be clear to anyone who has followed the discussion up to the present point.

TABLE OF THE LAGUERRE FUNCTIONS

Arg.	0	1	2	3	4	5
0	1.4142	−1.4142	1.4142	−1.4142	1.4142	−1.4142
.01	1.4001	−1.3721	1.3444	−1.3169	1.2898	−1.2629
.02	1.3862	−1.3307	1.2764	−1.2232	1.1710	−1.1199
.03	1.3724	−1.2901	1.2102	−1.1327	1.0577	−.98490
.04	1.3587	−1.2500	1.1457	−1.0456	.94957	−.85758
.05	1.3452	−1.2106	1.0829	−.96161	.84660	−.73766
.06	1.3312	−1.1714	1.0211	−.88010	.74791	−.62419
.07	1.3186	−1.1340	.96231	−.80294	.65532	−.51887
.08	1.3055	−1.0966	.90443	−.72808	.56670	−.41946
.09	1.2925	−1.0598	.84813	−.65610	.48255	−.32635
.1	1.2796	−1.0237	.79337	−.58692	.40274	−.23298
.2	1.1578	−.69472	.32420	−.03396	−.18711	.34900
.3	1.0477	−.41907	−.02095	.31011	−.48046	.55909
.4	.94797	−.18959	−.26543	.49800	−.57283	.54103
.5	.85766	.00000	−.42888	.55897	−.53610	.39993
.6	.77614	.15523	−.52777	.56503	−.42346	.20857
.7	.70228	.28091	−.57586	.50376	−.27337	.01251
.8	.63545	.38127	−.58461	.40838	−.11285	−.15969
.9	.57497	.45998	−.56347	.29438	.03990	−.29296
1.0	.52026	.52026	−.52026	.17342	.17341	−.38151
1.1	.47075	.56490	−.46134	.05398	.28123	−.42566
1.2	.42595	.59633	−.39188	−.05792	.36051	−.42952
1.3	.38542	.61667	−.31604	−.15828	.41114	−.39964
1.4	.34874	.62773	−.23714	−.24458	.43496	−.34331
1.5	.31555	.63111	−.15777	−.31555	.43389	−.26824
1.6	.28552	.62815	−.07995	−.37080	.41221	−.18152
1.7	.25838	.62005	−.00517	−.41061	.37341	−.08972
1.8	.23376	.60779	.06545	−.43574	.32129	.00161
1.9	.21169	.59273	.13124	−.44764	.25967	.08806
2.0	.19139	.57418	.19139	−.44658	.19140	.16587
2.1	.17318	.55417	.24672	−.43632	.12159	.23103
2.2	.15670	.53278	.29459	−.41410	.04821	.28694
2.3	.14179	.51043	.33745	−.38529	−.02188	.32743
2.4	.12829	.48752	.37462	−.34999	−.08845	.35427
2.5	.11608	.46434	.40630	−.30956	−.14995	.36759
2.6	.10504	.44116	.43276	−.26525	−.20522	.36820
2.7	.09504	.41819	.45431	−.21822	−.25343	.35704
2.8	.08600	.39559	.47127	−.16947	−.29414	.33558
2.9	.07781	.37351	.48400	−.11993	−.32703	.30522
3.0	.07041	.35205	.49287	−.07041	−.35205	.26657

TABLE OF THE LAGUERRE FUNCTIONS (Continued)

Arg.	0	1	2	3	4	5
3.1	.06371	.33129	.49820	−.02158	−.36932	.22407
3.2	.05764	.31129	.50037	.02596	−.37915	.17635
3.3	.05216	.29210	.49970	.07176	−.38193	.12589
3.4	.04720	.27374	.49651	.11541	−.37817	.07411
3.5	.04270	.25623	.49111	.15658	−.36834	.02208
3.6	.03864	.23958	.48379	.19506	−.35311	−.02889
3.7	.03496	.22377	.47481	.23067	−.33305	−.07794
3.8	.03164	.20881	.46443	.26331	−.30884	−.12413
3.9	.02862	.19466	.45287	.29289	−.28103	−.16692
4.0	.02590	.18131	.44273	.31946	−.25041	−.20549
4.1	.02344	.16875	.42702	.34300	−.21738	−.23959
4.2	.02121	.15693	.41311	.36357	−.18256	−.26899
4.3	.01919	.14583	.39874	.38125	−.14654	−.29341
4.4	.01736	.13543	.38406	.39619	−.10976	−.31264
4.5	.01571	.12568	.36919	.40848	−.07270	−.32676
4.6	.01421	.11656	.35424	.41824	−.03568	−.33598
4.7	.01286	.10804	.33931	.42563	3)88260	−.34042
4.8	.01164	.10009	.32448	.43081	1)36668	−.34032
4.9	.01053	1)92673	.30982	.43393	1)71381	−.33577
5.0	2)95289	1)85759	.29539	.43515	.10482	−.32718
5.1	2)86221	1)79323	.28125	.43462	.13677	−.31491
5.2	2)78016	1)73335	.26744	.43249	.16705	−.29929
5.3	2)70592	1)67768	.25399	.42892	.19554	−.28060
5.4	2)63874	1)62597	.24093	.42407	.22218	−.25933
5.5	2)57796	1)57796	.22829	.41805	.24683	−.23568
5.6	2)52296	1)53342	.21608	.41102	.26951	−.21021
5.7	2)47319	1)49212	.20432	.40307	.29017	−.18333
5.8	2)42816	1)45386	.19301	.39437	.30877	−.15501
5.9	2)38741	1)41841	.18216	.38501	.32539	−.12586
6.0	2)35055	1)38560	.17177	.37507	.34011	−.08625
6.1	2)31719	1)35524	.16182	.36475	.35263	−.06573
6.2	2)28701	1)32718	.15233	.35393	.36366	−.03615
6.3	2)25969	1)30125	.14329	.34294	.37267	−.00614
6.4	2)23498	1)27728	.13469	.33168	.38004	.02318
6.5	2)21262	1)25514	.12651	.32032	.38571	.05203
6.6	2)19238	1)23470	.11874	.30888	.38977	.08021
6.7	2)17408	1)21585	.11137	.29746	.39238	.10737
6.8	2)15751	1)19847	.10439	.28605	.39368	.13331
6.9	2)14252	1)18243	.09780	.27472	.39363	.15823
7.0	2)12896	1)16765	.09156	.26349	.39249	.18156
7.1	2)11669	1)15402	.08567	.25245	.39016	.20384
7.2	2)10558	1)14148	.08012	.24159	.38689	.22452
7.3	3)95536	1)12993	.07488	.23095	.38264	.24382
7.4	3)86444	1)11929	.06995	.22054	.37757	.26162
7.5	3)78218	1)10950	.06531	.21039	.37185	.27778

TABLE OF THE LAGUERRE FUNCTIONS (Continued)

Arg.	0	1	2	3	4	5
7.6	3)70775	1)10050	1)60951	.20053	.36535	.29274
7.7	3)64039	2)92214	1)56850	.19033	.35833	.30589
7.8	3)57945	2)84599	1)53006	.18166	.35080	.31774
7.9	3)52431	2)77599	1)49400	.17266	.34283	.32806
8.0	3)47441	2)71162	1)46016	.16775	.33445	.34724
	)42927	2)65249	1)42849	.15562	**.32579**	.34463
	)38841	2)59816	1)39883	.14757	**.31687**	.35091
	)35145	2)54827	1)37107	.13982	**.30774**	.35592
	)31801	2)50245	1)34511	.13239	**.29847**	.35971
	)28775	2)46039	1)32084	.12526	**.28910**	.36234
8.6	3)26036	2)42179	1)29817	.11844	**.27967**	.36389
8.7	3)23559	2)38636	1)27701	.11192	**.27021**	.36441
8.8	3)21317	2)35386	1)25725	.10569	**.26077**	.36399
8.9	3)19288	2)32404	1)23882	1)99720	**.25138**	.36265
9.0	3)17453	2)29670	1)22165	1)94071	**.24207**	.36046
9.1	3)15792	2)27162	1)20564	1)88673	**.23286**	.35752
9.2	3)14289	2)24863	1)19073	1)83535	**.22377**	.35386
9.3	3)12929	2)22756	1)17685	1)78654	**.21483**	.34955
9.4	3)11699	2)20824	1)16393	1)74017	**.20606**	.34466
9.5	3)10586	2)19054	1)15191	1)69619	**.19746**	.33923
9.6	4)95783	2)17432	1)14072	1)65447	**.18906**	.33332
9.7	4)86668	2)15947	1)13033	1)61496	**.18086**	.32701
9.8	4)78420	2)14586	1)12067	1)57754	**.17288**	.32029
9.9	4)70958	2)13340	1)11170	1)54217	**.16511**	.31328
10.0	4)64205	2)12199	1)10337	1)50872	**.15758**	.30958
10.1	4)58095	2)11154	2)95636	1)47712	**.15027**	.29845
10.2	4)52567	2)10198	2)88459	1)44729	**.14321**	.29073
10.3	4)47564	3)93226	2)81801	1)41915	**.13637**	.28286
10.4	4)43038	3)85216	2)75626	1)39262	**.12978**	.27487
10.5	4)38942	3)77886	2)69901	1)36761	**.12342**	.26681
10.6	**4)35236**	**3)71178**	**2)64596**	**1)34407**	.11730	**.25869**
10.7	**4)31883**	**3)65042**	**2)59679**	**1)32191**	.11141	**.25055**
10.8	**4)28849**	**3)59429**	**2)55125**	**1)30106**	.10575	**.24242**
10.9	**4)26104**	**3)54296**	**2)50908**	**1)28146**	.10032	**.23431**
11.0	**4)23620**	**3)49602**	**2)47003**	**1)26304**	1)95116	**.22626**
11.1	4)21372	3)45309	2)43391	1)24574	1)90109	.21827
11.2	4)19338	3)41384	2)40046	1)22950	1)85356	.21039
11.3	4)17498	3)37796	2)36952	1)21426	1)80831	.20259
11.4	4)15833	3)34515	2)34090	1)19997	1)76433	.19495
11.5	4)14326	3)31518	2)31445	1)18657	1)72270	.18743
11.6	4)12963	3)28778	2)28999	1)17401	1)68302	18005
11.7	4)11729	3)26273	2)26741	1)16226	1)64519	.17284
11.8	4)10613	3)23985	2)24652	1)15124	1)60918	.16577
11.9	5)96031	3)21896	2)22723	1)14093	1)57489	.15889
12.0	5)86892	3)19986	2)20976	1)13119	1)54251	.15215

TABLE OF THE LAGUERRE FUNCTIONS (Continued)

Arg.	0	1	2	3	4	5
12.1	5)78623	3)18241	2)19295	1)12228	1)51131	.14566
12.2	5)71141	3)16647	2)17776	1)11391	1)48190	.13932
12.3	5)64371	3)15192	2)16374	1)10597	1)45398	.13316
12.4	5)58245	3)13862	2)15081	2)98610	1)42751	.12720
12.5	5)52703	3)12649	2)13888	2)91738	1)40241	.12143
	5)47687	3)11540	2)12787	2)85323	1)37863	.11585
	5)43149	3)10528	2)11770	2)79337	1)35612	.11046
	5)39043	4)96046	2)10834	2)73751	1)33482	.10526
	5)35328	4)87613	3)99693	2)68803	1)31467	.10025
	5)31966	4)79914	3)91739	2)63687	1)29563	1)95420
1:	5)28924	4)72888	3)84400	2)59160	1)27764	1)90776
1:	5)26171	4)66475	3)77646	2)54943	1)26065	1)86312
1:	5)23681	4)60623	3)71417	2)51016	1)24462	1)82025
1:	5)21427	4)55283	3)65679	2)47358	1)22950	1)77912
1:	5)19388	4)50409	3)60394	2)43953	1)21524	1)74574
1:	5)17543	4)45963	3)55528	2)40784	1)20179	1)70190
1:	5)15874	4)41907	3)51047	2)37836	1)18907	1)66574
1:	5)14363	4)38206	3)46922	2)35093	1)17721	1)63113
1:	5)12996	4)34830	3)43125	2)32542	1)16598	1)59807
1·	5)11759	4)31750	3)39631	2)30171	1)15552	1)56654
14.1	5)10641	4)28942	3)36413	2)27967	1)14559	1)53630
14.2	6)96279	4)26379	3)33924	2)25918	1)13226	1)50552
14.3	6)87117	4)24045	3)30732	2)24017	1)12738	1)48013
14.4	6)78827	4)21914	3)28228	2)22249	1)11914	1)45399
14.5	6)71325	4)19971	3)25926	2)20608	1)11138	1)42918
14.6	6)64538	4)18245	3)23811	2)19085	1)10415	1)40539
14.7	6)58396	4)16584	3)21862	2)17671	2)97302	1)38292
14.8	6)52839	4)15112	3)20073	2)16359	2)90924	1)36153
14.9	6)47811	4)13768	3)18427	2)15141	2)84921	1)34117
15.0	6)43261	4)12546	3)16915	2)14012	2)79303	1)32189
15.1	6)39144	4)11431	3)15525	2)12965	2)74034	1)30357
15.2	6)35419	4)10414	3)14248	2)11994	2)69102	1)28614
15.3	6)32048	5)94863	3)13075	2)11094	2)64471	1)26965
15.4	6)28999	5)86417	3)11997	2)10260	2)60152	1)25401
15.5	6)26239	5)78718	3)11007	3)94874	2)56094	1)23932
15.6	6)23742	5)71702	3)10098	3)87712	2)52325	1)22525
15.7	6)21483	5)65308	4)92629	3)81092	2)48760	1)21194
15.8	6)19438	5)59482	4)84962	3)74936	2)45461	1)19947
15.9	6)17588	5)54173	4)77924	3)69248	2)42362	1)18756
16.0	6)15915	5)49336	4)71458	3)63983	2)39453	1)18148
16.1	6)14400	5)44929	4)65524	3)59109	2)36748	1)16578
16.2	6)13030	5)40914	4)60078	3)54599	2)34219	1)15578
16.3	6)11790	5)37256	4)55081	3)50425	2)31859	1)15198
16.4	6)10668	5)33924	4)50494	3)46564	2)29656	1)13744
16.5	7)96528	5)30889	4)46285	3)42994	2)27599	1)12903

TABLE OF THE LAGUERRE FUNCTIONS (Continued)

Arg.	0	1	2	3	4	5
16.6	7)87343	5)28125	4)42424	3)39691	2)25680	1)12111
16.7	7)79031	5)25606	4)38882	3)36637	2)23889	1)11365
16.8	7)71510	5)23312	4)35632	3)33814	2)22219	1)10661
16.9	7)64705	5)21223	4)32652	3)31204	2)20661	2)99985
17.0	7)58547	5)19273	4)29844	3)28722	2)19164	2)93520
17.1	7)52976	5)17588	4)27410	3)26563	2)17857	2)87874
17.2	7)47934	5)16010	4)25112	3)24502	2)16596	2)82348
17.3	7)43373	5)14573	4)23004	3)22600	2)15421	2)77151
17.4	7)39245	5)13265	4)21072	3)20843	2)14328	2)72264
17.5	7)35511	5)12074	4)19300	3)19220	2)13309	2)67669
17.6	7)32131	5)11310	4)17676	3)17721	2)12361	2)63352
17.7	7)29074	5)10001	4)16188	3)16336	2)11477	2)59295
17.8	7)26307	6)93390	4)14823	3)15059	2)10656	2)55486
17.9	7)23803	6)82836	4)13573	3)13879	3)98916	2)51909
18.0	7)21538	6)75385	4)12427	3)12791	3)91809	2)48553
18.2	7)17634	6)62425	4)10415	3)10860	3)79046	2)42447
18.4	7)14437	6)51687	5)87270	4)92171	3)68012	2)37077
18.6	7)11821	6)42790	5)73122	4)78191	3)58483	2)32359
18.8	8)96778	6)35421	5)61239	4)66299	3)50261	2)28219
19.0	8)79235	6)29317	5)51347	4)56197	3)42768	2)24788
19.2	8)64872	6)24262	5)42916	4)47613	3)37055	2)21407
19.4	8)53113	6)20076	5)35915	4)40325	3)31791	2)18624
19.6	8)43485	6)16611	5)30044	4)34141	3)27258	2)16521
19.8	8)35603	6)13743	5)25123	4)28893	3)23361	2 14065
20.0	8)29149	6)11368	5)21023	4)24443	3)20008	2)12209
20.5	8)17680	7)70719	5)14725	4)16067	3)13556	3)84623
21.0	8)10723	7)52003	6)85611	4)10539	4)91562	3)59589
22.0	9)39449	7)17318	6)34734	5)44633	4)41429	3)28638
23.0	9)14512	8)66612	6)14031	5)18969	4)18552	3)13575
24.0	10)53388	8)25092	7)56435	6)80081	5)82313	4)58138
25.0	10)19641	9)96238	7)22612	6)33600	5)36214	4)29425
26.0	11)72253	9)36849	8)90276	6)14021	5)15811	4)13589
28.0	12)97784	10)53781	8)14246	7)24048	6)29519	5)44859
30.0	12)13234	11)78078	9)22246	8)40535	7)53803	6)54553

THE WIENER RMS (ROOT MEAN SQUARE) ERROR CRITERION IN FILTER DESIGN AND PREDICTION*

By NORMAN LEVINSON

In the process of gathering or transmitting information by mechanical or electrical means the signal that contains the information frequently becomes distorted. Among the diverse sources of distortion there may be tracking errors, crosstalk, thermal noise, and poor characteristics of pickup, transmitting, or receiving equipment. When the distortion has random statistical features it is called noise.

The modification of a signal is sometimes necessary in order to remove the noise and recapture the original message. This process is called filtering. The determination of how much of the noise can be separated from the message contained in a signal is by no means simple. Cases exist where a crude filter will perform as well as an extremely complicated one. There are cases where the very best results require an elaborate filter but where only slightly inferior results can be obtained by using comparatively simple filters.

In this article a method will be presented for determining quantitatively the extent to which message and noise can be separated. Also will be given a method of designing a filter to carry out this separation. The close of the article will consider the problem of filtering and predicting simultaneously. The root mean square error approach used here is an approximation to and a simplification of the transcendental case developed by N. Wiener.

Wiener's work appeared in a book of limited circulation in February, 1942. An independent and similar but by no means identical work by Kolmogoroff had already appeared in *Bulletin de l'académie des sciences U.S.S.R.*, pp. 3-14, 1941.

A few months after Wiener's work appeared, the author, in order to facilitate computational procedure, worked out an approximate, and one might say, mathematically trivial procedure. This procedure is essentially that which appears in Secs. 2, 3, and 6 of the present paper. It is, actually, classical least squares.

* Reprinted from *Journal of Mathematics and Physics*, Vol. XXV, No. 4, January, 1947, pp. 261-278.

The basic idea underlying Wiener's work, rather than the intricate mathematical procedure for solving the transcendental problem, influenced work on smoothing and prediction in fire control work. Various classified documents have appeared some of which have lately been declassified. Of these the author has seen and been influenced [so far as minimizing the expression (35) of this paper is concerned] by the work of Phillips and Weiss, *Theoretical Calculation on Best Smoothing of Position Data for Gunnery Prediction*, NDRC Report 532, February, 1944.

Another relevant report which the author knows only by title is by Blackman, Bode, and Shannon, *Monograph on Data Smoothing and Prediction in Fire Control Systems*, NDRC Report, February, 1946.

1 Linear Filters

Here the discussion will be limited to linear filtering devices. The behavior of a linear filter may be expressed in terms of its impedance function. This impedance function gives the characteristic of the filter in terms of the relationship of the amplitude and phase of the output to those of any sinusoidal input. A dual way of indicating the behavior of the filter is in terms of the output corresponding to an input which is a unit-step function. If, when the input is $\begin{cases} 1, t > 0 \\ 0, t < 0 \end{cases}$, we denote the output by $A(t)$, then corresponding to any input $f(t)$ the output

$$F(t) = \int_0^\infty A'(\tau)f(t - \tau)\, d\tau + A(0)f(t). \tag{1}$$

By $A(0)$ is meant the limit of $A(t)$ as t approaches zero through positive values.

It is useful for many purposes to approximate to the integral in Eq. (1) by a sum. We have from Eq. (1) approximately, if h is small,

$$F(t) = h \sum_{n=1}^\infty A'(nh)f(t - nh) + A(0)f(t). \tag{2}$$

In case $A'(\tau)$ is small when τ is large the tail of the infinite series can be discarded. Using the notation $A_n = hA'(nh)$, $n > 0$, and $A_0 = A(0)$, we have approximately, for some suitably chosen M,

$$F(t) = \sum_{n=0}^M A_n f(t - nh).$$

This last result states that the output is given approximately by a certain linear combination of the input and a number of its past values. Or, to put it differently, $F(t)$ is given approximately by a weighted sum of a number of past values of the input. In case $F(t)$ and $f(t)$ are adequately determined by their values at $t = kh$, we find

$$F(kh) = \sum_{n=0}^{M} A_n f[(k - n)h].$$

Calling $F(kh)$, F_k, and $f[(k - n)h]$, f_{k-n}, we have

$$F_k = \sum_{n=0}^{M} A_n f_{k-n}. \tag{3}$$

2 Minimization of RMS Error

Let $f(t)$ be a signal containing a message $g(t)$ and noise. Clearly the noise is given by $f(t) - g(t)$.

Let us consider the output of an electrical circuit with input $f(t)$. If the circuit has the response $A(t)$ to a unit-step function, then referring to Eq. (1) we see that the output, with input $f(t)$, is given by

$$F(t) = \int_0^\infty A'(\tau)f(t - \tau)\,d\tau + A(0)f(t).$$

Our goal is to have $F(t)$ approximate as closely as possible the message $g(t)$. That is, we want to minimize $[F(t) - g(t)]$. As a criterion for measuring the difference between $F(t)$ and $g(t)$ we shall take

$$\lim_{T \to \infty} \frac{1}{2T} \int_{-T}^{T} [F(t) - g(t)]^2\,dt.$$

This is clearly the square of the rms value of $F(t) - g(t)$. The exact procedure for determining $A'(\tau)$ from the requirement that the rms value of $F(t) - g(t)$ be a minimum leads to an integral equation.

To avoid the transcendental analysis arising when the signal is treated as a continuous function, $f(t)$, we choose a time interval h sufficiently small so that $f(t)$ is well characterized by its values at the points $t = kh$, where k assumes integral values. If we denote $f(kh)$ by b_k then we can regard a signal as a sequence b_k. The message contained in the signal we shall denote by the sequence a_k, and noise, by the sequence of differences, $b_k - a_k$. It is our purpose to find the best way to treat the signal, that is, the b_k, so as to obtain the information, the a_k.

Let us try to determine the nature of a linear filter which, with input b_k, will have an output as close as possible to a_k. Using Eq. (3), we see that our problem is to determine the numbers A_n so that the

$$\sum_{n}^{M} A_n b_{k-n} \tag{4}$$

are as small as possible. What we shall do to try to make the ϵ_k as small as possible is to require that the A_n be so chosen that the average of the sum of the square of ϵ_k should be a minimum. This is equivalent to requiring that the rms of the ϵ_k be a minimum.

Stated in formula, we want to choose A_n so that

$$I = \lim_{N \to \infty} \frac{1}{2N+1} \sum_{k=-N}^{N} \left(a_k - \sum_{n=0}^{M} A_n b_{k-n} \right)^2 \tag{5}$$

should be a minimum. Equation (5) assumes a much simpler form if we introduce auto-correlation functions. The auto-correlation function is defined as

$$R_a(k) = \lim_{N \to \infty} \frac{1}{2N+1} \sum_{l=-N}^{M} a_l a_{l-k}.$$

It is an even function, that is, it has the property

$$R_a(k) = R_a(-k).$$

We shall also be concerned with the auto-correlation function

$$R_b(k) = \lim_{N \to \infty} \frac{1}{2N+1} \sum_{l=-N}^{N} b_l b_{l-k},$$

and the cross-correlation function

$$R_{ba}(k) = \lim_{N \to \infty} \frac{1}{2N+1} \cdot \sum_{l=-N}^{N} a_l b_{l-k}.$$

The cross-correlation function is not necessarily an even function of k.

It frequently happens that the message and noise are completely uncorrelated. In this case $R_{b-a,a}(k) = 0$ for all (k). Since

$$R_{ba}(k) = R_{b-a,a}(k) + R_a(k)$$

we see that if the message and noise have zero correlation $R_{ba}(k) = R_a(k)$.

When $R_{ba}(k)$ is itself zero, the signal and message have no correlation. This means that the noise cancels the message completely and leaves only a random residue, making it impossible to separate any part of the message from the signal by a linear device. Thus $R_{ba}(k) = 0$ is the worst situation that can arise.

We can write Eq. (5) as

$$I = \lim_{N \to \infty} \frac{1}{2N+1} \sum_{k=-N}^{N} a_k^2 - 2 \sum_{n=0}^{M} A_n \lim_{N \to \infty} \frac{1}{2N+1} \sum_{k=-N}^{N} a_k b_{k-n}$$
$$+ \sum_{n=0}^{M} \sum_{m=0}^{M} A_n A_m \lim_{N \to \infty} \frac{1}{2N+1} \sum_{k=N}^{N} b_{k-n} b_{k-m}.$$

Using the auto- and cross-correlation functions, we have

$$I = R_a(0) - 2 \sum_{n=0}^{M} A_n R_{ba}(n) + \sum_{n,m=0}^{M} A_n A_m R_b(m - n). \qquad (6)$$

If the A_n are chosen so as to make I a minimum we must have

$$\frac{\partial I}{\partial A_k} = 0, \quad k = 0, 1, \cdots, M.$$

Thus

$$\frac{\partial I}{\partial A_k} = -2R_{ba}(k) + 2 \sum_{n=0}^{M} A_n R_b(k - n) = 0.$$

$$\sum_{n=0}^{M} A_n R_b(k - n) = R_{ba}(k), \quad k = 0, 1, \cdots, M. \qquad (7)$$

We have derived Eqs. (7) as a necessary condition that the A_n make I a minimum. We shall have occasion to prove later, that with the A_n obtained from Eqs. (7), I actually assumes its minimum value.

Equations (7) are a linear system of $M + 1$ equations in the $M + 1$ unknowns A_n. From Eqs. (7) we see that the determination of A_n is dependent on the auto-correlation function of the b's and on the cross correlation of the a's and b's. It does not depend on the a's and b's directly as such. Thus, while the a's and b's may differ from one run to another, if the correlation functions do not, then a set of A_n's can be chosen once and for all which will work for all the runs. In other words, it is necessary for the sequences a_k and b_k to be elements of a stationary random process.

The advantage of dealing with the discrete sequences a_k and b_k rather than with the continuous functions $g(t)$ and $f(t)$ is that in the discrete case we face simply the linear algebraic problem [Eqs. (7)] as contrasted to an integral equation in the continuous case.

Using Eqs. (7) in (6), we see that the minimum value of I, I_m, is given by

$$I_m = R_a(0) - \sum_{n=0}^{M} A_n R_{ba}(n). \qquad (8)$$

The sum, $\Sigma A_n R_{ba}(n)$, on the right-hand side of Eqs. (7), cannot be negative since the choice $A_n = 0$ would in that case reduce I_m. This is an impossibility since I_m is already a minimum. Thus $\Sigma A_n R_{ba}(n) \geqq 0$. The worst case that can arise is for this expression to be zero. This happens when all the $R_{ba}(n)$ are zero. For the $R_{ba}(n)$ to be zero means that the signal and the message are completely incoherent. In this worst of all cases, $I_m = R_a(0)$. This suggests normalizing Eqs. (8) by dividing by $R_a(0)$:

$$\frac{I_m}{R_a(0)} = 1 - \sum_{n=0}^{M} A_n \frac{R_{ba}(n)}{R_a(0)}.$$

If we now call $I_m/[R_a(0)]$, V, and if we set

$$\frac{R_{ba}(n)}{R_a(0)} = \gamma_n,$$

then we have

$$V = 1 - E_M, \tag{9}$$

where

$$E_M = \sum_{n=0}^{M} A_n \gamma_n. \tag{10}$$

Obviously $V \leq 1$ since $I_m \leq R_a(0)$. On the other hand, since I_m is the average of a sum of squares, $I_m \geq 0$, and thus $V \geq 0$. We see then that

$$0 \leq E_M \leq 1.$$

The closer E_M is to one, the smaller is the rms value of ϵ_k, that is, the better the separation of the message from the noise. The value of E_M increases with M. Ordinarily, increasing M beyond a certain point will increase E_M only very slightly. There will be a value $\bar{E} = \lim_{M \to \infty} E_M$. beyond which it is impossible to increase E_M. If $\bar{E}$ is small compared to one, it means that even the best linear filter can effectuate only a poor separation of the noise from the message; if $\bar{E}$ is close to one, a considerable separation can be attained. The rms of ϵ_k for a given filter can be compared with $\sqrt{R_a(0)}\sqrt{1 - \bar{E}}$. If this rms value is almost as small as $\sqrt{R_a(0)}\sqrt{1 - \bar{E}}$, then the filter is close to optimum.

In finding E_M we use the A_n as found from Eqs. (7). It is convenient now to set

$$\frac{R_b(n)}{R_a(0)} = r_n.$$

We can write Eqs. (7) as

$$\sum_{n=0}^{M} A_n r_{k-n} = \gamma_k, \quad k = 0, 1, \cdots, M. \tag{11}$$

In practice it is usually impossible to build a filter with the A_n exactly as required. Moreover, over-all considerations may make it undesirable to do so. In case the filter selected has its characteristic response given by the sequence B_n rather than by the desired A_n the value of I will be affected. Let the difference $B_n - A_n$ be denoted by δ_n. In this case we have

$$I = \lim_{N \to \infty} \frac{1}{2N+1} \sum_{k=-N}^{N} \left(a_k - \sum_{n=0}^{M} B_n b_{k-n} \right)^2$$

$$= R_a(0) - 2 \sum_{n=0}^{M} B_n R_{ba}(n) + \sum_{n,m=0}^{M} B_n B_m R_b(n-m).$$

Using $B_n = A_n + \delta_n$ and dividing by $R_a(0)$ we find, denoting $I/[R_a(0)]$ by V, that

$$V = 1 - 2 \sum_{n=0}^{M} A_n \gamma_n + \sum_{n,m=0}^{M} A_n A_m r_{n-m} - 2 \sum_{n=0}^{M} \delta_n \gamma_n$$

$$+ 2 \sum_{n,m=0}^{M} A_n \delta_m r_{n-m} + \sum_{n,m=0}^{M} \delta_n \delta_m r_{n-m}.$$

Using Eqs. (11), we find

$$V = 1 - \sum_{n=0}^{M} A_n \gamma_n + \sum_{n,m=0}^{M} \delta_n \delta_m r_{n-m}.$$

Using Eqs. (10), this becomes

$$V = 1 - E_M + \sum_{n,m=0}^{M} \delta_n \delta_m r_{n-m}. \tag{12}$$

Thus the effect of using B_n instead of A_n is to increase V by

$$J = \sum_{n,m=0}^{M} \delta_n \delta_m r_{n-m}. \tag{13}$$

It is not difficult to show that $J \geqq 0$. In fact

$$r_{n-m} = \frac{1}{R_a(0)} \lim_{N \to \infty} \frac{1}{2N+1} \sum_{k=-N}^{N} b_{k+n} b_{k+m}.$$

Thus, heuristically we have from Eqs. (13)

$$J = \frac{1}{R_a(0)} \lim_{N \to \infty} \frac{1}{2N+1} \sum_{k=-N}^{N} \sum_{n,m=0}^{M} \delta_n \delta_m b_{k+n} b_{k+m}$$

$$= \frac{1}{R_a(0)} \lim_{N \to \infty} \frac{1}{2N+1} \sum_{k=-N}^{N} \left(\sum_{n=0}^{M} b_{k+n} \delta_n \right)^2.$$

Since the sum of squared terms is positive, we have $J \geqq 0$.

We have from Eqs. (12)

$$I = R_a(0)(1 - E_M + J).$$

Since $J \geqq 0$ we see that the minimum value of I, I_m is assumed when $J = 0$. When $\delta_n = 0$ we have $J = 0$. Thus choosing the A_n as the solution of Eqs. (11) does cause I to assume its minimum value.

3 Determination of the Weighting Function

We now turn our attention to a method for solving Eqs. (11) for the A_n. We recall that Eqs. (11) state

$$\sum_{n=0}^{M} A_n r_{k-n} = \gamma_k, \quad k = 0, 1, \cdots, M. \tag{11}$$

From the definition of $r_k = [R_b(k)]/[R_a(0)]$ we see that, since the $R_b(k)$ sequence is even, so is the r_k. This simplifies the process of solving Eqs. (11) for the A_n as we shall now see. In case $M = 3$, for example, we have

$$A_0 r_0 + A_1 r_1 + A_2 r_2 + A_3 r_3 = \gamma_0$$
$$A_0 r_1 + A_1 r_0 + A_2 r_1 + A_3 r_2 = \gamma_1$$
$$A_0 r_2 + A_1 r_1 + A_2 r_0 + A_3 r_1 = \gamma_2$$
$$A_0 r_3 + A_1 r_2 + A_2 r_1 + A_3 r_0 = \gamma_3.$$

Adding the first equation to the last, the second equation to the next to last, and in the general case proceeding further in this way, we have

$$(A_0 + A_3)(r_0 + r_3) + (A_1 + A_2)(r_1 + r_2) = \gamma_0 + \gamma_3$$
$$(A_0 + A_3)(r_1 + r_2) + (A_1 + A_2)(r_0 + r_1) = \gamma_1 + \gamma_2.$$

This is a pair of equations for the two unknowns $A_0 + A_3$ and $A_1 + A_2$.

Again subtracting the last equation from the first and the next to the last from the second, we get

$$(A_0 - A_3)(r_0 - r_3) + (A_1 - A_2)(r_1 - r_2) = \gamma_0 - \gamma_3$$
$$(A_0 - A_3)(r_1 - r_2) + (A_1 - A_2)(r_0 - r_1) = \gamma_1 - \gamma_2.$$

Here again we have two equations for the two unknowns $A_0 - A_3$ and $A_1 - A_2$.

Solving each of these two systems of equations, we get $A_0 + A_3$, $A_1 + A_2$, $A_0 - A_3$, and $A_1 - A_2$. Adding the first and the third of these quantities and dividing by two we get A_0, subtracting we get A_3. Proceeding similarly with the second and fourth we find A_1 and A_2.

The amount of work in finding the A_n is considerably reduced by this device. Thus when $M = 7$ there are eight unknowns, and solving Eqs. (11) is a formidable computation. By the procedure just discussed, this case is reduced to solving two systems of equations each in four unknowns. The latter problem is very tractable.

In case M is even, the device still works in a slightly modified form. Here we add the middle equation to itself and subtract it from itself. We then obtain two systems of equations, one with $[(M/2) + 1]$ and the other with $(M/2)$ unknowns.

We now turn to a procedure for getting the A_n by an iteration process. The method which we are about to develop will give some insight on the number of weights A_n needed for a good filter.

We have found that a measure of the effectiveness of the filter output

$$\sum_{k=0}^{M} A_k b_{n-k} \tag{14}$$

in representing the message a_n, was given by

$$E_M = \sum_{k=0}^{M} A_k \gamma_k.$$

The closer E_M is to one the more effectively (14) represents a_n.

It is an important practical question to decide how large to make M. Unless E_M increases appreciably when M is increased, it is not worth while to increase M. In practice this makes desirable a procedure which gives us E_1, E_2, E_3, etc., without undue computational difficulty. To distinguish between the various values A_n assumes as M changes, we introduce the more specific notation, $A_n^{(M)}$.

Thus Eqs. (11) and (10) become

$$\sum_{n=0}^{M} A_n^{(M)} r_{k-n} = \gamma_k \quad k = 0, 1, \cdots, M, \tag{15}$$

and

$$E_M = \sum_{k=0}^{M} A_k^{(M)} \gamma_k. \tag{16}$$

We shall now set up an iterative process by means of which we can proceed easily from $A_n^{(M)}$ to $A_m^{(M+1)}$. We introduce first an auxiliary sequence $C_k^{(M)}$ which we specify as follows:

$$\left. \begin{aligned} C_0^{(0)} &= \frac{r_1}{r_0} \\ C_0^{(M)} \left(r_0 - \sum_{k=0}^{M-1} C_k^{(M-1)} r_{M-k} \right) &= r_{M+1} - \sum_{k=1}^{M} C_{k-1}^{(M-1)} r_k \end{aligned} \right\} \tag{17}$$

$$C_k^{(M)} = C_{k-1}^{(M-1)} - C_0^{(M)} C_{M-k}^{(M-1)}, \quad k = 1, 2, \cdots, M. \tag{18}$$

Thus knowing $C_k^{(M-1)}$, $k = 0, 1, \cdots, M - 1$, we are able from Eq. (17) to find $C_0^{(M)}$ and then from Eq. (18) to find $C_k^{(M)}$, $k = 1, \cdots, M$.

Having determined the $C_k^{(M)}$, we find $A_{M+1}^{(M+1)}$ from the $C_k^{(M)}$ and $A_k^{(M)}$ by use of

$$\left.\begin{aligned} A_0^{(0)} &= \frac{\gamma_0}{r_0} \\ A_{M+1}^{(M+1)}\left(r_0 - \sum_{k=0}^{M} C_k^{(M)} r_{M+1-k}\right) &= \gamma_{M+1} - \sum_{k=0}^{M} A_k^{(M)} r_{M+1-k}. \end{aligned}\right\} \quad (19)$$

$$A_k^{(M+1)} = A_k^{(M)} - C_k^{(M)} A_{M+1}^{(M+1)}, \quad k = 0, 1, \cdots, M. \quad (20)$$

$$\left.\begin{aligned} E_0 &= \frac{\gamma_0^2}{r_0} \\ E_{M+1} &= E_M + A_{M+1}^{(M+1)}\left(\gamma_{M+1} - \sum_{k=0}^{M} C_k^{(M)} \gamma_k\right). \end{aligned}\right\} \quad (21)$$

Equations (21) are an immediate consequence of using Eq. (20) in the formula (16) for E_{M+1}. Thus on ascertaining $C_k^{(M)}$ and $A_{M+1}^{(M+1)}$ we can find at once how much larger E_{M+1} will be compared with E_M. This can be done even before using Eq. (20) to compute $A_k^{(M+1)}$, $k \leqq M$.

We now proceed with the proofs of Eqs. (19) and (20). We must show that with the $A_k^{(M)}$ determined from these equations, Eq. (15) is satisfied. First let us see what Eq. (20) gives when used in Eq. (15) with M replaced by $M + 1$. We have

$$\sum_{n=0}^{M} (A_n^{(M)} - C_n^{(M)} A_{M+1}^{(M+1)}) r_{k-n} + A_{M+1}^{(M+1)} r_{k-M-1} = \gamma_k,$$
$$h = 0, 1, \cdots, M + 1 \quad (22)$$

Using Eq. (15), we obtain from the above with $k < M + 1$,

$$\sum_{n=0}^{M} C_n^{(M)} r_{k-n} = r_{M+1-k}, \quad g = 0, 1, \cdots, M. \quad (23)$$

For $k = M + 1$ we get Eq. (19) from Eq. (22). Thus Eqs. (19) and (20) hinge on Eq. (23), which we proceed to prove by induction.

We now use Eq. (18) in Eq. (23) and obtain

This can be written as

$$\sum_{n=0}^{M-1} C_n{}^{(M-1)} r_{(k-1)-n} = r_{M-(k-1)} + C_0{}^{(M)} \left(\sum_{n=1}^{M} C_{M-n}{}^{(M-1)} r_{k-n} - r_k \right),$$

$$k = 1, 2, \cdots, M, \qquad (24)$$

and Eq. (17). But Eq. (23) with M replaced by $M - 1$ reduces Eq. (24) to

$$\sum_{n=1}^{M} C_{M-n}{}^{(M-1)} r_{k-n} = r_k, \quad k = 1, 2, \cdots, M. \qquad (25)$$

Replacing n by $M - m$, Eq. (25) becomes

$$\sum_{m=0}^{M-1} C_m{}^{(M-1)} r_{M-k-m} = r_k, \quad k = 1, 2, \cdots, M. \qquad (26)$$

If we set $M - k = j$ in Eq. (26) we get

$$\sum_{m=0}^{M-1} C_m{}^{(M-1)} r_{j-m} = r_{M-j}, \quad j = 0, 1, \cdots, M - 1. \qquad (27)$$

But Eq. (27) is the same as Eq. (23) with the index M replaced by $M - 1$. Thus Eq. (23) is true for the index M if it is true for $M - 1$. By induction, therefore, the validity of Eq. (23) is reduced to the case $M = 0$, $C_0{}^{(0)} r_0 = r_1$. This last equation is satisfied, being in fact the first equation of Eqs. (17).

4 Realization of Operator—Mathematical Formulation

It is convenient here again to regard the signal as a function of time, $f(t)$. The information which is to be extracted from the signal we again denote by $F(t)$, $F(t)$ being as close as possible to $g(t)$.

We shall consider the nature of a four-terminal linear passive network which, when its input voltage is $f(t)$, has $F(t)$ as its open-circuit ouput voltage. The complication inherent in the construction of satisfactory inductive elements makes the use of RC networks common. For this reason and for the sake of simplicity we shall *here restrict ourselves to RC networks.*

We denote by $A(t)$ the open-circuit output voltage of the network corresponding to an input voltage which is a unit-step function. We recall the relationship

$$F(t) = \int_0^\infty A'(\tau) f(t - \tau)\, d\tau + A(0) f(t).$$

We also shall require the Laplace transform of $A(t)$. Here we shall denote by $k(p)$ the Laplace transform of $A(t)$ multiplied by p. The function $k(p)$ is a transfer function. It is given by

$$k(p) = A(0) + \int_0^\infty A'(t)e^{-pt}\, dt. \tag{28}$$

In the case of a network free of inductances $k(p)$ is a rational function having its poles on the negative real axis of the complex p-plane. Moreover the poles of $k(p)$ are simple, and $k(p)$ is representable by a partial fraction expansion

$$k(p) = \alpha_0 + \sum_{m=1}^{K} \frac{\alpha_m}{p + \sigma_m}, \tag{29}$$

where $0 < \sigma_1 < \sigma_2 < \cdots < \sigma_K$ and the α_m are real. From Eq. (28) we see that Eq. (29) is satisfied if $\alpha_0 = A(0)$ and if

$$A'(\tau) - \sum_{m=1}^{K} \alpha_m e^{-\sigma_m \tau}. \tag{30}$$

We recall that in Eqs. (2) we used $hA'(nh) = A_n$. Thus we want A_n to be equal to

$$h \sum_{m=1}^{K} \alpha_m e^{-nh\sigma_m}, \quad n > 0. \tag{31}$$

The A_n, we recall, are already determined as in Sec. 3. Here we are trying to find $k(p)$. In general, to meet the requirement that A_n be given by Eqs. (31) exactly would require a filter of unwarranted complexity. Therefore, setting

$$B_n = h \sum_{m=1}^{K} \alpha_m e^{-nh\sigma_m}, \quad n > 0, \tag{32}$$

we require that $A_n - B_n$ be small. The extent to which we can make B_n close to A_n depends on how large we make K. If the successive A_n form a slowly changing sequence, K can be chosen much smaller than M. We recall that M is the number of A_n, $n > 0$. On the other hand, if the A_n change markedly from one value of n to the next it may be necessary to take K as large as M. The smaller K can be made, the simpler the filter. A plot of the values of A_n against n should be of great help in deciding how much the A_n fluctuate between successive values of n and therefore how large to take K.

Our problem is really one in approximation. We want to make Eqs. (31) represent A_n as closely as possible. We have at our disposal the choice of the σ_m and the α_m. It is inadvisable to choose σ_{m+1}/σ_m close to one since this introduces extremes in the sizes of the elements of the filter associated with $k(p)$. It is also inadvisable to take σ_K/σ_1 too large since this has no influence on the B_n except for small n.

In order to be able to carry our analysis further we shall now make the assumption

$$\sigma_m = \frac{\beta m}{Mh} \tag{33}$$

where β is a scale factor. A reasonable choice for β is 1. Under certain conditions a value of $\frac{1}{2}$ or 2 may provide a better fit of B_n to A_n for a given value of K. *The choice of σ_m as given in Eq. (33) is arbitrary and a quite different choice may be much more useful under certain conditions.* From here on, however, we shall proceed on the basis of the assumption in Eq. (33).

We have now to determine the α_m so that the $B_n - A_n$ are small. The effect of the terms $B_n - A_n$ on V as given in Eqs. (13) appears to be

$$\sum_{m,n=1}^{M} (B_n - A_n)(B_m - A_m) r_{n-m}. \tag{34}$$

This, however, is not complete in the present case because the B_n as given by Eqs. (32) are not zero for $n > M$. To prevent these $B_n, n > M$, from affecting the filter output, $F(t)$, too badly we require

$$\sum_{M+1}^{\infty} B_n{}^2$$

to be small. Recalling Eqs. (32), we can put this condition in more convenient form by requiring that

$$h \int_{Mh}^{\infty} [A'(\tau)]^2 \, d\tau \tag{35}$$

be small where $A'(\tau)$ is given by Eqs. (30). Combining this with Eq. (34), we choose the α_m so as to minimize

$$J = \sum_{m,n=1}^{M} (B_n - A_n)(B_m - A_m) r_{n-m} + \lambda h \int_{Mh}^{\infty} [A'(\tau)]^2 \, d\tau. \tag{36}$$

The value λ in Eq. (36) represents a positive number that is chosen large if it is important to make the influence of $f(t - \tau)$ on $F(t)$ small for $\tau > Mh$.

To see this, we recall that by Eq. (1)

$$F(t) = \int_0^{Mh} A'(\tau) f(t - \tau) \, d\tau + A(0) f(t) + H$$

where

$$H = \qquad A'(\tau) f(t - \tau) \, d\tau.$$

Choosing λ large emphasizes Expression (35) in J, and thus, when the α_m are determined by minimizing J, Term (35) will be small. Making Expression (35) small will make H small, and therefore $F(t)$ is determined mainly by $f(t - \tau)$, $0 < t < Mh$. Thus, as soon as $t > Mh$, $F(t)$ is largely independent of any aberrations in $f(t)$ that occurred when $t < 0$.

In cases where this transient aspect is of little importance, λ is given a smaller value determined by the size of r_n when n is near M in size.

Once a value of λ is decided upon we again have only the α_m to determine. In terms of α_m we have, using Eqs. (30) in Eqs. (36),

$$J = \sum_{m,n=1}^{M} (B_n - A_n)(B_m - A_m)r_{n-m} + \lambda h \sum_{p,q=1}^{K} \frac{\alpha_p \alpha_q e^{-(\sigma_p+\sigma_q)Mh}}{\sigma_p + \sigma_q} ; \quad (37)$$

to minimize J we set $\partial J/\partial \alpha_s = 0$. Finding $\partial J/\partial \alpha_s$, we have

$$\frac{\partial J}{\partial \alpha_s} = 2 \sum_{m,n=1}^{M} (B_n - A_n)r_{n-m}\frac{\partial B_m}{\partial \alpha_s} + 2\lambda h \sum_{p=1}^{K} \frac{\alpha_p e^{-(\sigma_p+\sigma_s)Mh}}{\sigma_p + \sigma_s} .$$

Or, setting $\partial J/\partial \alpha_s = 0$ and finding $\partial B_m/\partial \alpha_s$ from Eqs. (32), we have

$$h \sum_{m,n-1}^{M} (B_n - A_n)r_{n-m}e^{-mh\sigma_s} + \lambda h \sum_{p=1}^{K} \frac{\alpha_p e^{-(\sigma_p+\sigma_s)Mh}}{\sigma_p + \sigma_s} = 0, \quad s = 1, 2, \cdots, K.$$

And again using Eqs. (32), we obtain

$$\sum_{p=1}^{K} \alpha_p \left(h^2 \sum_{n,m=1}^{M} e^{-nh\sigma_p - mh\sigma_s}r_{n-m} + \lambda h \frac{e^{-(\sigma_p+\sigma_s)Mh}}{\sigma_p + \sigma_s} \right)$$
$$= h \sum_{m,n=0}^{M} A_n r_{n-m}e^{-mh\sigma_s}, \quad s = 1, \cdots, K. \quad (38)$$

Here we have K equations to determine the K numbers α_p. We can write Eqs. (38) as

$$\sum_{p=1}^{K} C_{s,p} \alpha_p = d_s, \quad s = 1, \cdots, K, \quad (39)$$

where using Eq. (33),

$$d_s = \sum_{m,n=1}^{M} A_n r_{n-m}e^{-m\beta(s/M)}, \quad s = 1, \cdots, K,$$

and

$$C_{s,p} = \lambda Mh \frac{e^{-\beta(p+s)}}{(p+s)\beta} + h \sum_{n,m=1}^{M} e^{-\beta(np+ms)/M}r_{n-m}.$$

We have in Eqs. (39) a system of equations for determining the α_m.

Once the α_m are determined we have the problem of choosing a network for which $A'(\tau)$ is given by Eqs. (30), or what is equivalent, $k(p)$, by Eqs. (29).

5 RC Filter

Here we begin by summing up the characteristics of a four-terminal linear passive network with only resistors and condensers for its elements.†

We denote $\sigma + j\omega$ by p. Let $Z_{11}(p)$ be the driving-point impedance at the input terminals with the output an open circuit. Similarly $Z_{22}(p)$ is the open-circuit driving-point output-terminal impedance. Finally $Z_{12}(p)$ is the transfer impedance between one end with the other an open circuit. Using the subscripts I and 0 to denote the input and output terminals respectively, we have the well-known relationship,

$$V_I = Z_{11}I_I + Z_{12}I_0;$$
$$V_0 = Z_{12}I_I + Z_{22}I_0. \tag{40}$$

If V_I is a complex number denoting the input voltage at some frequency $\omega/2\pi$ and V_0 is the output voltage on open circuit, then it follows from Eq. (40) that

$$V_0 = V_I \frac{Z_{12}(j\omega)}{Z_{11}(j\omega)}$$

In terms of p we have

$$V_0(p) = V_I(p) \frac{Z_{12}(p)}{Z_{11}(p)}. \tag{41}$$

In the notation of the previous section $V_0(p)$ is the Laplace transform of $F(t)$ and $V_I(p)$ of $f(t)$. We have as the Laplace transform of Eq. (1), $V_0(p) = k(p) \cdot V_I(p)$. Comparing this with Eq. (41), we get

$$\frac{Z_{12}(p)}{Z_{11}(p)} = k(p). \tag{42}$$

We have already determined $k(p)$. In this section we shall determine $Z_{11}(p)$ and $Z_{12}(p)$ so that Eq. (42) is satisfied.

It is necessary and sufficient for Z_{11}, Z_{22}, and Z_{12} to satisfy the following criteria in order to characterize a four-terminal linear passive network free of inductances:

$Z_{11}(p)$ [and $Z_{22}(p)$] have simple zeros and poles which lie on the νe real axis in the p-plane. Zeros and poles separate each other. Moreover the smallest pole lies to the right of the smallest zero. For positive p, $Z_{11}(p)$ and $Z_{22}(p)$ are positive.

2. $Z_{12}(p)$ has simple poles and is real for real p.

3. A pole of $Z_{12}(p)$ must also be a pole of $Z_{11}(p)$ and $Z_{22}(p)$. In fact, if $p = -\sigma'$ is a pole of Z_{12} with residue α_{12} and if α_{11} and α_{22} are the residues of Z_{11} and Z_{22} at $p = -\sigma'$, then it is necessary for

$$\alpha_{11}\alpha_{22} - \alpha_{12}^2 \geqq 0. \tag{43}$$

We shall choose the poles of Z_{12} coincident with those of Z_{11}. Therefore, we see from Eq. (42) that the zeros of $Z_{12}(p)$ are the zeros of $k(p)$ and the zeros of $Z_{11}(p)$ are the poles of $k(p)$. The zeros of Z_{11} are therefore $-\sigma_k$ where $0 < \sigma_1 < \sigma_2 < \cdots < \sigma_K$. As the poles of Z_{11} and Z_{12} we choose $-\sigma_k'$, where

$$0 < \sigma_1' < \sigma_1 < \sigma_2' < \sigma_2 < \cdots < \sigma_K' < \sigma_K. \tag{44}$$

We can take

$$\sigma_1' = \tfrac{1}{2}\sigma_1, \quad \sigma_2' = \tfrac{1}{2}(\sigma_1 + \sigma_2), \quad \sigma_3' = \tfrac{1}{2}(\sigma_2 + \sigma_3), \text{ etc.}$$

Thus we have

$$Z_{11}(p) = e\,\frac{(p + \sigma_1)(p + \sigma_2) \cdots (p + \sigma_K)}{(p + \sigma_1')(p + \sigma_2') \cdots (p + \sigma_K')}, \tag{45}$$

where e is a positive constant that can be chosen to help make the size of the elements of the network physically reasonable. Using Eq. (42), we see that, having determined $Z_{11}(p)$, $Z_{12}(p)$ is given by

$$Z_{12}(p) = k(p)Z_{11}(p). \tag{46}$$

It is convenient to choose $Z_{22}(p) = Z_{11}(p)$, thus making the four-terminal network symmetric. In general, such a choice may cause Eq. (43) to be violated. This can be avoided by reducing $k(p)$ by some constant factor, g, and then compensating for this reduction by any one of several amplifying devices. Equation (43) then becomes

$$\alpha_{11}^2 - g^2\alpha_{12}^2 \geqq 0. \tag{47}$$

Clearly g can be chosen so that this condition is satisfied at all the poles, $-\sigma_k'$, of Z_{12}.

Having chosen

$$Z_{11}(p), \; Z_{12}(p), \text{ and } Z_{22}(p) \; [= Z_{11}(p)],$$

all to within an arbitrary coefficient e, we can now follow Guillemin‡ in finding a four-terminal network with the desired characteristics. Briefly,

‡ *Op. cit.*

in the symmetric network shown in Fig. 1, it is necessary for

$$Z_a = Z_{11} - Z_{12}$$
$$Z_b = Z_{11} + Z_{12}$$

(48)

in order for the network to have Z_{11}, Z_{12}, and Z_{22} as its open-circuit impedances. In this manner the problem is reduced to finding Z_a and Z_b.

The quantities Z_a and Z_b are two-terminal impedances. To see this we observe first that (44) and (45) assure that

$$\alpha_{11,m} > 0, \qquad (49)$$

FIG. 1.

in the partial fraction expansion

$$Z_{11}(p) = e + \sum_{m=1}^{K} \frac{\alpha_{11,m}}{p + \sigma_m'}. \qquad (50)$$

From Eq. (46) we observe that, since the poles of $k(p)$ are canceled by the zeros of $Z_{11}(p)$, we have

$$Z_{12}(p) = ek(\infty) + \sum_{m=1}^{K} \frac{\alpha_{12,m}}{p + \sigma_m'}.$$

Using the modified $gk(p)$ in place of $k(p)$, this becomes

$$Z_{12}(p) = egk(\infty) + \sum_{m=1}^{K} \frac{g\alpha_{12,m}}{p + \sigma_m'}. \qquad (51)$$

We see from Eq. (28), incidentally, that $k(\infty) = A(0)$.

Using Eqs. (50) and (51), we have

$$Z_a = Z_{11} - Z_{12} = e - egk(\infty) + \sum_{m=1}^{K} \frac{\alpha_{11,m} - g\alpha_{12,m}}{p + \sigma_m'}.$$

By (47) and (49) we see that $\alpha_{11,m} - g\alpha_{12,m} \geqq 0$. Moreover, by further adjusting g if necessary, $e - egk(\infty) \geqq 0$. Thus Z_a is of the form

$$a_0 + \sum_{m=1}^{K} \frac{a_m}{p + \sigma_m'}, \qquad (52)$$

where

$$a_m \geqq 0, \quad \sigma_m' < 0,$$

which is precisely the necessary and sufficient condition for Z_a to be a two-terminal impedance containing resistances and condensers only. The same argument applies to Z_b.

A two-terminal impedance as given

structed. Since a resistor R in parallel with a condensor C has an impedance

$$\frac{1/C}{p + (1/RC)},$$

we see that by choosing $C = 1/a_m$ and $R = a_m/\sigma_m{}'$ we obtain an impedance $a_m/(p + \sigma_m{}')$. Arranging K of these in series and adding a resistor a_0, we obtain a two-terminal impedance of the desired form. With the choice of a large value of e in Eq. (45) a_m is large, and therefore $1/a_m$, the capacitance, can be made reasonably small.

6 Prediction and Lag with and without Noise

In Sec. 2 the problem of separating a message, represented by a sequence a_n, from a signal, represented by a sequence b_n, was considered. The sequence $b_n - a_n$ is called noise. There the optimum set of numbers A_n was determined in order that a_k should be represented as closely as possible by

$$\sum_{n=0}^{M} A_n b_{k-n}. \tag{53}$$

In Eq. (53) we utilize b_k and earlier values such as b_{k-1}, b_{k-2}, etc., in deriving a_k. There are situations where on the basis of knowing b_k, b_{k-1}, b_{k-2}, etc., we must use Eq. (53) to represent not a_k but a_{k+s}, where s is a positive integer. Here we have a problem involving not only filtering, that is, the separation of message from noise, but also prediction. In other words, even if there were no noise, there would still be the problem of determining a_{k+s} from a knowledge of a_k, a_{k-1}, etc. This problem arises in fire control where it is necessary to point a gun not at where the target is but at where it is likely to be by the time the shell arrives.

Proceeding as in Sec. 2, we now choose the A_n so as to minimize the rms of

$$\epsilon_k = a_{k+s} - \sum_{n=0}^{M} A_n b_{k-n}. \tag{54}$$

Instead of Eq. (5) we find

$$I = R_a(0) - 2 \sum_{n=0}^{M} A_n R_{ba}(n + s) + \sum_{n,m=0}^{M} A_n A_m R_b(m - n).$$

Minimizing I, we obtain

$$\sum_{n=0}^{M} A_n r_{k-n} = \gamma_{k+s}, \quad k = 0, 1, \cdots, M, \tag{55}$$

in place of Eq. (10), where r_k and γ_k are defined as in Sec. 2.

In determining the effectiveness of Eq. (53) in representing a_{k+s}, we get now, instead of Eqs. (9) and (10),

$$V = 1 - E_M \tag{56}$$

$$E_M = \sum_{n=0}^{M} A_n \gamma_{n+s}. \tag{57}$$

The method given at the beginning of Sec. 3 for solving two systems each of about half the order of Eq. (11) in place of Eq. (11) applies equally well to Eq. (55). The iteration formulas given in Sec. 3 can also be generalized to cover the case of predicting together with filtering, and we now turn to this problem.

In place of Eqs. (55) and (57) we have, in more explicit notation,

$$\sum_{n=0}^{M} A_n(M) r_{k-n} = \gamma_{k+s}, \quad k = 0, 1, \cdots, M, \tag{58}$$

$$E_M = \sum_{n=0}^{M} A_n{}^{(M)} \gamma_{n+s}. \tag{59}$$

We observe that the only difference between these equations and Eqs. (14) and (15) is in the index of γ which is now increased by s. Thus the only change in Eqs. (16) to (20) is an increase in the index of γ by the number s. Equations (17) and (18) remain unchanged since they do not contain γ, and we rewrite them as before

$$C_0{}^{(M)} \left(r_0 - \sum_{k=0}^{M-1} C_k{}^{(M-1)} r_{M-k} \right) = r_{M+1} - \sum_{k=1}^{M} C_{k-1}{}^{(M-1)} r_k, \tag{60}$$

$$C_k{}^{(M)} = C_{k-1}{}^{(M-1)} - C_0{}^{(M)} C_{M-k}{}^{(M-1)}, \quad k = 1, 2, \cdots, M. \tag{61}$$

Equation (19) is modified to

$$A_{M+1}{}^{(M+1)} \left(r_0 - \sum_{n=0}^{M} C_n{}^{(M)} r_{M+1-n} \right)$$
$$= \gamma_{M+1+s} - \sum_{n=0}^{M} A_n{}^{(M)} r_{M+1-n}, \tag{62}$$

whereas Eq. (20) remains unchanged as

$$A_k{}^{(M+1)} = A_k{}^{(M)} - C_k{}^{(M)} A_{M+1}{}^{(M+1)}, \quad k = 0, 1, \cdots, M. \tag{63}$$

In place of Eq. (21) we have

$$E_{M+1} = E_M + A_{M+1}{}^{(M+1)} \left(\gamma_{M+1+s} - \sum_{n=0}^{M} C_n{}^{(M)} \gamma_{n+s} \right). \tag{64}$$

It is extremely useful to observe that, by Eqs. (60) and (61), the $C_k{}^{(M)}$ are independent of the choice of s. It is also helpful to observe that the same combination appears in the bracket in the left-hand side of Eqs. (60) and (62) except for the index M in one case and $M + 1$ in the other. The $A_k{}^{(M)}$ depend of course on s. In some cases the range of prediction is taken as far ahead as is possible without causing E_M to fall below some preassigned value. Under such conditions the $A_k{}^{(M)}$ and E_M must be recomputed for several choices of s. The fact that $C_k{}^{(M)}$ is independent of s greatly facilitates the computation.

So far, for the sake of being definite, we have considered the case $s > 0$ and discussed the prediction problem. The case $s < 0$ also is of considerable importance. By taking $s < 0$ it is possible to improve the separation of message from noise. If such improvement turns out to be appreciable and if the lag in obtaining the sequence a_{k+s}, $s < 0$, instead of a_k, is not important, then of course it is worth while to take $s < 0$. *All* the formulas given here are valid for any integer value of s, whether positive or negative.

MASSACHUSETTS INSTITUTE OF TECHNOLOGY.

A HEURISTIC EXPOSITION OF WIENER'S MATHEMATICAL THEORY OF PREDICTION AND FILTERING*

By NORMAN LEVINSON

Consider the function of time $f(t)$ which is the sum of a function $g(t)$ and a disturbance, $f(t) - g(t)$. How can we best extract $g(t)$ from $f(t)$? This is the problem of filtering.

More generally, how can we best determine $g(t + h)$ from $f(t - \tau)$, $0 \leqq \tau < \infty$? If $h > 0$ we have here a problem in prediction as well as in filtering.

In case $f(t) = g(t)$ then there is no problem of filtering, but there may still be a prediction problem, that is, finding of $f(t + h)$ from $f(t - \tau)$, $0 \leqq \tau < \infty$.†

An explicit solution to this problem was given by N. Wiener in 1942 in a document not publicly available.‡ Here we shall present an expository account of Wiener's linear theory, making several minor departures from Wiener's procedure. Moreover we shall deal mainly with the analytic rather than the statistical aspects.

The theory developed here will apply if the function, $f(t)$, possesses an auto-correlation function,

$$\varphi(t) = \lim_{T \to \infty} \frac{1}{2T} \int_{-T}^{T} f(t + \tau) f(\tau) \, d\tau;$$

if $g(t)$ possesses an auto-correlation function $\gamma(t)$; and if the cross-correlation function, $\chi(t) = \lim_{T \to \infty} \frac{1}{2T} \int_{-T}^{T} g(t + \tau) f(\tau) \, d\tau$ exists. The importance of the auto-correlation function will be seen from Sec. 1, which follows. In case $f(t) = g(t)$ then $\chi(t) = \gamma(t) = \varphi(t)$. We shall further assume that $\varphi(t)$ and $\chi(t)$ are continuous and that each has a

---

* Reprinted from *Journal of Mathematics and Physics*, Vol. XXVI, No. 2, July, 1947, pp. 110–119.

† For further background on this problem see the introduction in an earlier paper of the author, The Wiener RMS Error Criterion in Filter Design and Prediction, *Journal of Mathematics and Physics*, Vol. XXV, pp. 261–278, 1946.

‡ The book to which this article is appended appears here in its first publicly available form. ED.

Fourier transform. These requirements eliminate from the scope of the theory such functions as $f(\tau) = 1$, $-\infty < \tau \leq t$ or $f(\tau) = \sin a\tau$, $-\infty < \tau \leq t$. Each of these functions has a $\varphi(t)$ which does not tend to zero as $|t| \to \infty$ and therefore has no Fourier transform. In fact, these requirements exclude all elementary functions. However, all the elementary functions are perfectly predictable, and therefore their exclusion involves no real loss.

It is necessary to subtract the perfectly predictable component from a function, $f(t)$, before applying the theory presented here. Thus, if the average of $f(t)$ is not zero, it should be subtracted from $f(t)$.

1 The Auto-correlation Function

In the linear theory of prediction and filtering we attempt to express $g(t + h)$ in terms of a linear combination of values of $f(t - \tau)$ where $\tau \geq 0$. One way of doing this would be to select several values of τ, $\tau_n \geq 0$, and try to choose coefficients, a_n, so that

$$\sum_0^N a_n f(t - \tau_n) \tag{1.0}$$

gives an optimum prediction of $g(t + h)$. This procedure has much to recommend it in practice and is easy to carry through. A more general procedure is to attempt to predict the value of $f(t + h)$ by means of

$$\int_0^\infty f(t - \tau)\, dK(\tau). \tag{1.1}$$

This latter expression involves only the past of $f(t)$ since $\tau \geq 0$ in (1.1).

Another example of an operation on the part of $f(t)$ is

$$\sum_0^N a_n f^{(n)}(t - \tau_n), \quad \tau_n \geq 0, \tag{1.2}$$

where $f^{(n)}$ denotes the nth derivative of f.

It will be convenient for purposes of exposition to use the form

$$\int_0^\infty f(t - \tau) K(\tau)\, d\tau \tag{1.3}$$

which appears to be more restrictive than (1.1) and not to include (1.2). Actually the method of treatment used will be such that the result will come out as an operator on $f(t - \tau)$. This operator may be of the form of (1.3), but it also can be more general in nature and can include the cases (1.1) and (1.2). Thus our assumed form (1.3) is no real restriction.

The question we ask is: How shall we choose the operator $K(\tau)$ so that, for a prescribed $h \geq 0$,

$$g(t + h) - \int_0^\infty f(t - \tau)K(\tau)\, d\tau \qquad (1.4)$$

is as small as possible? Before answering this question we must decide what we mean by the phrase "as small as possible." Here we shall mean that the average (with respect to t) of the square of (1.4) should be a minimum. To be precise, let

$$I[K] = \lim_{T \to \infty} \frac{1}{2T} \int_{-T}^{T} \left[g(t + h) - \int_0^\infty f(t - \tau)K(\tau)\, d\tau \right]^2 dt. \quad (1.5)$$

Our question now becomes: What choice of $K(\tau)$ will make I a minimum?

If we expand the right member of (1.5) we get, inverting limits freely,

$$I[K] = \lim_{T \to \infty} \frac{1}{2T} \int_{-T}^{T} g^2(t + h)\, dt$$

$$- 2 \int_0^\infty K(\tau)\, d\tau \lim_{T \to \infty} \frac{1}{2T} \int_{-T}^{T} g(t + h)f(t - \tau)\, dt$$

$$+ \int_0^\infty K(\tau_1)\, d\tau_1 \int_0^\infty K(\tau_2)\, d\tau_2 \lim_{T \to \infty} \frac{1}{2T} \int_{-T}^{T} f(t - \tau_1)f(t - \tau_2)\, dt,$$

$$(1.6)$$

the last term of which arises from the

$$\lim_{T \to \infty} \frac{1}{2T} \int_{-T}^{T} \left(\int_0^\infty K(\tau)f(t - \tau)\, d\tau \right)^2 dt. \qquad (1.7)$$

Incidentally, since (1.7) is non-negative, it follows that the last term of (1.6) is also non-negative.

The right-hand member of (1.6) becomes considerably simplified if we introduce the auto-correlation functions φ, χ, and γ. A consequence of the existence of $\varphi(t)$ is that for any a, b, and c

$$\varphi(t - c) = \lim_{T \to \infty} \frac{1}{2T} \int_{-T+a}^{T+b} f(t + \tau)f(\tau + c)\, d\tau.$$

A similar result is true for χ and γ. This last result can be used to show that $\varphi(t)$ and $\gamma(t)$ are even functions. We also use it to rewrite (1.6) as

$$I[K] = \gamma(0) - 2 \int_0^\infty K(\tau)\chi(h + \tau)\, d\tau$$

$$+ \int_0^\infty K(\tau_1)\, d\tau_1 \qquad (1.8)$$

Since our problem is to find $K(\tau)$ so as to minimize I, we see from (1.8) that the question of what K to choose so as to get an optimum value for $g(t + h)$ does *not depend on* $f(t)$ *and* $g(t)$ *directly but rather on* $\varphi(t)$ *and* $\chi(t)$, the correlation functions. This is a most important point. Finding K depends on knowing two statistical functions of f and g rather than on knowing f and g themselves. If we find two ensembles of functions $\{f(t)\}$ and $\{g(t)\}$, having the same correlation functions, φ, γ, and χ, then we can choose a $K(\tau)$ that will give us the best prediction of $g(t + h)$ in terms of the past of $f(t)$ for every g and f in the respective ensembles.

Since the last term in (1.6) is non-negative it follows that the last term in (1.8) to which it is equal must also be non-negative. Thus, for any K and any auto-correlation function,

$$\int_0^\infty K(\tau_1) \, d\tau_1 \int_0^\infty K(\tau_2)\varphi(\tau_1 - \tau_2) \, d\tau_2 \geq 0. \qquad (1.9)$$

2 The Integral Equation

If $K(\tau)$ actually makes I a minimum this means that replacing $K(\tau)$ by $K(\tau) + \epsilon M(\tau)$, where ϵ is a real number and $M(\tau)$ is a function of τ, must increase I. That is

$$I(K + \epsilon M) \geqq I(K).$$

From (1.8) we have

$$I[K + \epsilon M] = I[K] - 2\epsilon \int_0^\infty \chi(\tau + h)M(\tau) \, d\tau$$

$$+ 2\epsilon \int_0^\infty M(\tau) \, d\tau \int_0^\infty K(\tau_1)\varphi(\tau - \tau_1) \, d\tau_1$$

$$+ \epsilon^2 \int_0^\infty M(\tau) \, d\tau \int_0^\infty M(\tau_1)\varphi(\tau - \tau_1) \, d\tau_1.$$

Or

$$I[K + \epsilon M] = I[K] - 2\epsilon J_1 + \epsilon^2 J_2, \qquad (2.0)$$

where

$$J_1 = \int_0^\infty M(\tau) \left(\chi(\tau + h) - \int_0^\infty \varphi(\tau - \tau_1)K(\tau_1) \, d\tau_1 \right) d\tau$$

and

$$J_2 = \int_0^\infty M(\tau) \, d\tau \int_0^\infty \varphi(\tau - \tau_1)M(\tau_1) \, d\tau_1.$$

Now, if for some $M(\tau)$, $J_1 \neq 0$, then, by changing the sign of $M(\tau)$ if necessary, we have $J_1 > 0$. Writing (2.0) as

$$I[K + \epsilon M] = I[K] - 2\epsilon(J_1 - \tfrac{1}{2}\epsilon J_2), \qquad (2.1)$$

we see that since $J_1 > 0$ we can, by making ϵ small enough, make $J_1 - \frac{1}{2}\epsilon J_2 > 0$. Thus (2.1) gives us

$$I[K + \epsilon M] < I[K],$$

which is impossible. Therefore $J_1 = 0$ for any $M(\tau)$.

Clearly we will have $J_1 = 0$ for any $M(\tau)$ if

$$\chi(t + h) - \int_0^\infty \varphi(t - \tau)K(\tau)\,d\tau = 0, \quad t \geq 0. \qquad (2.2)$$

It is important to note that (2.2) need hold only for $t \geq 0$ since $M(\tau) \equiv 0$, $\tau < 0$. Conversely, the fact that $J_1 = 0$ for any $M(\tau)$ implies (2.2). Thus, if $K(\tau)$ minimizes $I[K]$, then (2.2) must hold.

With (2.2) valid, $J_1 = 0$ and (2.0) becomes

$$I[K + \epsilon M] = I[K] + \epsilon^2 J_2.$$

As we saw in (1.9), $J_2 \geq 0$. This implies that $I[K + \epsilon M] \geq I[K]$. We see then that (2.2) is not only a necessary but is also a sufficient condition for $I[K]$ to be a minimum. The problem has thus been reduced to the solution of the integral equation (2.2) for the function K.§

3   The Modified Integral Equation

Since the second term in (2.2) is in the form of a convolution, it is natural to conclude that this equation can be solved for $K(\tau)$ by use of the Fourier transform theorem. However, because of the requirement that (2.2) holds only for $t \geq 0$, this conclusion is false. To see precisely why the Fourier transform does not work, let us try it.

Multiplying both sides of (2.2) by e^{iut} and integrating for $t > 0$, we have

$$\int_0^\infty \chi(t + h)e^{iut}\,dt = \int_0^\infty e^{iut}\,dt \int_0^\infty K(\tau)\varphi(t - \tau)\,d\tau. \qquad (3.0)$$

§ In the integral equation (2.2), K is unknown, and χ and φ are known. The equation might be called a Wiener-Hopf integral equation of the first kind. In the Wiener-Hopf equation itself it is necessary to restrict the kernel φ to be exponentially small in magnitude. When transforms are taken this provides a strip in the complex plane in which to match up factors. In the present case no such strip is available, and, as will be seen, factorization is carried out on the real axis of the complex plane. The W-H equation of the first kind also arises in some problems of electromagnetic theory as has been shown by Schwinger. (See for example, the Reflection of an Electromagnetic Plane Wave by an Infinite Set of Plates I, by J. F. Carlson and A. E. Heins, *Quarterly of Applied Mathematics*, Vol. 4, p. 313, January, 1947.) However in the equation discussed by Carlson and Heins, there is available a strip of regularity for matching factors. Therefore their method of solution follows that of the original W-H equation.

But the right member above is equal to

$$\int_0^\infty K(\tau)\, d\tau \int_0^\infty e^{iut}\varphi(t-\tau)\, dt.$$

Setting $t = s + \tau$, we get for (3.0)

$$\int_0^\infty \chi(t+h)e^{iut}\, dt = \int_0^\infty K(\tau)e^{iu\tau}\, d\tau \int_{-\tau}^\infty e^{ius}\varphi(s)\, ds. \quad (3.1)$$

Now in the usual case the limits in the last integral would not involve τ but would be fixed. In that case the last equation could be solved for $\int_0^\infty K(\tau)e^{iu\tau}\, d\tau = k(u)$ from which $K(\tau)$ can be determined. Here, however, there is no simplification. Nevertheless, since $\tau \geqq 0$, *notice that the last integral would not involve τ if $\varphi(t) = 0$, $t < 0$.* Of course this last requirement is impossible, but the general idea can be exploited as we shall now proceed to do.

We replace φ by a function which vanishes for negative t. This is achieved as follows. We introduce the functions $\psi_1(t)$ and $\psi_2(t)$ such that

$$\psi_1(t) = 0, \quad t < 0, \quad\quad\quad\quad (3.2)$$

$$\psi_2(t) = 0, \quad t > 0, \quad\quad\quad\quad (3.3)$$

$$\varphi(t) = \int_{-\infty}^\infty \psi_2(\tau)\psi_1(t-\tau)\, d\tau \quad\quad\quad (3.4)$$

Of course it is necessary to show that this is possible. This we shall do later. Using (3.4) in (2.2) and also using (3.3), we get

$$\chi(t+h) = \int_{-\infty}^0 \psi_2(\tau)\, d\tau \int_0^\infty \psi_1(t-\tau-s)K(s)\, ds, \quad t > 0. \quad (3.5)$$

Now, if it is possible to find an $\alpha(t)$ such that

$$\chi(t) = \int_{-\infty}^0 \alpha(t-\tau)\psi_2(\tau)\, d\tau, \quad\quad\quad (3.6)$$

then (3.5) becomes

$$\int_{-\infty}^0 \alpha(t+h-\tau)\psi_2(\tau)\, d\tau = \int_{-\infty}^0 \psi_2(\tau) \int_0^\infty \psi_1(t-\tau-s)K(s)\, ds,$$
$$t > 0.$$

From this we find

$$\int_{-\infty}^0 \psi_2(\tau)\left[\alpha(t+h-\tau) - \int_0^\infty \psi_1(t-\tau-s)K(s)ds\right] d\tau = 0, \quad t \geqq 0.$$

Clearly this equation, and therefore also (2.2), will hold if

$$\alpha(t + h - \tau) - \int_0^\infty \psi_1(t - \tau - s)K(s)\,ds = 0, \quad t > 0, \quad \tau < 0.$$

Or, since $t - \tau > 0$, the above is equivalent to

$$\alpha(t + h) = \int_0^\infty \psi_1(t - s)K(s)\,ds, \quad t > 0. \tag{3.7}$$

Therefore, we have only to solve (3.7) for $K(\tau)$ in order to minimize I. The equation (3.7) has the same form as (2.2) except that $\psi_1(t) = 0$, $t < 0$, and consequently (3.7) *will yield to the Fourier transform method.*

Of course everything depends on our being able to find a ψ_1, and ψ_2 satisfying (3.2), (3.3) and (3.4). We observe that (3.4) is an integral equation of the ordinary convolution type which we want to solve for two functions ψ_1 and ψ_2 subject to auxiliary conditions (3.2) and (3.3). Since (3.4) and (3.6) involve ordinary convolutions, they can be simplified by use of the Fourier transform.

4   The Factorization Problem

We proceed now to find ψ_1, ψ_2, and α. Once this is done, solving (3.7) for K will be a simple and routine Fourier transform problem. Let

$$\int_{-\infty}^\infty \varphi(t)e^{iut}\,dt = \Phi(u). \tag{4.0}$$

Then by the Fourier transform theorem

$$\varphi(t) = \frac{1}{2\pi}\int_{-\infty}^\infty \Phi(u)e^{-iut}\,du. \tag{4.1}$$

Similarly if

$$\int_0^\infty \psi_1(t)e^{iut}\,dt = \Psi_1(u), \tag{4.2}$$

then

$$\psi_1(t) = \frac{1}{2\pi}\int_{-\infty}^\infty \Psi_1(u)e^{-iut}\,du, \tag{4.3}$$

and an analogous result holds for $\psi_2(t)$. Multiplying (3.4) by e^{iut} and integrating, we have

$$\Phi(u) = \int_{-\infty}^\infty \psi_2(\tau)\,d\tau \int_{-\infty}^\infty e^{iut}\psi_1(t - \tau)\,dt.$$

Setting $t - \tau = s$, we get

$$\Phi(u) = \Psi_1(u)\Psi_2(u). \tag{4.4}$$

The equation (4.2) gives us, if $w = u + iv$,

$$\Psi_1(w) = \int_0^\infty \psi_1(t)e^{-vt}e^{iut}\,dt, \tag{4.5}$$

and

$$\Psi_1'(w) = \int_0^\infty it\psi_1(t)e^{-vt}e^{iut}\,dt. \tag{4.6}$$

In the upper half-plane $v > 0$, $\Psi_1'(w)$ is determined as a finite function, since for $v > 0$, the term e^{-vt} in (4.6) assures the convergence of the integral. Thus $\Psi_1(w)$ defined by (4.5) is an analytic function of w in the upper half-plane $v > 0$. Also $\Psi_1(w)$ is a bounded function in the upper half-plane $v \geqq 0$. We observe then that *the Fourier transform of a function vanishing over* $(-\infty, 0)$ *is analytic and bounded in the upper half-plane.* Also the Fourier transform of a function vanishing over $(0, \infty)$ is analytic and bounded in the lower half-plane.

The converse of this result is also true. For suppose that $\Psi_1(w)$ is analytic and bounded. Then the integral

$$\psi_1(t) = \frac{1}{2\pi}\int_{-\infty}^\infty \Psi_1(w)e^{-iwt}\,dw$$

can be shown to be zero for $t < 0$ simply by closing the path of integration in the upper half-plane and using Cauchy's integral theorem. The fact that e^{vt} is small for $t < 0$ and large v makes this step legitimate. Thus we conclude that if a *function is analytic and bounded in the upper half-plane its Fourier transform vanishes over* $(-\infty, 0)$. Similarly the Fourier transform of a function analytic and bounded in the lower half-plane vanishes over $(0, \infty)$.

Combining this fact with (4.4), $\Phi(u) = \Psi_1(u)\Psi_2(u)$, we see that the *problem of finding* $\psi_1(t)$ *is reduced to the problem of factoring* $\Phi(u)$ *into two factors,* $\Psi_1(u)$ *and* $\Psi_2(u)$, *such that* $\Psi_1(u + iv)$ *is analytic and bounded in the upper half-plane* $v > 0$, *and* $\Psi_2(u + w)$ *is analytic and bounded in the lower half-plane,* $v < 0$.

Before attempting to factor $\Phi(u)$, we observe that $\Phi(u) \geqq 0$. [This result is established in Wiener's theory of generalized harmonic analysis, *Acta Mathematica*, Vol. 55, pp. 117–258, 1930. In fact $\Phi(u)$ is the density of the energy of $f(t)$ at frequency u. Thus it must be positive.] If $\Psi_1(u + iv) = P(u, v) + iQ(u, v)$ is analytic for $v > 0$, then it follows at once from the Cauchy-Riemann equations that $\Psi_2(u + iv) = P(u, -v) - iQ(u, -v)$ is analytic for $v < 0$. Moreover using the bar to denote the conjugate complex number, we see that $\Psi_1(u) = \overline{\Psi}_2(u)$, so that $\Psi_1(u)\Psi_2(u) \geq 0$. In other words, by choosing $\Psi_2(u, v)$ as $P(u, -v)$

$-iQ(u, -v)$, we satisfy the requirement $\Phi(u) > 0$. Moreover, since

$$\Psi_1(u)\Psi_2(u) = |\Psi_1(u)|^2 \equiv \Phi(u)$$

we see that

$$|\Psi_1(u)| = \sqrt{\Phi(u)}. \tag{4.7}$$

Thus the problem of finding $\psi_1(t)$ has now been reduced to the problem of finding $\Psi_1(u + iv)$ analytic and bounded in the upper half-plane $v \geqq 0$, knowing the value of $|\Psi_1(u)|$.

5 The Functions ψ_1, ψ_2, and α

We introduce the function

$$\lambda(w) = \log \Psi_1(w).$$

If we write $\lambda(w)$ in terms of its real and imaginary parts, then $\lambda(u + iv)$ $= p(u, v) + iq(u, v)$. The requirements on Ψ_1 are certainly fulfilled if $\lambda(w)$ is analytic for $v > 0$, if $e^{p(u,v)}$ is bounded for $v > 0$, and if

$$p(u, 0) = \tfrac{1}{2} \log \Phi(u). \tag{5.0}$$

This last requirement is (4.7). The condition that $\lambda(w)$ be analytic for $v > 0$ is equivalent to the condition that $p(u, v)$ be a harmonic function for $v > 0$. In this way all our requirements can be specified in terms of $p(u, v)$.

The determination of the harmonic function, $p(u, v)$, taking on specified values on the real axis, as is indicated in (5.0), is well known. In fact

$$p(u, v) = \frac{1}{\pi} \int_{-\infty}^{\infty} \frac{\tfrac{1}{2} v \log \Phi(s)}{(u - s)^2 + v^2} \, ds \tag{5.1}$$

will be harmonic‖ and will satisfy (5.0). The integral (5.1) is the well known Poisson integral, and $e^{p(u,v)}$ is a bounded function for $v > 0$. Thus all requirements on $p(u, v)$ are fulfilled. We shall also have occasion to use the fact that, with $p(u, v)$ determined by (5.1), $e^{-p(u,v)}$ is very limited in magnitude for $v > 0$. (It is certainly $0(e^{\epsilon|w|})$ for any $\epsilon > 0$.)

If R denotes "real part of," then

$$\frac{v}{(u - s)^2 + v^2} = R\left\{\frac{i}{w - s}\right\}.$$

Thus (5.1) can be written as

$$p(u, v) = R\left\{\frac{i}{2\pi} \int_{-\infty}^{\infty} \frac{\tfrac{1}{2} \log \Phi(s)}{w - s} \, ds\right\}.$$

‖ If the integral (5.1) diverges
fectly from its past.

Taking account of the fact that $\Phi(s)$ is an even function, we have

$$p(u, v) = R\left\{\frac{i}{\pi} \int_0^\infty \frac{w \log \Phi(s)}{w^2 - s^2} ds\right\}. \tag{5.2}$$

Since $p(u, v) = R\{\lambda(w)\}$ it follows from (5.) that

$$\lambda(w) = \frac{i}{\pi} \int_0^\infty \frac{w \log \Phi(s)}{w^2 - s^2} ds. \tag{5.3}$$

We recall that

$$\Psi_1(w) = e^{\lambda(w)}.$$

Thus we have completely determined Ψ_1, and with it, from (4 .3 also) $\psi_1(t)$ Not only is $\Psi_1(w)$ analytic and bounded in the upper half-plane, but $1/\Psi_1(w) = e^{-\lambda(w)}$ is also analytic in the upper half-plane. This last relationship, which appears to be incidental here, is in fact a basic requirement as we shall see.

We turn next to (3 6) .

$$\chi(t) = \int_{-\infty}^\infty \psi_2(\tau)\alpha(t - \tau) \, d\tau. \tag{5.4}$$

Introducing the Fourier transforms,

$$A(u) = \int_{-\infty}^0 \alpha(t) e^{iut} dt \quad \text{and} \quad X(u) = \int_{-\infty}^\infty \chi(t) e^{iut} dt,$$

we get from (5) $X(u) = A(u)\Psi_2(u)$. Thus $A(u) = X(u)/\Psi_2(u)$ is determined. We find $\alpha(t)$ from $\alpha(t) = \frac{1}{2\pi} \int_{-\infty}^\infty A(u) e^{iut} du$. Thus $\psi_1(t)$, $\psi_2(t)$ and $\alpha(t)$ are determined.

6 The Prediction Operator

We return now to Eq. (3 .7),

$$\alpha(t + h) = \int_0^\infty \psi_1(t - \tau)K(\tau) \, d\tau, \quad t \geqq 0.$$

Multiplying the equation by e^{iwt} and integrating for $t \geqq 0$, we find

$$\int_0^\infty \alpha(t + h)e^{iwt} \, dt = \int_0^\infty K(\tau) \, d\tau \int_0^\infty \psi_1(t - \tau) e^{iut} dt.$$

Or setting $t - \tau = s$,

$$\alpha(t + h)e^{iwt} \, dt = \int_0^\infty \tag{6.0}$$

If for $v \geq 0$,

$$k(w) = \int_0^\infty K(\tau)e^{iw\tau} \, dt, \tag{6.1}$$

where $w = u + iv$, then we have from (6.0)

$$k(w) = \int_0^\infty \frac{\alpha(t+h)e^{iwt}}{\Psi_1(w)} \, dt. \tag{6.2}$$

We have thus found the Fourier transform, of $K(\tau)$.

In order that $K(\tau)$ as determined from its Fourier transform, $k(w)$, shall be null for $t < 0$, it is necessary for $k(w)$ to be analytic and of limited growth in the upper half w-plane. Now the integral on the right side of (6.2) defines a bounded analytic function for $v \geq 0$. As has already been indicated by the remark in the paragraph following (5.1), $e^{-\lambda(w)}$ is limited in magnitude in the upper half-plane. Thus $k(w)$ as given by (6.2) is analytic and limited in magnitude in the upper half-plane $[0(e^{\epsilon|w|})$ for any $\epsilon > 0]$. We may conclude, therefore, that $K(\tau)$ as determined from $k(w)$ will be null for $\tau < 0$. Strictly speaking, $k(u)$ often will not have a Fourier transform in the orthodox sense but is rather the transform of an operator which deals only with the interval $(0, \infty)$.

For example the best representation of $g(t + h)$ may be given by $f'(t)$ and not by $\int_0^\infty f(t - \tau)K(\tau) \, d\tau$ at all. In this case if we apply $\left[-\dfrac{d}{d\tau}\right]_{\tau=0}$ to $f(t - \tau)$ we get $f'(t)$ as desired. If we apply $\left[-\dfrac{d}{d\tau}\right]_{\tau=0}$ to $e^{iw\tau}$ we get $-iw$. Thus in this case we would find $k(w) = -iw$.

Again if $f(t - a)$ should be used in the representation of $g(t)$ this is the result of taking $[f(t - \tau)]_{\tau=a}$. Doing this to $e^{iw\tau}$, we get e^{iwa}. More generally then, if we find as a result of using (6.2) that

$$k(w) = -w^2 + 2iwe^{iw} - e^{\frac{1}{2}iw} + \frac{i}{w+i},$$

then in place of an operation on $f(t - \tau)$ of just the form $\int K(\tau) \, d\tau$ we get

$$\frac{d^2}{d\tau^2}f(t - \tau)\bigg]_{\tau=0} + 2\frac{d}{d\tau}f(t - \tau)\bigg]_{\tau=1} - f(t - \tau)\bigg]_{\tau=\frac{1}{2}}$$

$$+ \int_0^\infty f(t - \tau)e^{-\tau} \, d\tau = f''(t) - 2f'(t - 1) - f(t - \tfrac{1}{2})$$

We can check this by using $e^{iw\tau}$ in place of $f(t-\tau)$, getting

$$-w^2 + 2iwe^{iw} - e^{\frac{1}{2}iw} + \int_0^{\infty} e^{iw\tau}e^{-\tau}\,d\tau,$$

which is in fact $k(w)$.

Massachusetts Institute of Technology

INDEX

M.I.T. Press paperbacks — the first ten

Printed in the United States
by Baker & Taylor Publisher Services